D1611487

MANHATTAN
IN MAPS
1527-2014

Duytsche Mylen Tot 15 voort Een graet

MANHATTAN IN MAPS
1527-2014

Paul E. Cohen   Robert T. Augustyn

Foreword by
Tony Hiss

New Introduction by
Marguerite Holloway

"Manhattan As It Once Was" by
Eric W. Sanderson

DOVER PUBLICATIONS, INC.
Mineola, New York

FOR PHYLLIS, KATIE & WILL

Bibliographical Note

Manhattan in Maps 1527–2014, first published by Dover Publications, Inc., in 2014, is an unabridged republication of the work originally published by Rizzoli International Publications, Inc., New York, in 1997. A new Introduction by Marguerite Holloway and an essay, "Manhattan As It Once Was," by Eric W. Sanderson, with an accompanying graphic illustration by Mr. Sanderson and Markley Boyer, have been specially prepared for the Dover edition.

International Standard Book Number

ISBN-13: 978-0-486-77991-1
ISBN-10: 0-486-77991-2

Manufactured in the United States by Courier Corporation
77991201   2014
www.doverpublications.com

CONTENTS

NIEUW AMSTERDAM
op t Eylant Manhattans.

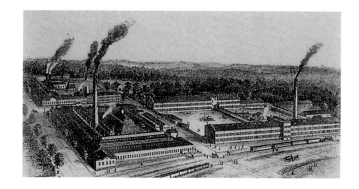 

ACKNOWLEDGMENTS

This book has been in the works for several years, and we have been helped and encouraged by many people along the way. Our biggest debt of gratitude goes to Asher Jason, our agent, and Alice Hudson, the head of the Map Division at The New York Public Library. They both had great faith in our project and on several occasions rescued it from oblivion. Alice Hudson is the best-informed curator of New York City maps, and she is exceedingly generous in sharing her knowledge and providing assistance.

Many librarians helped in acquiring photographs and locating facts and details about the maps in their collections. At the Library of Congress we have relied on the expertise of Ralph Ehrenberg, Gary Fitzpatrick, Jim Flatness, and Ron Grim. Mariam Touba of the New-York Historical Society was always ready to drop whatever she was doing to assist with the remarkable resources at that institution. Tony Campbell of the British Library made valuable suggestions, and the staff of the map department helped us acquire transparencies of the many important New York City maps in England. Jim Corsaro of the New York State Library informed us about maps we otherwise would have missed. We were constantly calling upon the librarians at The New York Public Library: Roberta Waddell of the Print Room, Jennifer Lee of the Rare Book Department, and Tom Bourke of the Map Division. We were in regular communication with Nancy Kandoian of the Map Division of The New York Public Library, who fielded our many questions with agility.

We have enjoyed many months of working with David Morton and Megan McFarland of Rizzoli International Publications; we thank them for their perceptive suggestions, long hours of work, and indulgence with us. We also wish to thank our first editor on this project, Alan Axelrod, who was one of the first to recognize the merit in a book about New York City maps.

Our colleagues and coworkers have supported and put up with us as we toiled away on Manhattan maps: Richard Arkway, Richard Lan, Seyla Martayan, Engela Brondum, Mead Cain, Anne De Mare, Seth Fagen, Ben Jones, Milton Mendez, and Jennifer Woodward.

We thank Richard Brown, Bill Ginsberg, Robert Goelet, Norman Hubbard, Joep De Koning, Allison Eckardt Ledes, Glen McLaughlin, Kenneth and Brian Quintenz, David Rumsey, Donald Schnabel, Arthur O. Sulzberger, Sr., Chase Viele, and Charles Wendell.

We would like generally to thank the private collectors we work with every day, whose interest and curiosity are in many ways the inspiration for this book.

We have also called upon Barbara Cohen of New York Bound Bookstore; Bob Lorenzson, photographer extraordinaire; Lynn de Marco, Bruce Altshuler, Jean Ashton, Georges Cohen, Joseph Montebello, Deborah Nadler, John Tauranac, Louis De Vorsey, and the late Constance Cohen, who would loved to have seen this book.

PREFACE

In many ways New York City conceals its past. Even though it is in fact America's oldest major city, Boston and Philadelphia, which still preserve many of their colonial buildings, feel older. In New York there is almost no physical evidence of the city's long colonial history from the period 1625–1783. Several conflagrations and the city's need to build ever taller buildings in order to expand have all but obliterated structures built before 1800. Even less evident on the slender island of Manhattan, now almost entirely covered with pavement and cement, is a sense of the natural world, or indications of what the island was like prior to development.

Yet an avenue to New York's past does exist, though it is one that is relatively unknown: the history of the city through maps. No other medium provides, at a glance, so many vital clues to reconstructing the past. Some of the oldest maps preserve on paper the virgin landscape of Manhattan with its lakes, streams, and hills. Others follow the evolution of the island over the centuries—from the promising harbor on a sixteenth-century Italian map, to Dutch trading outpost, then to village, city, and finally, metropolis. It is only through maps that we can see this story unfold so graphically.

Despite the wealth of material and the intriguing subject, there has never been an illustrated book devoted exclusively to the mapping of Manhattan. Many of the maps that follow have not been reproduced before; others have not been reproduced for almost a century. It should be pointed out that at the beginning of the twentieth century, I. N. Phelps Stokes first published many of the important maps of New York City in a work that all students of Manhattan must acknowledge: the six-volume *Iconography of Manhattan Island* (1915–1928). Stokes's *Iconography* has been called "the greatest single reference work about any American city," and the numerous references to him throughout this book are a testament to our indebtedness to his remarkable research.

Stokes had one of the world's best collections of prints and maps relating to America (it is now housed at The New York Public Library) and ultimately he compiled the most thorough book on the subject. Despite its excellence, the *Iconography* is cumbersome to use, has long been out of print, and its reproductions are unsatisfactory by current standards. We felt that a new book should present the maps individually and in color and include items uncovered since Stokes or not reproduced by him. Frederick Law Olmsted and Calvert Vaux's original plan for Central Park, "Greensward," (see p. 118) has never been published before in color, and John Randel, Jr.'s original manuscript of New York's comprehensive plan for the city's development, The Commissioners' Plan of 1811 (see p. 86) has not been photographed since Stokes. In addition, we have tried to expand the commentary that many of these maps have received to date. By learning as much as we could about the circumstances under which each map was created, we have been able to present them as multifaceted works that

DETAIL: Watercolor view of New York from Governors Island (model for engraved view on The Ratzer Map). Capt. - Lt. Thomas Davies, 1760. Private collection.

record much more than simple geographical data.

The richness of New York's cartographic heritage is unique among the major cities of the world. Most important European and Asian cities are so old as to preclude the existence of their earliest maps. American cities of an age comparable to New York's have not been as fortunate in the survival of maps and plans dating from their earliest days. In addition to sheer luck, several other factors contributed to New York's cartographic wealth. Its first European settlers, the Dutch, were a mapping people. Concurrent with the Dutch colonial period in the early and mid-seventeenth century was the golden age of mapmaking, when Holland was the international hub of cartographic activity. The most accurate and lavish maps, atlases, and globes came from the printing presses of Amsterdam at the same time that Manhattan, or New Amsterdam, was a fledgling colony. The nature of the Dutch settlement on Manhattan—a commercial enterprise managed from overseas by the Dutch West India Company—also fostered map production. The

Company demanded maps from leaders of the colony, like Peter Minuit, in order to monitor commercial development. Maps such as the Minuit Chart, the Manatus Map, and the Castello Plan (see pp. 10, 14, and 24) permit us to see what Manhattan's earliest European settlers discovered.

When the British seized Manhattan in 1664, they surveyed and mapped their prize. The English colonial period, however, produced fewer maps than the Dutch, most likely because New York grew slowly under English rule and was not administered as closely as it had been from Amsterdam. After the French and Indian War (1763), England won clear title to her North American possessions and English cartographic activity increased. Many maps of New York were produced during the American Revolution, making the city at war's end the most thoroughly mapped urban area in America. This was because Manhattan and its immediate environs were a battleground during the war, and many campaign maps, such as the Faden Campaign Map and the Holland Map (see pp. 64 and 68), were produced. Also,

throughout the war, New York was the command center for British forces, and constant fear of attack by American forces prompted the production of numerous maps to aid in the defence of the city.

We have searched libraries and private collections throughout the world to locate the most significant and best copies of maps. The most important repositories are The New York Public Library, the New-York Historical Society, the Library of Congress, and the British Library. We found significant works in archives in Italy, the Netherlands, and Spain. In fact, the only contemporary cartographic record of Henry Hudson's exploration of the New York area is on a manuscript map, the Velasco Map, in the General Archives of Simancas, Spain (see p. 6). It was brought to Spain in the seventeenth century by the Spanish ambassador to England, who must have obtained it from a spy in the English court. The sole surviving copy of a fine street plan of New Amsterdam made in 1660, the Castello Plan, was found in a villa in Florence. Private col-

lectors are often the proud possessors of unusual items or especially interesting copies of significant maps. For example, we discovered two majestically colored maps by Lt. Bernard Ratzer that were once part of an eighteenth-century military archive and are now in a private collection (see p. 59). Our debt to private collectors can be appreciated by the number of maps we have illustrated from their collections.

In 1931, Daniel C. Haskell published a carto-bibliography entitled *Manhattan Maps,* listing nearly two thousand entries from the early seventeenth century to 1930. It is incorrect to think that there are this many different maps of the city, as most of the entries enumerate various printings of the same map or derivative maps. We have made an effort to include only maps that are landmarks in the mapping of the city or maps that made a distinct contribution to shaping the city by providing new geographical information. We have also included maps that offer unique perspectives, such as Mrs. Buchnerd's Plan of 1735, which illuminates the social history of its period, and the Midtown Vice Map of 1973.

Urban mapping demands the highest skills of the surveyor, the artist, and the engraver. After selecting and studying the maps in this book, we were left with tremendous admiration for the mapmakers of New York City. These surveyors and cartographers often devoted the better part of their lives to enormous mapping projects of the island. The highly skilled English military mapmakers of the revolutionary war period—Montresor, Ratzer, Holland, Sauthier, and Hill—brought to the mapping of Manhattan a professional exactitude that resulted in cartographic masterpieces. John Randel, Jr. spent nearly thirteen years measuring every inch of Manhattan island and laying out the streets of the famous grid. After several decades of delineating the topography of the island, Egbert Ludovicus Viele knew the location of every stream and hill that ever existed in Manhattan. And John Tauranac is still perfecting the subway maps he began in the 1970s. Their achievements have resulted in the most complete and thorough cartographic record of any city in history.

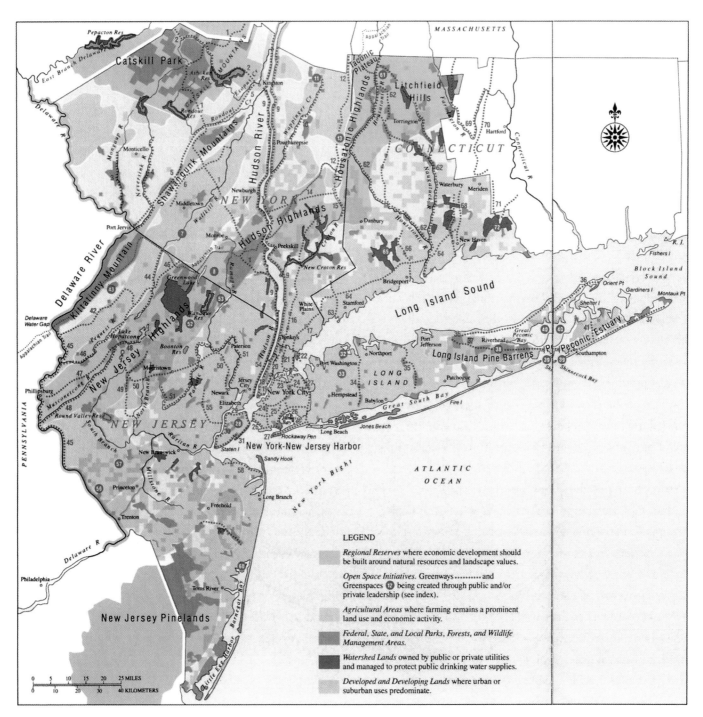

LEGEND

Regional Reserves where economic development should be built around natural resources and landscape values.

Open Space Initiatives. Greenways ·········· and Greenspaces 🟢 being created through public and/or private leadership (see index).

Agricultural Areas where farming remains a prominent land use and economic activity.

Federal, State, and Local Parks, Forests, and Wildlife Management Areas.

Watershed Lands owned by public or private utilities and managed to protect public drinking water supplies.

Developed and Developing Lands where urban or suburban uses predominate.

DETAIL: Metropolitan Greensward Summary Map, 1995. *Regional Plan Association, New York. Published in* A REGION AT RISK, *Third Regional Plan (New York: Regional Plan Association, 1996).*

FOREWORD: A CLOSER LOOK
BY TONY HISS

Finally, the library of New York has some completeness. Notable books about the city have been accumulating for centuries, capped just two years ago by the publication of Kenneth T. Jackson's thirteen-hundred-page *Encyclopedia of New York City*. Now that first-rate reference work has a superb companion volume, the city's first atlas of historical maps, Paul E. Cohen and Robert T. Augustyn's *Manhattan in Maps*. It is a book that is destined to have a profound and positive influence on twenty-first-century New York. Had it been published, say, 215 years ago, just after the halfway point in the city's long history, it might already have altered the course of New York's evolution, perhaps even giving us a city where today trees, grasses, and streams would be visible outside every one of New York's millions of windows.

How could one new book bring about changes when the hundreds already printed have such modest effects? I see a kind of rough mathematical equation at work. If one picture has the impact of a thousand words, a good map— those of us who are map lovers would argue—can be five times more powerful than that, in terms of the intensity with which it reaches the mind and the imprint it leaves behind. That is because a well-crafted map, which by its nature carefully combines pictures and words into a single, integrated, often unforgettable and even dazzling eye-burst of information, is more than just an enjoyably efficient way of presenting knowledge about the world around us.

Modern cartography has been honed and refined ever since the Renaissance to further practical day-to-day concerns, helping sailors, for instance, stay afloat by warning them of the exact whereabouts of hidden rocks and reefs. Overtly, any map we look at is a neutral document—an annotated catalog of patterns, a table of contents with graphics, an objective record of our understanding of the world. But look again! Maps are evocative, provocative; they nudge and push. Every time we pore over one, it is subtly urging us to do more with ourselves, to get out and about, to take better care of the communities and landscapes it has recorded.

Maps give us an instantaneous God's-eye view of our surroundings, and this built-in hanging-down-from-heaven distortion sets up an odd kind of tension, simulcasting both to our pride and to some more humble ways of looking around us. On the one hand, maps flatter outrageously, exaggerating human importance in the scheme of things, tempting us to think, like Dr. Seuss's Yertle the Turtle, that if we can see something, that makes us the king of it. At the same time, maps endow the world with urgent and beguiling voices, because when they set up face-to-face encounters with a place, they are showing us, at a glance, all that is worth caring for in a city, or perhaps a whole region, or even an entire continent. Maybe the baby effect is at work, too—by making us big and the world small, maps make the world seem more vulnerable, helpless, and in need of our protection. Maps also tug at our memories, flashing miniature life histories before our eyes—that's where I learned to swim; and that's where I learned to lie on my back and look at the clouds.

And I think the best maps also look forward, summoning hopes as effectively as memories or obligations. After reading through this book, I can see for the first time New York's first great turning point. In 1783, at the conclusion of the American Revolution, British troops, who had occupied New York throughout the war, evacuated the city, leaving in their wake appalling scenes of destruction—a quarter of the city had burned, including most of its landmarks, such as the charming, gabled, century-old red-brick Dutch houses that had survived from early New Amsterdam. Most of Manhattan's extensive woods had been leveled for firewood and to build forts and stockades. But the most devastating part of the British pullout, an act hidden from view until the publication of *Manhattan in Maps,* was that the soldiers took with them their crowning achievement— an enormous, three-square-yard map of Manhattan Island that compellingly presented the case, two hundred years before such concepts became commonplace, for respecting and celebrating the watersheds and ecosystems of the twelve-mile island as the city pushed northward from its original settlement near the Battery.

This 1782 map, the British Headquarters Map (see p. 70), painstakingly delineates, as the commentary to the map indicates, "every stream, pond, swamp, marsh, elevation, and contour of shoreline" that then existed on Manhattan. Because the map was designed as a practical exercise to help British commanders decide which spots to fortify and where to deploy their forces, the landscape is visualized as a key British ally. They needed to know which hills were tall enough and which streams and marshes were wide enough to slow down any invading American forces, as well as which valleys might be deep enough to trap them. Accordingly, the original rolling, water-threaded topography of the island becomes the central feature of this huge image. Every hillside is colored with such intense dark shading and every brook is so brightly blue that the entire map takes on a very three-dimensional, bumpy, and quite drenched look.

The Headquarters Map, which has languished in London ever since American independence—stashed first at the War Office and transferred more recently to the care of the Public Records Office—has never appeared previously in any book. So the city has had to grow without it—a ludicrous situation, as if the only maps of the beauties and intricacies of Yellowstone and Yosemite were locked in a drawer somewhere in Calcutta. Because the gigantic Headquarters Map does not hang in a place of honor in the City Hall rotunda, supplemented by smaller wall map copies in every New York public office and classroom, New York is no longer a spectacular setting of hills and kills—"kills" being the original Dutch name for the area's many tidally influenced streams. Instead, under the notorious waffle-iron influence of a second map, the 1811 Commissioners' Plan (see p. 86), Manhattan was squashed, flattened, dried, degreened, and gridded with right-angle streets and avenues; landfill killed every hill and kill.

In this two-dimensional vision of the city, every marsh and stream was a receptacle waiting to be smothered by a displaced hilltop. New York was placed in the artificial position of creating an economy and a society that had almost no connection to its underlying environment—and at the turn of the last century this concept was exported almost as successfully into the Bronx, Brooklyn, Queens, and Staten Island, and the counties in New York State and New Jersey just beyond the city limits (see The Risse Map, p. 130). The 1811 Manhattan vision held together for well over a century only because of a bold, mid-nineteenth-century afterthought—Central Park (see p. 116)—which reclaimed for greenery a piece of Manhattan big enough to be claimed as common ground by the entire New York community.

But now another century dawns. And what is New York, which for so long was so proud to call itself "the city of the twentieth century," to do next? Words and pictures can help craft a new vision of a city where economy, society, and environment support each other. But I have a hunch that, as we step forward, we will turn to new maps of hope to help us chart our course. The Regional Plan Association's 1995 Metropolitan Greensward Summary Map of the entire greater New York/New Jersey/Connecticut metropolitan area (see p. xiv), is perhaps a prototype for a twenty-first-century cartography of New York. Like the 1782 British Headquarters Map, the new

Greensward map makes intact landscapes its indelible focus. In this new formulation, Manhattan at first seems almost insignificant, and Central Park even smaller. But when you look closely, it is still at the center of the picture, a force to be reckoned with, an organizing principle that gives focus to a community of twenty million people.

And with a book like *Manhattan in Maps* to guide us, we might be headed for smoother sailing at last.

INTRODUCTION TO THE DOVER EDITION

This beautiful book is more than a collection of maps of Manhattan—it is itself a map, for maps depict routes and landscapes and ways to or through them, and this book does just that. It provides its viewers a path through five centuries across an ever-shifting landscape.

When it was first published in 1997, *Manhattan in Maps* brought into public view rare maps and maps previously unknown beyond a relatively small group of people who collected them, used them for civic ends, or were intimate with New York City history. By making such maps available, *Manhattan in Maps* inspired discovery, a richer relationship with the island for many New Yorkers, and some new maps. New Yorkers know their way around a thing or two, most particularly their famous island. But every now and then, even the savviest, grid-grounded person becomes lost, and the familiar becomes unfamiliar and is seen anew. These maps of the past lives of the city engender fresh perspective: they are familiar, and yet not. They give viewers a tether and a carabiner by which they can attach to a known landmark or era and then set out to explore high above the landscape or to rappel into its particulars—perhaps with Colton's Topographical Map (pages 106–107), which depicts the city in 1836 from aerial perspective, or with Bernard Ratzer's 1766–1767 map (pages 60–61), which shows the young city down to the level of individual trees.

Just a year after *Manhattan in Maps* appeared, landscape ecologist Eric W. Sanderson happened upon a copy in the Strand Bookstore and was inspired to undertake such an adventure. He was mesmerized by the British Headquarters Map (circa 1782, on pages 71–73), which had never appeared in a book before except in the early twentieth century as a somewhat crude black-and-white reproduction. In color and in richer detail, the British Headquarters Map is revelatory. The dramatic topography it records shows Manhattan naked to the rock, without its thick bristly coat of buildings. Seeing that raw landscape, a landscape alive with geologic dimensionality, sparked Sanderson's idea for the Mannahatta Project, a compelling work of science and imagination that has given New Yorkers a new map (pages xxii–xxiii): a depiction of the island before Europeans arrived in 1609—a depiction of an island as varied in its ecosystems as in its topography.

Some of the other maps in this book similarly marry fact and imagination. The Mangin-Goerck Plan of 1803 (pages 82–83) bore slight resemblance to the city it was supposed to depict, but did memorialize its creators in named streets. The 1811 Commissioners' Plan (pages 86–87), surveyed and drawn by John Randel Jr., charted a nearly eight-mile street grid—with some streets running through water—for a grand metropolis that didn't yet exist. Those maps present a vision of what individuals or governments wanted to see the island become: they are possibility maps, dreams of a future city. A vibrant city always needs new maps for the future. As climate change occurs, the city's true nature increasingly will be revealed: it is water-bounded and water-laced, the southern end is low lying, and a terra infirma of landfill has padded the island, pushing it out into the rivers beyond its natural profile. Engineers have long been familiar with the watery nature of the city, often turning to Egbert Viele's 1865 Water Map (pages 116–117) to understand the flooding caused by submerged springs and creeks that still flow through ancient terrain beneath the city. Today, post Hurricane Sandy, many more New Yorkers know Viele's map, and many think about the necessity of integrating ecology and topography into the fabric of urban planning, into the city's next maps. Perhaps, as some designers have suggested, the island needs to recover its ring of wetlands or oyster reef barriers to defuse wave surges.

A few years after the genesis of Mannahatta, geographer Reuben Skye Rose-Redwood discovered *Manhattan in Maps*. The map that spoke to him was Randel Farm Map No. 27 (page 97), created more than three decades after the British Headquarters Map and at a time when New York was growing rapidly. Rose-Redwood became entranced by the detail captured on that map, which shows rocks along the shore of Turtle Bay and property lines and houses for the Beekman, Bayard and other families, as well as a stream running under the winding Eastern Post Road. A single beautiful map such as this can bring to life the daily routines and landscape of a lost neighborhood.

Map No. 27 is one of 92 maps of Manhattan created by Randel, the surveyor who set the 1811 street grid on the island. Together, the Randel farm maps extend 50 feet long and 11 feet wide—a map unlike any other of New York City, and one that does not seem to have a nineteenth-century counterpart except perhaps in the work of Japanese cartographer Inō Tadataka. Rose-Redwood studied the farm maps, examining every one of the 1,865 structures they depicted—ice houses, root cellars, dairies, stables, and forts, among them; the street grid, he noted, would destroy or displace some 700 of those buildings. He also examined the elevations Randel had recorded at many intersections of the anticipated grid. Using these elevations—the northwest corner of First Avenue and 50th Street, for instance, was 52.9 inches above tide level (the midpoint between average high and low tides)—Rose-Redwood created a new map. His map showed the original topography of the island and made clear that although the West Side had lost some elevation and the East Side had gained some, Manhattan's original shape is still there. The overall features of the island of many hills endure. One of those features—a great boulder—survived the sculpting and engineering that created Central Park and still holds an iron bolt, the record of an intersection never constructed.

The little-known Randel farm maps became central to an exhibit at the Museum of the City of New York honoring the bicentennial of the 1811 Commissioners' Plan. The maps were digitized and stitched into one grand map that lives on the web. Now anyone can travel across the island of the early 1800s and see what the land looked like, to whom it belonged, and perhaps, see the spot where their building stands today.

Manhattan in Maps assembles the island rich's cartographic history, stitching maps together into a whole that animates New York's past and encourages travel—on foot, by bicycle, in the mind's eye—and an escape from the all-too-familiar. When the first map in this collection was drafted—the Maggiolo map of 1527 (page 3)—maps were rare and belonged to the realm of royalty, explorers, entrepreneurs, and armies. Until the late eighteenth and early nineteenth centuries, when state cartographers and printers began to produce and distribute atlases, most Americans did not own maps of their country or region or even city. Today, nearly everyone has a map. The idea of a map and the possession of a map are so commonplace that they have become largely invisible in their ubiquity; they are the dull-colored, infrastructure-centric background that pins drop on or dots slide across. The story those computer-generated maps tell is often one of an individual moving with purpose toward a particular destination. Not so the maps in this collection. These maps tell intricate, layered stories and have inspired new ones. They lead us out of the flatland of the familiar, everyday maps of our devices, out of our one-dimensional relationship with location, and into a colorful, evocative, endlessly recreated island. May you have the very good fortune to get lost in these maps.

Marguerite Holloway

MANHATTAN AS IT ONCE WAS

Cities are habitats for people. But what was the habitat before the city? I often wondered about that after moving to New York City in 1998 to work as a landscape ecologist for the Wildlife Conservation Society, headquartered in the Bronx Zoo. My job took me around the world to conserve the kinds of animals one normally sees only in a zoo or aquarium—elephants, tigers, and whales—but my weekends took me to the concrete canyons of late twentieth century Manhattan, to marvel at the crowded streets, tall buildings, art museums and concert halls. One day I wandered into the Strand, a bookstore on Twelfth Street and Broadway and picked up an earlier edition of the book you are holding now. I happened to flip to the British Headquarters Map (reproduced on pages 71–73) and was immediately entranced. Not by the fortifications and emplacements of the occupying British Army, not by the irregular blocks of the old colonial city clustered at the tip of the island, but by the streams and hills and beaches . . . of Manhattan!

In conservation, we grab onto any piece of information that will help us save wildlife. Here was a piece of information to save the world: Manhattan full of critters and no cars. My thought was to georeference the map; that is, to transform it to fit a modern geographic coordinate system so that other maps—of the buildings and sidewalks, for example—could be overlaid and compared. After I had obtained a high-resolution image from the National Archives in Kew, England, and collected nearly two hundred ground control points, I was able to match the modern and the historic with a geographic precision of less than one city block (heading uptown.) The foundation had been laid, not just to analyze the late Revolutionary era, but to derive the basis for an expedition into the past to reconstruct and visualize the landscape of the island as it appeared to Henry Hudson, who, arriving on September 12, 1609, set in motion the city-making that Manhattan takes for granted today.

In Hudson's time, maps were something you could hold in your hand. In our time, maps are computer databases, held in geographic information systems, and increasingly served up through the Internet. Teams of students and volunteers helped me extract layers of streams, shorelines, and wetlands from the British Headquarters Map and from earlier documents like the Carwitham Plan (pages 43–45) and the Nicolls Map (pages 30–31). We added geological information and set off on a long quest via the Randel Farm Map (page 96) to scale the heights of the hills and with nautical charts like the DesBarres (page 55) to plumb the depths of the sea. We summarized the archaeology of Manhattan's Lenape people from the Late Woodland and Contact Periods and modelled their occupation patterns and uses of fire and horticulture. We listed species derived from surveys dating back to the early nineteenth century and documented habitat relationships in a novel networking structure called Muir webs. Spatially-enabled computer code connected habitats of this with

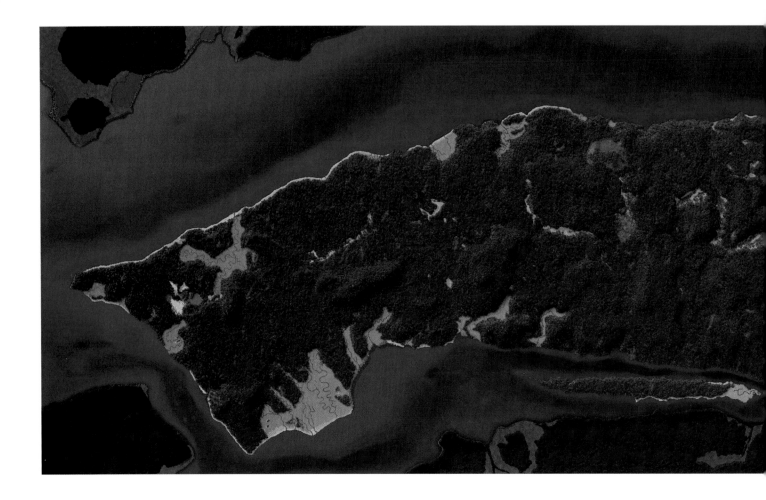

distributions of that to produce maps of beavers, wolves, and the Hudsonian godwit, slimy sculpin, and northern black racer (respectively, a bird, a fish, and a snake). All told, 1,001 species of plants and animals, likely inhabiting 55 distinct ecological communities, were compiled in a database of more than 1,600 layers.

Along the way, I met Markley Boyer, a silversmith, a cartographer, and most recently, a drone master, who helped me reconstruct views of the old island like the one you see here. Boyer used a piece of software called Visual Nature Studio, which, unlike most of the tools of Hollywood moviemakers, actually knows something about real geography, and thus enables us to peer out any window in Manhattan and reconstruct a particular view of the past. An activated webmap, now part of welikia.org (Welikia means "my good home" in Lenape and refers to our project to reconstruct the historical ecology of all of New York

City), enables anyone to click on any block of Manhattan and see what life once flowered, slithered, swam or walked where offices or apartment buildings now stand. Soon we will be adding Brooklyn, Queens, the Bronx and Staten Island, too.

There is no going back, of course, but there remains the search for the kind of sustainability and resilience that Mannahatta took for granted. Ecosystems don't fear hurricanes or financial crises; they thrive and adapt in ways that The City, and any city, can learn from. As I wrote in *Mannahatta: The Natural History of New York City* (Abrams, 2009), nearly a decade after first browsing *Manhattan in Maps* in the Strand: "The goal of the Mannahatta Project has never been to return Manhattan to its primeval state. The goal of the project is to discover something new about a place we know so well, whether we live in New York or see it on television, and through

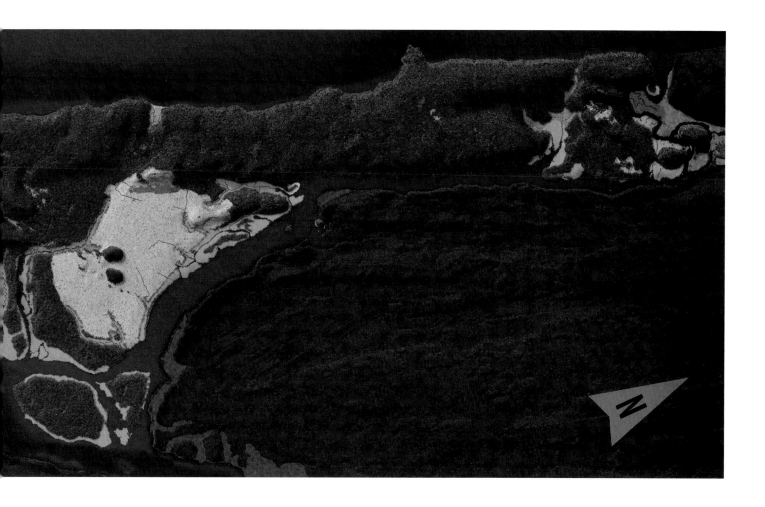

that discovery, to alter our way of life. New York does not lack for dystopian visions of its future; King Kong, climate change, war, and disease have all had their cinematic moments tearing the Big Apple down. But where is the vision of the future that works? Might it lie in Mannahatta, the green heart of New York, and with a new start to history, a few hours before Hudson arrived that sunny afternoon four hundred years ago?"

Eric W. Sanderson

The Mannahatta Project
Title: Mannahatta as Henry Hudson Might Have Seen It
Date Depicted: September 12, 1609
Date Drawn: 2009
Cartographers: Markley Boyer and Eric W. Sanderson
Publisher: Wildlife Conservation Society
[format] Digital image, 5.14" x 18.19" at 300 dots per inch
[owner] Wildlife Conservation Society

MANHATTAN
IN MAPS
1527-2014

THE LOST FIRST MAP
THE MAGGIOLO MAP

Untitled

DATE DEPICTED: 1527 (?)

DATE DRAWN: *Original, 1527; facsimile (one sheet of four depicted here), 1905*

CARTOGRAPHER: VESCONTE DE MAGGIOLO

Original, *Pen and ink and watercolors on vellum, 24 x 71¼ inches; facsimile, lithographic print, four sheets 19 x 24 inches each*

Harvard Map Collection

Before it was destroyed during World War II, The Maggiolo Map was the earliest map to provide a representation of the New York City area. The island of Manhattan itself would not be depicted on a map until nearly a century later, on Block's Map of the Northeast (see p. 8). Dated 1527, just three years after Verrazano's brief reconnaissance of New York Harbor, this splendid, hand-drawn map of the world was the work of Vesconte de Maggiolo, member of a prominent Genoese family of cartographers. Although produced not long after Verrazano's exploration, Maggiolo's mapping of the east coast of the United States was at some remove from Verrazano's original data and likely derived from an unknown prototype. There is some question as to what is represented at any particular point on the map; however, the location of New York Harbor can be determined with some certainty: it appears slightly to the west of an island identified as "luisa," which most believe to be Block Island. Shown on the map near what is thought to be New York Harbor are versions of two place-names that Verrazano was known to have applied to the area, "B.S. Margarita" and "Anguileme." The configuration of this area on Maggiolo's map—two bays divided by headlands, with a river emptying into the northernmost of the two—approximates that of the actual harbor. Although produced decades later, the small Gastaldi Map (see p. 4) provides a considerably more precise view of the New York area than the one found here. The Maggiolo map was housed at the Biblioteca Ambrosiana in Milan when it was destroyed.

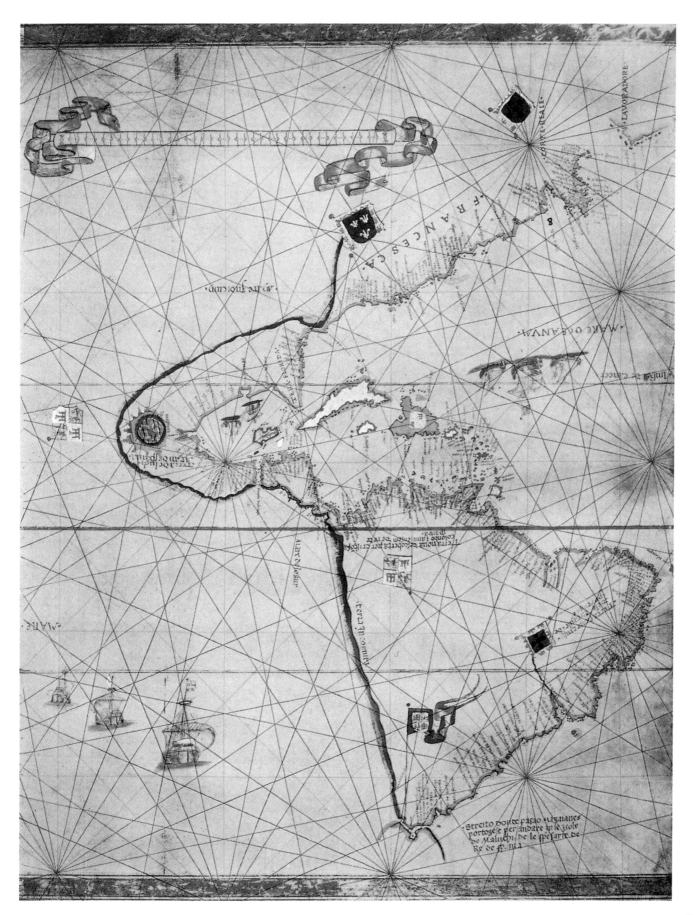

CORTE-REALE

FRANCESCA

MARE OCEANVM

MARE AQVILONIA

A.LAVORADORE

TERRA DE FLORIDA

TERRA DEL LABORA DE REI DE SPAGNA

MARE DEL SVR

terra incognita

MARE

Streto pou de pasio di manes
portoges e per andare ale isole
de Maluchi de le spesarie de
Re de spana

3

MANHATTAN FOUND AND LOST
THE GASTALDI MAP

Untitled
CARTOGRAPHER: GIACOMO DI GASTALDI
PUBLISHED: J. B. RAMUSIO, *Viaggi*, VOL. 3,
VENICE, 1556
Woodblock engraving, 10½ x 14¼ inches
Private collection

We found a very agreeable situation located within two small prominent hills, in the midst of which flowed to the sea a very great river. . . . The people . . . clothed with feathers of birds of various colors, came toward us joyfully, uttering very great exclamations of admiration. . . .
—Verrazano's description of his entry into New York Harbor in 1524.

In April 1524, Giovanni da Verrazano became the first known European to glimpse Manhattan and explore its superb harbor. The best surviving early map to register this momentous episode is Gastaldi's small, seemingly crude work, published over thirty years after the event. The Gastaldi Map provides a better depiction of the New York area than even that found on both the now lost 1527 Maggiolo map (see p. 2) and the 1529 hand-drawn map of the world by Verrazano's brother, Gerolamo, housed in the Vatican Library— the very first existing map on which the New York area is shown. Gastaldi's map was based directly on Verrazano's report of his voyage, which was ignored by most map-makers of the day. The report was, in fact, printed for the first time in the book in which the map itself appeared, although it had circulated earlier in manuscript copies. The map was most likely a sketch drawn from this description, which may account for its crude look. In any case, it effectively reveals that Verrazano carefully observed the general features of New York Harbor. Its two large bays, separated by the Narrows now spanned by the bridge named after Verrazano, and the Hudson River entering from the north all unmistakably appear at the far left on the map. The bays are, however, incorrectly aligned on an east-west rather than a north-south axis. Naturally, there are several other distortions that are to be expected on a map of this period. The size of the New York area is propor-

tionately much too large, perhaps reflective of the emphasis Verrazano placed on it in his report. To the north, an abbreviated Hudson River intersects with the St. Lawrence River, which was discovered by Jacques Cartier about the same time Verrazano found the Hudson. Also, just east of "Port du Refuge" on the map, which most likely designates Buzzards Bay south of Cape Cod, one soon encounters "c breton" (Cape Breton Island) in Nova Scotia, Canada! This contraction of hundreds of miles of coastline is a reminder of just how groping the cartography of the northeast was in the sixteenth century.

Verrazano, a Florentine sailing under the French flag, entered the Lower Bay of New York Harbor in the *Dauphine,* a hundred-ton, three-masted vessel, which is possibly the ship illustrated at the lower left on the map. Wary of the dangerously shallow water of the Lower Bay (indicated by speckles on the map), Verrazano anchored his ship and approached the shore of Staten Island in longboats, led by welcoming Indians. Although Staten Island is not identifiable on the map, it is presumably indicated by the appearance of the Narrows. The Indians may be depicted as three figures on the map to the right of the New York area; one of them is pointing with his arm. It is believed that Verrazano and his men came ashore in Tompkinsville on Staten Island. From here they proceeded to pass through the Narrows, and then entered what Verrazano described as the "beautiful lake"

of the Upper Bay, where Verrazano sighted the Hudson River ("a very great river, which was deep within the mouth"). At this point, he must have also seen Manhattan, but as is apparent from the map, which shows no insular or peninsular land mass, he had no idea it was an island or in any way distinct from the mainland.

Verrazano's exploration was then cut short by a sudden storm, which forced him and his men to return to the *Dauphine* and quickly sail away. Despite the brevity of his visit, Verrazano came away from the area with at least a glimmer of what its future would hold: he "left the said land," he reflected in his letter, "with much regret because of its commodiousness and beauty, thinking it was not without some properties of value."

The favorable impression the area made on the explorer is further registered in the place-names he applied to it, Angouleme and Santa Margarita (not on the map). As was the case with all the names he used in the course of his voyage, these two relate to the family of his employer, Francis I of France. However, the two chosen for the New York area are of special significance. *Angouleme*, which was meant to denote the New York area generally, refers to the king's title before ascending the throne; he had been the duke of Angoulême. *Santa Margarita*, Verrazano's name for the harbor itself, refers to the king's sister, an accomplished author who furthered the Renaissance in France. These place-names,

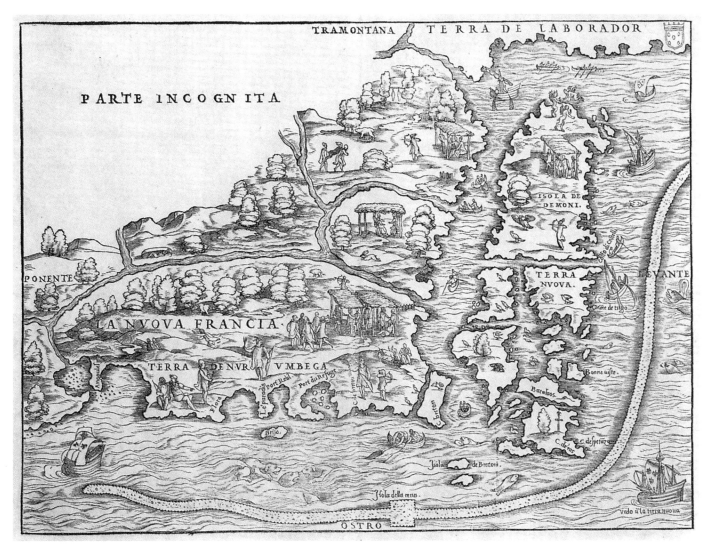

however, were shortlived and disappeared from maps by the end of the sixteenth century.

Despite Verrazano's positive account of the New York region, the area would not be sought out again for eighty-five years. This is all the more remarkable given that Gastaldi's map was relatively accessible in its day. It appeared in a popular work, Ramusio's *Viaggi*, the first comprehensive collection of exploration accounts relating to the New World, which went through three editions: 1556, 1565, and 1606. There were several factors that contributed to the failure of Europeans to follow up Verrazano's discovery of New York. Although his voyage was a momentous accomplishment—Europeans gained for the first time a sense of the actual size of North America, thereby greatly expanding their conception of the size of

the earth—his discovery did not yield the passage to the East Indies, and so his voyage was judged a failure. Moreover, the mineral samples and materials he brought back from the New World proved to be of little worth. Another factor explaining why New York was virtually forgotten after Verrazano's discovery has to do with the difficulties of mapping North America in the sixteenth century. One historian has observed that the Northeast from New York to Massachusetts became a "lost coast." Most sixteenth-century mapmakers simply ignored Verrazano's report of his explorations and instead drew upon the discoveries of Estéban Gómez, a Portuguese who sailed along the eastern seaboard about the same time as Verrazano. Gómez, however, had sailed too far off the coast in the New York to Massachusetts area and missed it altogether. Yet, Gómez's

incomplete chart was accepted by most mapmakers because he was sailing on behalf of the Spanish, who were believed to have the most advanced geographic knowledge of the day. In part because Verrazano was employed by the French, the latest entrants in the field of exploration, his broadly accurate mapping of New York and the Northeast went largely ignored.

Although New York and much of the Northeast had simply vanished as far as sixteenth-century Europeans were concerned, a desire for a shorter route to the East did not vanish. Early in the following century, another great navigator, Henry Hudson, also employed by an emerging nation, would try unsuccessfully again to find a water passage through North America. Instead, he would reencounter the unclaimed prize of the "lost coast."

HUDSON REDISCOVERS MANHATTAN
THE VELASCO MAP

Untitled
DATE DEPICTED: 1610
DATE DRAWN: 1610
Pen and ink with watercolor on paper, 31 ½ x 43 ⅝ inches
General Archives of Simancas, Spain

A Spanish spy in the court of the English monarch James I produced or obtained The Velasco Map, which is the only surviving, contemporaneous map recording Manhattan and its vicinity as seen by Henry Hudson in 1609. The basis of the map was a confidential document prepared for the king in order to provide a comprehensive picture of English possessions in America based on the most current information. Don Alonso de Velasco, the Spanish ambassador to England, acquired or copied the map and sent it off to his own king with a coded letter explaining its contents. The Spanish were naturally concerned about English colonial activities in North Carolina and Virginia, just to the north of their own North American possessions.

The Velasco Map is especially precious because none of Hudson's original charts or even copies of them have survived. On his return from the New World, Hudson was captured by the English and his charts confiscated, never to be seen again. However, there is little doubt that this map's delineation of the New York area and the Hudson River was based on his lost charts. The journal of Hudson's first mate, Juet, has survived in printed form, and the descriptions there and the details on the map correspond in virtually all particulars.

On the map, versions of Manhattan's present name (*Manahatin and Manhatta*) appear for the first time. While there would be numerous permutations of the word on early maps, these first instances were the closest to its eventual form. Most believe the word to be a contraction of the Indian words for "island" and "hills" or "island of the hills," which accurately describes Manhattan's originally rugged, glacially formed topography. The other possibility is that Manhattan was derived from the name of the local Indian tribe.

Although the New York area does not appear well-detailed on the map, a closer look reveals a great deal about Hudson's experience there. The generally accurate mapping of the Lower Bay of New York Harbor reflects the seven days spent there by Hudson and his men. He entered the Lower Bay on September 2, 1609, in longboats, having anchored his main vessel, the *Halve Maen*, (Half Moon) just off Sandy Hook at the entrance of the harbor. It is clear from the map that Hudson also explored to some extent the two small rivers that enter the Lower Bay, the Raritan and the Arthur Kill, which can be seen on the map.

Moving north, the mapping becomes less accurate, although the small islands of the Upper Bay (Liberty, Ellis, and Governors) are roughly indicated, along with a fourth, which may have existed at the time. Hudson clearly did not discern that Manhattan was an island, which may seem a surprising oversight by someone noted to have been a careful explorer. However, Manhattan is actually a kind of peninsular island, barely separated from the mainland at its northern end by a very nar-row strait. Therefore, Hudson would have had to sail completely around it to ascertain its insularity. Obviously, he bypassed it in some haste. One reason for his hurry must have been the fatal confrontation with Indians in the Lower Bay, which left one of Hudson's men dead with an arrow through his throat. Hudson did apparently notice both the mouth of the Harlem River at the northern end of Manhattan, which he in fact entered on his return trip, and that of the East River to the south. A close examination of the map reveals two indentations in the approximate locations of the mouths of the two waterways.

Hudson's cursory exploration of Manhattan becomes even more understandable in light of the primary purpose of his voyage. Although an Englishman, Hudson was employed (against the wishes of his king) by a Dutch commercial organization, the Dutch East India Company, which monopolized the lucrative spice and silk trade in the East Indies. The profitability of the trade would be increased if a shorter route to the East Indies could be found. The Dutch had been required to sail west around Europe, then around Africa, and finally across the Indian Ocean to reach the East Indies. Therefore, when Hudson embarked on his voyage from Holland in 1609, his orders were to sail to the northeast over and around Russia and down the Asian mainland in the hope that a shorter route lay in this direction. Shortly into the voyage, his way was blocked by ice, and in defiance of his orders, he turned west and headed for America. His decision was motivated by the same thinking that had impelled most early voyagers to America, including Verrazano: there must be an easy passage somewhere through America leading to the East.

Looking again at the Velasco Map, one can see why Hudson was drawn to the

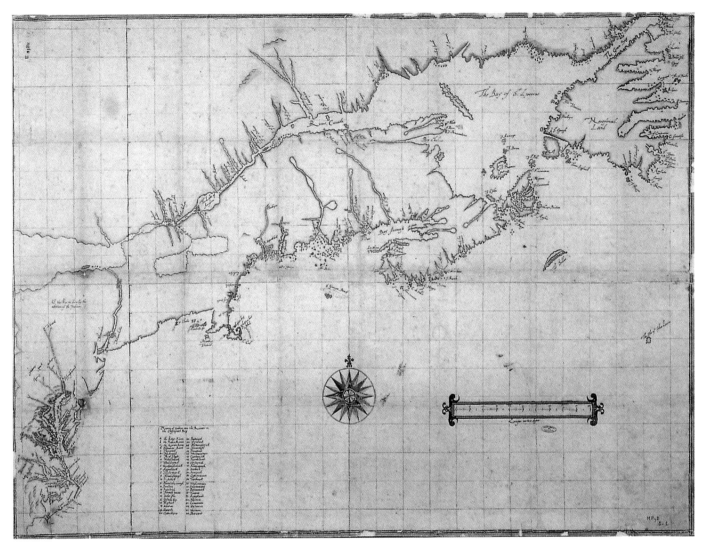

New York area to find this route to the East. It was in the center of the least-detailed, thus least-explored, stretch of the eastern seaboard below Canada, precisely the area that has been called the "lost coast." Although this area had been explored by Verrazano to some extent, it had literally faded from the map and European consciousness by the end of the sixteenth century.

Another factor in Hudson's decision to sail to the New York area was that his friend Captain John Smith had told Hudson that there was a river leading to the Western, or Pacific, Ocean at around 40 degrees latitude, nearly the exact location of New York Harbor. Therefore, when Hudson entered the harbor and soon after saw the majestic river emptying there, he must have felt that he had indeed found the gateway to the Pacific Ocean. Hudson followed the river to the northern limit of its navigability, just above the present town of Cohoes, at the confluence of the Mohawk River, which can be detected on the map.

Hudson's discoveries attracted neither the Dutch nor the English in significant numbers to the New York area in the years immediately following his voyage. From the point of view of the Dutch East India Company, the best that could be said for Hudson's explorations was that he eliminated two areas where a short cut to the East might be found. The English, on the other hand, as the existence of this map testifies, garnered precious cartographic data from Hudson's voyage, which illuminated a large, unclaimed territory with a great river and harbor at its center. However, domestic and foreign troubles prevented them from acting upon this advantage. Yet one piece of information brought back by Hudson eventually proved motivating to the Dutch: he reported that there was an abundance of beaver and other fur-bearing animals where he had explored. The pelt of the North American beaver, far superior to the European variety, had long been harvested by the French in Canada. The Dutch, who had been forcibly kept out of Canada by the French, saw the opportunity to acquire a territory of their own in the New York area.

The Velasco Map was discovered at the General Archives of Simancas, Spain, by Alexander Brown in the 1880s. Brown was a pioneering American historian, primarily of Virginia, who uncovered many previously unknown, primarily historical documents in archives throughout the world.

THE INVENTION OF NEW NETHERLANDS
BLOCK'S MAP OF THE NORTHEAST

Untitled
DATE DEPICTED: 1614
DATE DRAWN: 1614
CARTOGRAPHERS: ADRIAEN BLOCK AND CORNELIS DOETSZ
Pen and ink and watercolors with gold on vellum, 25 x 18⅛ inches
State Archives, The Hague, the Netherlands

Adriaen Block, a Dutch lawyer turned merchant-explorer, sailed back from America in 1614 with two items of great significance for the future of Manhattan: a full cargo of beaver pelts and a map. The rich fur of the North American beaver, long traded in European markets by the French, would provide the Dutch with the commercial incentive to colonize Manhattan. The map, in turn, was a declaration in graphic form of the creation of New Netherlands and was the cornerstone for the Dutch claim to the area. Not only was it the first map to depict Manhattan as an island, but it was also the earliest to illuminate and hence open up to the Dutch one of the most valuable stretches of coastline in the world. The map also preserves the names and original locations of all the Indian tribes of the area as they existed just prior to European settlement. Block was also the first European to explore and chart the Connecticut shoreline and river, Long Island Sound, and parts of Rhode Island, and to establish the insularity of Long Island.

Dutch merchants, desiring the wealth the New World had created for Spain and France, had long hoped to find an unclaimed territory that held an easily harvested, profitable product. Word of the beaver pelts carried back by Hudson drew their attention to the New York area. By 1614, four Dutch companies in New York Harbor were in rancorous competition for beaver pelts, Block's among them. On his return to the Netherlands, Block and his partners sought exclusive rights to the trade. The States General, the legislative body that could grant such a monopoly, was amenable to such an arrangement because competition among the companies had grown so violent as to threaten the trade altogether. The policy of the States General was to give preference to the company that explored and charted new areas and thereby expanded the sources of the pelts.

This map, most likely a contemporaneous copy of Block's original, was presented before the States General as documentation on October 11, 1614, to secure the monopoly of the beaver trade. Emblazoned in large letters across the entire northeastern portion of the finely drawn map was "NIEV NEDERLANDT", which must have played upon the territorial ambitions of the Dutch leadership. The States General declared that the area between 40 and 45 degrees latitude (most of the Northeast, including New York) would henceforth be called New Netherlands. At the suggestion of Block's Map, the Dutch province in the New World was simply asserted into existence. The States General also granted Block and his partners a charter allowing them the exclusive right to trade in the area through January 1, 1618.

Although Block is remembered mostly by the small island near the entrance of Long Island Sound bearing his name, he deserves to be ranked among the great explorers of North America as is demonstrated by what this chart records. Also,

New Yorkers may even recognize one of their own in his improvisational flair and tenacity. Shortly after Block reached New York Harbor in late summer of 1613, his ship, the *Tiger*, caught fire at anchor and burned down to its hull. Block and his men, with the help of Indians then constructed four huts in which to pass the winter, becoming the first known white people to build a settlement on Manhattan. The following spring they constructed a small ship (16 tons, 44½ feet in length) most likely from the surviving timbers of the *Tiger*. Called the *Onrust*, meaning "Restless," it was the first European vessel built on Manhattan.

It is likely that Block did not carefully survey Manhattan itself, which is crudely delineated on the map in a triangular shape. (The island of Manhattan on the map is designated by the word *Manhates*, which was not yet a true place-name but referred most likely to the Indian tribe that lived there.) This shape for the island would not be corrected on printed maps until c. 1655 in the Jansson-Visscher Map (see p. 18). A possible reason for Block's hasty treatment of Manhattan on the map is that his primary concern was to reach the uncharted coastal areas east of Manhattan.

From Manhattan, Block set off up the East River, negotiating its daunting tidal current, which he aptly named "Helle-gatt" (Hell Gate). From the East River, he entered Long Island Sound ("Groote Bay"), being the first known European to approach it from this direction. He explored the Connecticut coastline and entered the Connecticut River, following it until probably just north of Hartford. He named it the Fresh ("Versche") River, possibly to distinguish it from the briny Hudson. From here he veered back south to Long Island (which is shown as divided into three islands), followed its coast, and rounded Montauk Point, thereby proving that Long Island was indeed an island. He then sailed to the north, rounded Cape Cod, which is curiously bisected on the map, and went as far as Nahant Bay, just north of Boston. He even investigated Plymouth Bay six years before the Pilgrims landed there. As a result of this voyage, the eastern seaboard from New York to Massachusetts, formerly the "lost coast," was at last truly found again.

Despite Block's careful exploration and mapping, it would be another ten years before the Dutch actually sent colonists to the area. However, his map probably did affect the Dutch method of settlement. Instead of concentrating colonists in one location, the Dutch placed them throughout the lower Northeast, possibly because the area had been so well mapped by Block.

Block's Map remained the prototype for the depiction of the Northeast until the middle of the seventeenth century. The most popular Dutch printed map of the Northeast of the period, Willem Janszoon Blaeu's handsome "Nova Belgica et Anglia Nova" (1635), is nearly an identical copy of Block's Map. Even the great Jansson-Visscher Map, published c. 1655, relied on Block's Map for its general outlines.

Block's work was discovered in 1853 by the American historian J. R. Brodhead in the State Archives in The Hague, where it remains. Recent research has demonstrated that the map was not prepared by Block alone. It is now believed that Cornelis

Doetsz, a cartographer from Edam, prepared the general outline of the map and that Block provided the detail. This is borne out by the divergent styles of lettering and drawing found on the manuscript.

As an archeological postscript to Block's story, a part of what is possibly the charred hull of his original ship, the *Tiger*, was found in 1916 by workers excavating a subway extension in the vicinity of Greenwich and Dey streets. This artifact is now housed in the Museum of the City of New York. However, it was reported in 1916 that only part of the hull was recovered and that a good portion of it still remained at the site. In the mid and late 1960s, the foundation of the World Trade Center was being dug in the area of the original discovery. An effort was made to find the remainder of the hull, but only two cannons that might have belonged to the *Tiger* were found.

EARLY RECONNAISSANCE
THE MINUIT CHART

TITLE: Noort Rivier in Niew Neerlandt
DATE DEPICTED: c. 1630
DATE DRAWN: c. 1660
CARTOGRAPHER: PETER MINUIT(?)
Pen and ink with watercolor on paper, 18¾ x 27⅛ inches
Library of Congress

Copied from a lost original drawn just six years after the initial settlement of Manhattan, the Minuit Chart is the only surviving cartographic record from the first years of New Amsterdam. It demonstrates how quickly the Dutch achieved cartographic command over the Manhattan area and the lower Hudson River. The chart preserves the original place-names the Dutch applied throughout the area, which otherwise would be unknown to us, since most were not permanently adopted. Manhattan and the Hudson River valley are seen on the chart during the brief period when the Dutch were the only European power holding sway in the area. All future maps would show English settlements in the midst of those of the Dutch, portending the inevitable collapse of the New Netherlands.

Unlike the Pilgrims' religiously driven quest to find refuge in the New World, the Dutch settlement of Manhattan in 1624 was a speculative commercial venture. It was sponsored by the Dutch West India Company, a unique private trading company, which had a sanctioned monopoly to develop various areas in North America. Therefore, the first colonists who disembarked in Manhattan from the appropriately named ship the *Nieu Nederland* were employees of the company. This commercial impetus behind the city's settlement would color the entire Dutch experience there, and for that matter, the personality of the city throughout its history.

The product that was intended to be the mainstay of the colony and enrich the company was the fur of the beaver and other animals, which Adriaen Block and other Dutch merchants had already traded successfully. A good chart of the complex waterways of the area where the beaver made its home would have been a necessity. Peter Minuit, who is best remembered for his purchase of Manhattan for sixty guilders ($24) in trinkets, was a highly skilled cartographer. As the colony's second director general and also as an individual who sought private gain from the beaver trade, Minuit was expected to chart every river, bay, and inlet (or kill) in the Dutch purview. The original of this map was surely one result of this effort, although Minuit's precise connection to it is not known.

On the map, which is oriented with north to the right, Manhattan is called Manatuns Houck. This usage indicates that the word is here being applied clearly as a true place-name for the island. A four-bastioned fort, named Fort Amsterdam, is shown on the southern tip, or upper left, of the island. Originally an ambitious pentagonal fort was planned for the location. This proved too great an undertaking, and the simpler structure represented on the chart was decided upon in 1627 or 1628. However, the lines for the pentagonal fort were laid out by the engineer Crijn Frederikszoon in 1625. It has recently been shown that the configuration of present-day Pearl, Beaver, State, and Stone streets

corresponds to that of the walls of this originally planned fort. What were to have been its walls must have instead been used as roads by the original settlers.

One should not be misled by the distorted triangular shape of Manhattan on the chart; this is a most remarkable map for its period. Both the complex channel through New York's large, double-bay harbor and the Hudson River, the area's two key waterways, are mapped with impressive accuracy. To the north is shown Fort Orange, later Albany, a key outpost for Dutch traders and their earliest permanent settlement in North America. The chart terminates at the confluence of the Hudson and Mohawk rivers near present-day Troy. (The northern stretch of the Hudson River appears below the southern section on the chart.) For most of the river, dotted lines mark off its navigable sections, and continuous depth soundings are given. Some scholars claim that Minuit's is the earliest map to provide depths in a continuous manner.

The chart takes great pains to help the mariner enter and navigate through New York Harbor's two large bays. Since simply finding its entrance must have caused difficulty at the time, a guiding landmark is given in the note just below Sandy Hook along the upper left-hand portion of the chart. In translation, it reads: "This is the High hook of the bay and may be easily recognized as one approaches from the South." This refers to the Navesink Highlands, which act as a convenient signpost for the harbor. Although there is an enticingly wide berth between Sandy Hook and Rockaway Point in Brooklyn through which the harbor might be entered, nearly the entire way is blocked by dangerous shoals that are indicated on the chart. (Sandy Hook is shown as an island, which it may have been at the time.) Once in the Lower Bay ("Landt Bay"), the pilot is

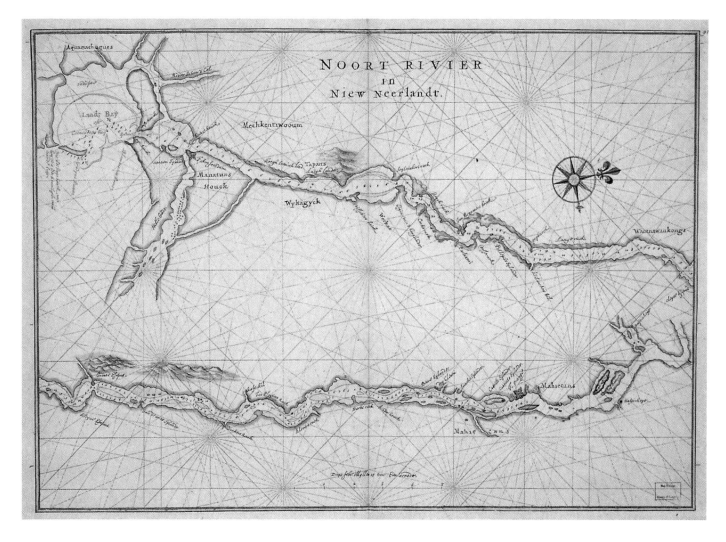

shown the channel by means of the direction of the depth soundings that take him through the Narrows to the Upper Bay.

The path of the soundings continues up the Hudson River along the west side of Manhattan, which was probably the preferred side for anchoring. At the time the map was drawn, New Amsterdam did not have a pier or dock, so all shipping was forced to anchor. The reason for the possible preference for the west side is clearly seen in the several crosses marked along the eastern shore of Manhattan indicating the very treacherous currents and eddies of the aptly named Hell Gate, an original Dutch appellation that has survived. However, two invitingly large bays (Kips and Turtle) are shown along the lower shore of the east side; they also could have been used as anchorages. Although the chart greatly exaggerates the sizes of the two bays, it

gives some sense of how large they were before being filled in.

New Amsterdam in its early years was a sputtering enterprise. It was little more than a commercial outpost with no design for self-sufficiency and permanence. By 1629, the population had only reached about three hundred. Most settlers remained for only as long as their contracts with the Dutch West India Company obligated them. Also, once they arrived in the challenging environment of the Northeast, most gravitated toward the lucrative fur trade instead of agriculture or other productive activities that would have bolstered the colony. Evidence of the individualism embraced by many of the first settlers is that Minuit himself abandoned New Amsterdam only to return to the New World some years later to direct a rival Swedish settlement on the Delaware River.

To help remedy this situation, the Dutch West India Company introduced in 1629 the "patroon" system. It in effect privatized the process of settlement by granting large tracts of land to prominent Hollanders (mostly company directors). The land in turn would be subleased to emigrants, who would develop it and share in the profits. The most famous and long-lasting of these patroonships (and the only one even marginally successful) was that of Kiliaen van Rensselaer (not shown on the chart). For several reasons the patroon system did not work, the chief one probably being the lure of quick profit held out by the fur trade that continued to draw colonists away from farming. As a result, New Amsterdam would continue to struggle throughout its first two decades of existence.

SPREADING THE NEWS OF NEW AMSTERDAM
The De Laet-Gerritsz Map

TITLE: Nova Anglia, Novum Belgium Et Virginia
DATE DEPICTED: c. 1625–30
CARTOGRAPHER: HESSEL GERRITSZ
PUBLISHED: JOHANNES DE LAET, *De Nieuwe Wereldt ofte*
Beschrijvinghe van West-Indien, SECOND EDITION, LEYDEN, 1630
Copperplate engraving, 11 x 14⅛ inches
Private collection

Many educated Europeans of the seventeenth century first became geographically acquainted with Manhattan through the simple but well-drawn De Laet-Gerritsz Map. It was the first map with a generally correct view of Manhattan and its surroundings to appear in a commercially published work. It was, in fact, the first widely circulated map to correctly delineate Manhattan as an island. A few earlier works did also show an insular Manhattan, namely Willem Janszoon Blaeu's two large maps of the Atlantic seaboard—the "West Indische Paskaerts" of about 1617 and 1621—as well as Adriaen Block's chart of 1614 (see p. 8). Also, Blaeu's large globe of 1622 had Manhattan as an island on it. However, the circulation of these works was limited to an official and commercial elite. The De Laet-Gerritsz Map is also the earliest on which the name of the fledgling settlement of New Amsterdam appeared. As in the case of the Minuit Chart (see p. 10), the word for Manhattan on this map, *Manbattes,* no longer referred to the tribe of Indians living there but had come to stand for the place itself.

Geopolitically, the map reflects the relative comfort briefly enjoyed by the Dutch vis-à-vis their English neighbors in the early years of the New Netherlands enterprise. On the map, ample buffer zones are suggested to exist between New Netherlands and its English neighbors to the south and northeast, Virginia and New England. The latter is seen here as obligingly confined to the coastal area. This sense of comfort, both actual and cartographic, would soon dissipate, and regional maps produced a few decades later would show English settlements well within what is here an unsullied Dutch sphere.

The De Laet-Gerritsz Map follows the Block Map in its triangular delineation of Manhattan and in giving short shrift to Staten Island in relative size. Nevertheless, several place-names are seen for the first time on the De Laet-Gerritsz Map in addition to the ones mentioned above. They are "Noordt Rivier" for the Hudson River, an appellation that persisted until early in the nineteenth century, and "Zuyd Rivier" for the Delaware River. "Coenraed Bay" for Raritan Bay and "Godyns punt" for Sandy Hook are also names seen for the first time.

This map and the book in which it appeared were the work of two of the most important figures in Dutch expansion of the period. No cartographer played a more central role in mapping Dutch colonial efforts at their most dynamic moment than Hessel Gerritsz (1581/82–1632), the actual maker of this map. His connection with the New York area extended back to Henry Hudson, as Gerritsz was the first to publish in 1612 a report of his voyage, on which Manhattan was rediscovered. In 1617, Gerritsz was appointed the official cartographer of the Dutch East India Company. In this position, he reviewed all the charts of returning captains, thus giving him access to the latest cartographic informa-

tion. The austere style of this map is typical of Gerritsz, who did not work in the florid manner of many Dutch mapmakers of the period, as most of the maps he produced were intended for use at sea by merchant captains rather than for the armchair sailor.

In 1636, Johannes Jansson reengraved a larger format version of this map with the same title but added the decorative flourishes more characteristic of the Dutch style. It was virtually an exact copy save for two changes. A quite important one is the addition of a stretch of river at the northern terminus of the Hudson River that could represent the Mohawk River or the beginning east-west stretch of the Hudson River. The other change is slightly more coverage in the northeastern corner of the map with the addition of a few place-names. Also, Blaeu's famous and beautifully engraved map of the northeast, "Nova Belgica et Anglia Nova," first published in 1635, while based primarily on the Block chart, nevertheless adopted many of the new place-names that were first seen on the De Laet-Gerritsz Map.

Johannes De Laet (1583–164?), author of the text that accompanied the map, was a prime mover in the founding of New Netherlands. He was one of the so-called Heeren XIX, or the nineteen lord directors of the Dutch West India Company, which sponsored the colony. Moreover, he had a direct financial and personal interest in the area as co-patroon of Rensselaerswyck, a vast grant of land occupying hundreds of

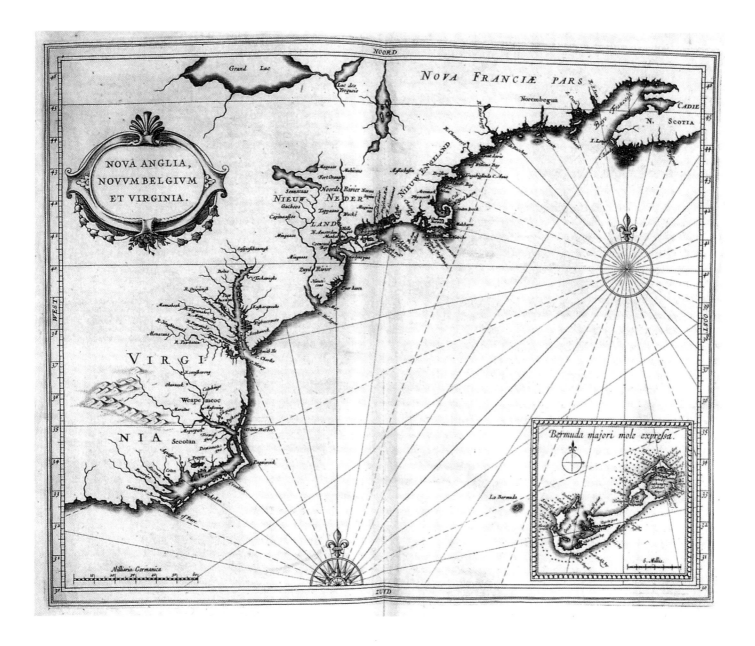

square miles around Fort Orange, near present-day Albany. His daughter and son-in-law had settled in the area. However, De Laet, like most other patroons, never traveled to New Netherlands. De Laet's book is still regarded as one of the best sources on the Dutch colonies. He was able to draw upon the files of the West India Company, including material such as Block's logbooks, as well as upon personal correspondence. The first edition of the work, which was in Dutch, was published in Leyden in 1625 and entitled *Nieuwe Wereldt ofte Beschrijvinghe van West-Indien. . . .* This edition had ten maps but did not

include this one. The second edition of 1630 added this map of the Northeast and three others. In 1633, a Latin translation appeared with the same maps, and in the same year a French translation of the Latin was also issued. As a result of these various editions, knowledge of New Amsterdam reached seventeenth-century readers of travel and exploration narratives, who were typically merchants, officials, and the intellectually curious.

It is initially baffling that the Dutch would be so forthcoming about their colonial efforts to the extent of allowing the publication of a book about them. The

Iberian nations, for example, forbade the publication of maps relating to their New World colonies. The openness of the Dutch perhaps sprang from a need to excite interest in the Dutch people for colonization. From the very first, when Manhattan was settled for the Dutch by French-speaking Walloons and Huguenots, refugees from what is today Belgium, few Dutchmen could be coaxed to emigrate. A book like De Laet's would therefore have had the effect of making the New World less forbidding to the reluctant Dutch. Moreover, as a co-patroon, De Laet needed to find potential colonists to profit from his land grant.

13

METROPOLIS IN EMBRYO
THE MANATUS MAP

TITLE: Manatus Gelegen op de Noot Rivier
DATE DEPICTED: 1639
DATE DRAWN: c. 1665–70
Pen and ink and watercolor on paper, 26⅝ x 18¼ inches
Library of Congress

Not discovered until the late nineteenth century, the hand-drawn Manatus Map is something of a Rosetta stone for the early history of Manhattan. It was the result of the first careful survey of Manhattan and the surrounding area conducted by its early settlers. As one of the greatest students of the city's history, I. N. Phelps Stokes, has observed: "There is, perhaps, no other city in the world, having equal claims to antiquity, that can boast such a record of the early years of its existence." The map yields the names of all the early settlers who had large landholdings or farms (called *bouweries* by the Dutch) just fifteen years after initial settlement. Also included is an inventory of the few structures on Manhattan during its initial period of development, most of which are described as still under construction. It also displays the dispersed pattern of settlement that marked the early years of the colony's existence.

When originally drawn in 1639, the Manatus Map provided for the first time the generally correct shape of Manhattan. Also, the smaller waterways in the area, in particular the Harlem River along the northern part of the island, are well-delineated for the first time. The map also conveys a sense of Manhattan's originally rugged and hilly topography, which has been planed nearly flat in the course of the city's development. In fact, the word *Manatus*, an early name for Manhattan, is believed to mean "island of the hills." The map shows that Manhattan originally had

several bays and deeply penetrating inlets, or kills as the Dutch called them. These, too, have been eradicated by development and are now remembered only through neighborhood names like Kips and Turtle bays. Visible also on the map (and shown with dotted lines) is the large lake called Collect Pond or Fresh Water that originally occupied a considerable area in lower Manhattan.

It is possible that the original of this map was prepared by the colonists at the request of the directors of the Dutch West India Company to display the pattern of settlement resulting from the institution of the patroon system (see p. 11). What the map reveals is a remarkably dispersed configuration of settlements. In addition to Manhattan, settled areas include what are today the four outer boroughs and parts of New Jersey, Long Island, and Westchester. Thus, even at this early date, the map presents in embryo the suburban network that would form the greater metropolitan area. This decentralized approach to settlement characterized the Dutch enterprise from the very beginning. Of the 130 original colonists, it is believed that only eight settled on Manhattan, while the remainder fanned out as far as the Delaware River valley, Connecticut, and Albany. Later colonists arriving in the 1630s also followed this trend. It may have been this picture of unfocused settlement on the map that prompted the directors in 1643 to order the colonists to consolidate themselves into a

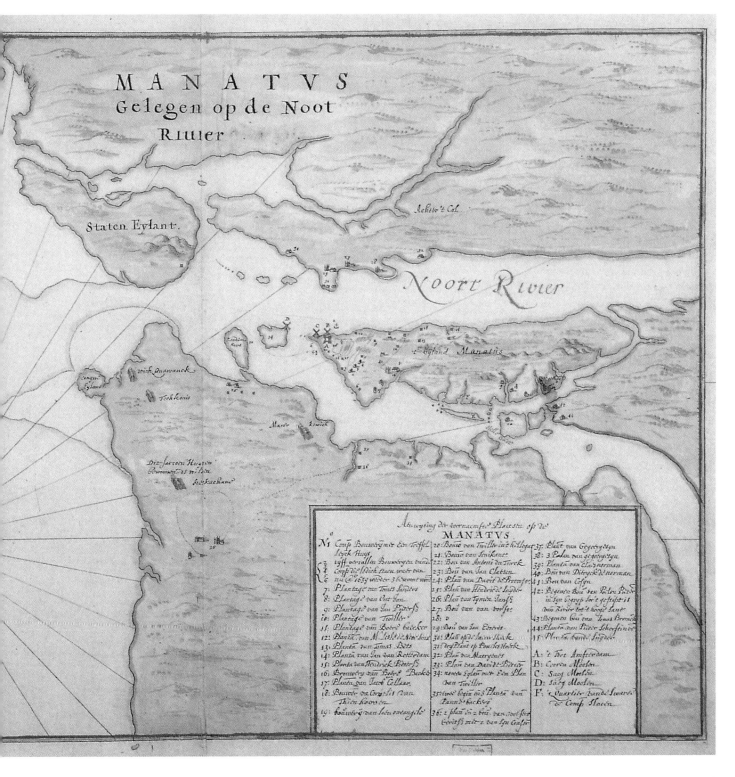

town in the area of the fort seen on the map at the southern tip of the island. This would allow for more effective defense against Indian attacks, enable more orderly growth, and provide a market center.

The names of the city's first landowners appear in the legend in the bottom right corner of the map. For the most part these names are not familiar and have not been memorialized in the city's history. One exception is Jonas Bronck, after whom the Bronx is named. Many of these early settlers viewed their foray to the New World as temporary employment from which they would eventually return home. Further, the West India Company's policies attracted land speculators, who often quickly sold off their grants. The list of names also reveals that ethnic diversity characterized the city's population from the beginning. On it are several English, a Norwegian, a Dane (Bronck), and even a Moroccan. One reason for such diversity was that not enough Hollanders could be enticed to emigrate from the mother country, which was enjoying its Golden Age, making it necessary to recruit colonists from other countries. A chilling note is struck by the presence of slave quarters in stark isolation on the map (F in the legend) in the area of present-day Sixty-third Street near the East River.

New Amsterdam at the period of the map contrasted sharply with the orderly homeland. Roads, indicated on the map by dashed lines, were haphazardly laid, being merely muddy farm lanes filled with sheep and pigs. Nearly all houses at the time were ramshackle timber-constructed affairs, roofed with reed and straw, and arranged in no particular order. Even the fort, although begun shortly after the first settlers arrived, was continually in disrepair. With too many fur traders and sailors and too few productive farmers in the population, New

Amsterdam was a rough, brawling place. By 1639, there had already been executions for manslaughter and convictions for robbery. Even more respectable citizens dissipated their energies through numerous lawsuits. Yet, as often has been the case through most of its history, many in Manhattan in 1639 managed to prosper. Already the harbor teemed with the ships of many nations. The map indicates with two anchors and the numbers 2 and 3, one each in the Hudson and East rivers, where ships anchored for loading. Also, faintly drawn lines indicate the routes followed by ships through the harbor.

The map pictured here is a copy of the 1639 original which is now lost, and was made about 1665–70. The date of the original is indicated in number 6 in the legend below the map, which reads in translation: "Five bouweries of the company, three of which are now (anno 1639) again occupied." The copy of the map reproduced here surfaced in the late nineteenth century and was donated to the Library of Congress in 1911 by the collector Henry Harrisse. Early in this century, another copy of the map, nearly identical to this one and thought to have been drafted at about the same time, was discovered, remarkably, on the walls of the Villa Castello near Florence. (See p. 26 for details on how this map came to find its way to Italy.)

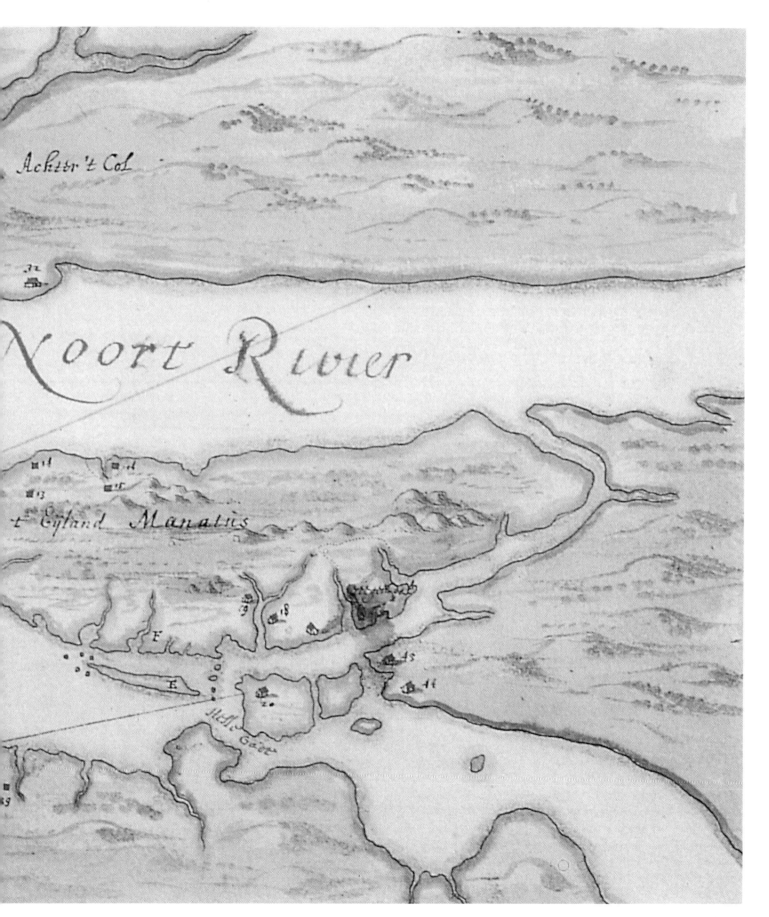

Achter 't Col

Noort Rivier

't Eyland Manatus

Helle Gate

THE COLONY IN CRISIS
THE JANSSON-VISSCHER MAP

TITLE: Novi Belgii Novaeque Angliae Nec Non Partis Virginiae Tabula
DATE DEPICTED: c. 1651–53
CARTOGRAPHER: AUGUSTINE HERMANN(?)
PUBLISHED: CLAES JANZOON VISSCHER, *Atlas Contractus*, AMSTERDAM,
UNDATED (C. 1655–77)
Hand-colored copperplate engraving highlighted with gold, 18⅜ x 21⅞ *inches*
Private collection

The masterful and beautiful Jansson-Visscher Map showed educated Europeans of the mid-seventeenth century for the first time what New Amsterdam looked like and also provided them with a remarkably precise idea of its geographic context. Unlike most of the previously illustrated maps, which were one-of-a-kind works, the Jansson-Visscher Map was something of a best-seller that reached a broad audience. It appeared in thirty-one issues that were published as late as the mid-eighteenth century in several countries.

One reason for the map's long publication life was simply its high quality. Its cartography was so exact that one historian observed that most areas of Europe were not better mapped at the time. The Jansson-Visscher Map was the first printed map to delineate the shape of Manhattan correctly. It was the summation of all the surveys of New Netherlands conducted by Dutch colonists since their arrival and is believed to include every place-name in use in 1650 in the Northeast. Evidence of the high regard for the map in its day was that in 1685 an example of it was used by William Penn to settle the boundary between Pennsylvania and Maryland.

The probable origins of the Jansson-Visscher Map are interwoven with a pivotal period of New Amsterdam's history. By the mid-1640s the settlement was on the verge of collapse. Incompetent directors, virulent Indian attacks, lack of public education, onerous taxes, and crumbling defenses made it increasingly unlivable. The colonial leadership attributed most of the problems to shortsighted, avaricious management by the Dutch West India Company. Finally, in 1649 a contingent of New Amsterdam residents led by Adriaen van der Donck sailed to the mother country to bring their protest against the rule of the company to the States General, the legislative body of the Netherlands. In Van der Donck's *Remonstrance*, the document containing the colonists' protests and proposals, there is a reference to a "perfect map of the country and its situation." Moreover, all the place-names and geographic details referred to in the *Remonstrance* can be found on the Jansson-Visscher Map. Van der Donck was therefore most likely using a manuscript prototype of the Jansson-Visscher Map to support his case to the States General. Although he did not succeed in wresting control of New Amsterdam from the company, many crucial reforms were enacted that helped save the colony.

With Van der Donck's protest, which was carried out in widely circulated and inflammatory pamphlets, New Amsterdam, about which little had been known in Europe, suddenly became a cause célèbre. Ambitious Dutch map publishers, eager to put forth a map of the area, would naturally have been drawn to the one presented by the colonists in their protest. What was most likely a reduced version of this map was then published anonymously in separate sheets. (The map's association with the colonial protest made it an embarrassment to the still-powerful Dutch West India Company.) Next, Johannes Jansson, one of the leading cartographic publishers in the Netherlands, included a copy of the map (but without the bird's-eye view) in his atlas of 1652. Since he was the first publisher of the unsigned map, he is often mistaken as its author. Another Dutch publisher, Claes Jansoon Visscher, actually engraved the map. (Some historians have conjectured that the actual author of the map was Augustine Hermann, one of the most able and prosperous citizens of New Amsterdam.) In 1655, Visscher himself then published in his own atlas a corrected version of the map that included the bird's-eye view, which is reproduced here. Again, Visscher has erroneously been credited with the authorship of the view, the actual artist of which is unknown. Visscher produced five states of the map, which were followed by at least twenty-five others by various mapmakers and publishers.

The Visscher View is a somewhat idealized but generally accurate look at New Amsterdam roughly twenty-five years after its initial settlement. Its perspective is from Governors Island, southeast of Manhattan. While it shows the structures that are known to have existed in New Amsterdam at the time (and identifies them in a key below the view), it does not convey the deterioration that had befallen parts of the town. For example, the fort, which was in a state of disrepair at the time, is seen here fully intact. A detail in the view that has puzzled historians is the two-posted structure (G) just to the left of the tall crane in the center foreground. It is identified as a gallows, although there is no record of such a structure in the city during the Dutch Period. In any case, someone or something can be seen hanging from the structure in the view. One source says it is a tarred corpse left hanging to warn potential wrongdoers.

Despite its general accuracy, the Jansson-Visscher Map misleads in a most important way. The size and breadth of the lettering of NOVA BELGICA NIEUW NEDERLANDT in relation to NOVA ANGLIA NIEUW ENGELANDT on the map is most deceptive

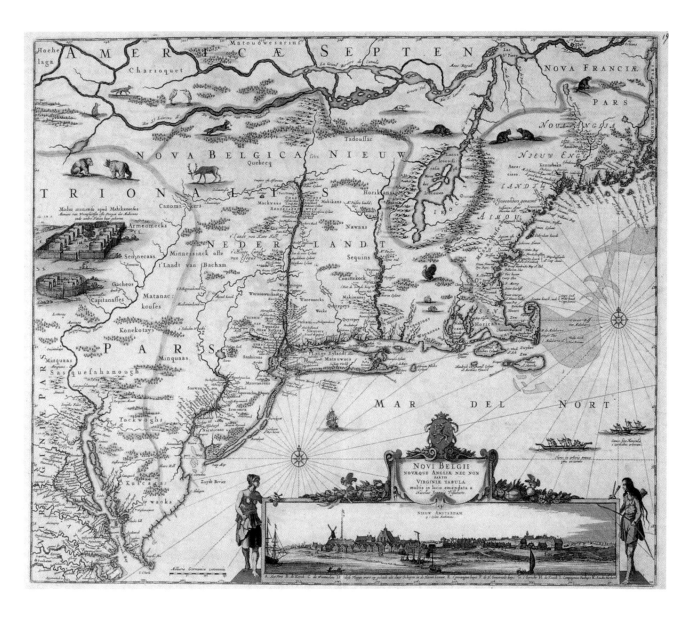

in regard to the relative strength of the Dutch and the English in the Northeast at the time. In 1650, Peter Stuyvesant, then the director general of New Netherlands, signed a treaty with English colonial leaders, the terms of which delineate the actual situation when the map was published. The agreement put the eastern limit of Dutch territory at a line drawn north from the Greenwich-Stamford area of Connecticut and forced the Dutch to cede all of Long Island east of Oyster Bay. While the treaty was very costly to the Dutch, Stuyvesant regarded it as a diplomatic triumph to have induced the much more powerful English to agree to a border of any kind. The map does, however, accurately show the extent

to which the English had dispersed throughout the Northeast, even well within Dutch strongholds. Hartford ("Herfort") and New Haven had grown into thriving English towns. The more recent English towns along the Connecticut shore can be seen closing in on New Amsterdam: Gilfort, Milfort, Stratford, and Stamford. Even closer to home were the English settlements in Queens and Long Island: Flushing, Heemstee (Hempstead), Hamton, Greenwyck (Greenswick), Gravesant, and Mispat. Although the map depicted the areas fourteen years prior to the English capture of New Amsterdam, one can read on it the inevitability of the Dutch demise.

A possible reason for the map's false

presentation of Dutch strength in the New World was again the need to lure potential emigrants. The attractively engraved map with its view of the bucolic village of New Amsterdam was just one of many instances of the deceptive marketing of America in the Netherlands. Because of the difficulty of attracting Dutch citizens willing to emigrate to New Netherlands, the West India Company resorted to unscrupulous promises and claims to lure colonists. Another factor explaining the map's overstatement of Dutch power was that Stuyvesant did not inform his superiors in the Netherlands of the treaty with the English until 1652. By that time, the map was most likely already engraved.

NEW LISBON
THE JOLLAIN VIEW

TITLE: Nowel Amsterdam En LAmerique, 1672
PUBLISHED: GÉRARD OR FRANÇOIS JOLLAIN, PARIS, 1672(?)
Hand-colored copperplate engraving, 12⅜ x 19¾ inches
Collection of Leonard Milberg

Despite the many editions of the Jansson-Visscher Map (see p. 18) with its accurate bird's-eye view of New Amsterdam, most Europeans of the seventeenth century would still have been unaware of what the settlement actually looked like. An indication of this is a curious view and map that was issued by Jollain in France, a country where the Jansson-Visscher Map was not published. As one looks for identifying landmarks and structures on the Jollain View, it quickly becomes apparent that the place depicted has nothing whatsoever to do with New Amsterdam. Jollain's work is a complete fabrication. He has even misnamed the place; New Amsterdam had been New York for eight years when the view was published. Jollain must have felt that a representation of a relatively recent American settlement would enhance the marketability of his atlas of city views and plans that contained the view. Since only about a half-dozen copies of the view are known to exist, Jollain's duplicity apparently did not result in commercial success.

Particularly amusing are the little touches on the view meant to enhance its credibility. For example, the area map inset in the upper left-hand corner is just slightly more accurate than the view itself. While it does show New Amsterdam at the mouth of a river, the town is enclosed by an elongated Long Island that stretches to meet the New Jersey coast. Hellegaet (Hell Gate), the water passage between the East River and Long Island Sound, is shown as a siz-

able region northeast of the city. For some reason, Jollain placed Quebec and Le Chateau de Nassau on hills overlooking the town. Also, the body of water fronting the city is called Mer du Nort, an early name for the North Atlantic Ocean, rather than Rivière du Nort, one of several names at that time for the Hudson River.

The question remains, If the Jollain View is not of New Amsterdam, what, if anyplace, is depicted? In a rather audacious example of self-plagiarism, there is in Jollain's atlas a view of Lisbon that is nearly identical to the one of New Amsterdam. Moreover, Jollain's plan of Lisbon was copied from yet another view of that city done a few years earlier by the Dutch cartographic publisher Frederick de Wit. It, in turn, was copied from a work by Braun and Hogenberg, which appeared at the end of the sixteenth century. Therefore, the prototype for a supposed 1672 view of New Amsterdam is a view of Lisbon from about 1580.

While Jollain's is perhaps the most spectacular of the fictional views of New York, it was not the only one. As late as 1776, F. X. Habermann in Augsburg published a series of five engravings chronicling events of the American Revolution that occurred in New York City, the settings of which were completely fabricated.

NOWEL AMSTERDAM

EN L'AMERIQVE * 1672.

la Iustice

Le Chateau de Nassau

Quebec

A. het Tuchthuys
c'esta dire Maison de
Dicipline, aussi en icele
et renfermoi des
aus que l'on fait travailler.

Eglise ou Temple
de Bikerque

Hospital

Place
de la
Bourse

Maison de Ville

Bureau des
Entrées

L'amirauté

Grand Ritlay

Mer du Nort

NEW AMSTERDAMERS IN NEW JERSEY
THE GOOS CHART

TITLE: Paskaerte Van de Zuydt en Noordt Revier in Nieu Nederlant . . .
DATE DEPICTED: c. 1656
PUBLISHED: PIETER GOOS, *Zee-Atlas ofte Water-Wereld*, AMSTERDAM, 1666
Hand-colored copperplate engraving, 19⅞ x 23⅝ inches
Private collection

At the height of the Dutch Golden Age, numerous shops could be found along the bustling waterfront of Amsterdam selling charts, atlases, and pilot books of the far-flung territories touched by Dutch commerce. Among the busiest of the shops was the one evocatively called In the Golden Sea Mirror, owned by Pieter Goos. There one would have encountered a strikingly diverse clientele of hard-bitten seamen and ruddy-faced pilots side by side with prosperous shipowners and merchants. Goos's success derived precisely from his talent for producing atlases and pilot guides that appealed to the armchair sailor at least as much as to the working one. Remarkably, he accomplished this while, for the most part, republishing the work of others. With the exception of the work illustrated here and a few others, all of the charts in the atlas that contained this one were copied from an earlier work by Hendrik Doncker. Despite this, Goos was able to succeed in the highly competitive Dutch chart trade in part because of the sheer beauty of his work. Like the present example, his charts had rich but never overpowering ornamentation; exquisite hand-coloring, often with the lavish use of gold; and paper of the highest quality, which was often doubled to give greater thickness. Moreover, like the name of his shop, his charts were able to call up the romance of the sea and faraway lands for the armchair sailor. This, after all, has always been one of the great lures of maps, especially of finely wrought early

maps. The appeal of Goos's charts has endured, as they are eagerly sought after by collectors today.

Clever marketing seems to have been another factor in Goos's success. That he quite consciously aimed his charts at both the armchair and actual sailor is revealed by a bit of disingenuous promotion found on the frontispiece of his atlas. In some copies of the atlas, the frontispiece states that the atlas is very useful for sailors and pilots, as well as for all gentlemen and merchants; on others, however, the order of intended users is reversed.

The Goos Chart is an admirably spare, uncluttered effort, perhaps reflective of its maker's intention to include only verified detail. Moreover, its depiction of Manhattan and vicinity is better than that found on any printed map or chart that preceded it. Although the scale is quite small, one can still see that the shape of Manhattan is correct save for the northern area being a bit too wide. It has a new variant spelling of Manhattan, "Mannathans." Also, the Bronx is here called Broncken, an intermediate version of the word on its way to its final form. The chart also reveals other place-names in the New York area that had their origin in the Dutch period, for example, Hoboken, Maspeth, Red Hook, the Arthur Kill, and the Raritan River. Other parts of the harbor and vicinity are generally correct, except that the Harlem River is too wide, the Upper Bay too narrow, and Staten Island quite misshapen. The chart is

also valuable as a record of the several small rivers, or kills, that flowed at one time into the East River and Upper Bay from Queens and Brooklyn.

Among the numerous charts of the Northeast produced by Dutch map publishers of the period, only this one and Arent Roggeveen's of 1675 focus specifically on the New York City/New Jersey area. In fact, Goos's is the earliest printed map to focus on what would become New Jersey. Displaying these particular areas on a single chart, however, did make sense, since New Jersey, and, in particular, the Delaware River area, were of great interest to the Dutch through the entire history of New Netherlands. In fact, Dutch presence on the Delaware River, which originated with the construction of Fort Nassau (shown on the chart on the southern side of the river at the point of its elbowlike bend) in 1623, predated the founding of New Amsterdam by two years.

An ambitious colony called New Amstel was planned for the area in 1656 under the sponsorship of the city of Amsterdam. There was great excitement generated by this venture, which many hoped would yield valuable timber for masts as well as the always desirable animal pelts. In fact, the colony was the subject of an intensive publicity campaign, and it was as a part of this effort that Goos's chart focusing on the intended location of the colony was most likely issued. This is borne out by the chart's cartouche enclosing the title, which incorporates the arms of the colony. With the exception of the beaver pelts draped along the bottom of the cartouche, its design is identical to that of the arms of the small village of Nieuwer Amstel outside of Amsterdam, after which the colony was named. The chart itself, however, does not show New Amstel, which was not settled until 1657; presumably an exact

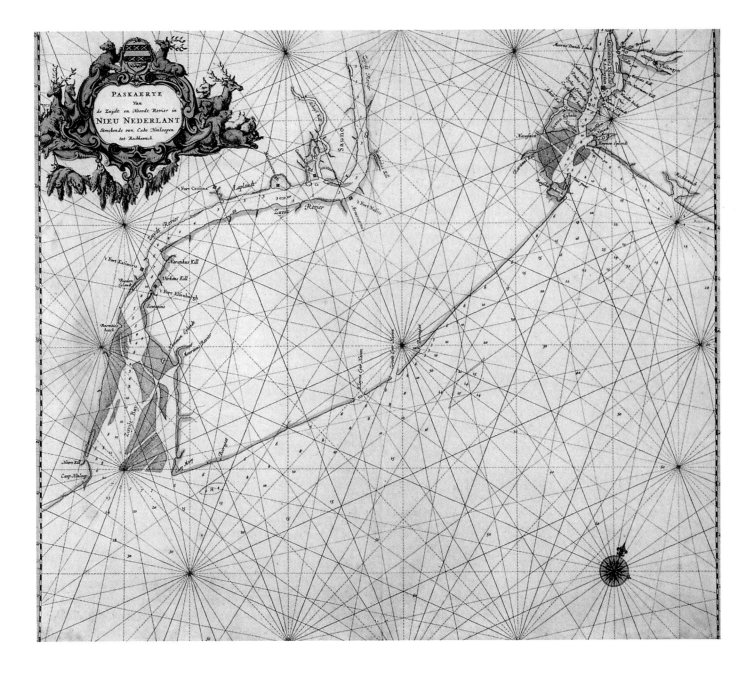

location was not selected for the colony while it was being promoted.

The Goos chart was therefore most likely first published separately in 1656 before being included in Goos's 1666 atlas. This is further supported by the facts that the chart is found in only some copies of the atlas and that it is significantly larger than all of the other charts in the atlas. (As a result, individual examples of the chart that have been extracted from the atlas had often been cropped by the binder to conform to the sizes of the atlas' other charts.) It was

therefore an already existing chart that was inserted in some copies of the atlas.

The publishing of a map with ten-year-old cartography, as was the case here, was not at all unusual in the seventeenth century. Therefore, even though Goos's chart appeared two years after the British conquest of New Netherlands, it is not surprising that there is absolutely no suggestion of the event on the chart. Dutch maps, in fact, were exceptionally slow to acknowledge the loss of New Netherlands and generally did not begin to do so for about fifteen years

after the event. Even a number of Dutch maps published in the following century continued to show New Netherlands. This is another example of the way that maps can disguise reality by perpetuating a nation's fantasies about its power. It also suggests that the Dutch, once the master cartographers of the world, began to produce derivative and uncorrected maps in the late seventeenth and early eighteenth centuries. Therefore, it seems that the fortunes of the Dutch as both colonizers and cartographers roughly paralleled each other.

THE BRAVE PLACE
THE CASTELLO PLAN

TITLE: Afbeeldinge van de Stadt Amsterdam in Nieuw Neederlandt
DATE DEPICTED: 1660
DATE DRAWN: c. 1665–70
CARTOGRAPHER: ORIGINAL BY JACQUES CORTELYOU; THIS COPY BY UNKNOWN ARTIST
Pen and ink with watercolor on paper, mounted on canvas, 18⅝ x 25 inches
Biblioteca Medicea Laurenziana, Florence, Italy

This place, the Manhattans, is quite rich of people, and there are at present, full over 350 houses, so that it begins to be a brave place.

—Jacob Jansen Hays, captain of the Nieu Amstel, September 30, 1660

ADAMS-STOKES'S REDRAWING OF THE CASTELLO PLAN, 1916

TITLE: Redraft of The Castello Plan New Amsterdam in 1660
DATE DEPICTED: 1660
DATE DRAWN: 1916
DRAFTSMEN: JOHN WOLCOTT ADAMS & I. N. PHELPS STOKES
Pen and ink on paper, 33½ x 45⅞ inches
The New York Public Library, I.N. Phelps Stokes Collection

The Castello Plan is the most richly detailed, contemporaneous image of New Amsterdam during the Dutch Period. In 1916, a still-more-detailed version of the plan was recreated by John Wolcott Adams under the supervision of I. N. Phelps Stokes, author of a comprehensive work on the depiction of the city through history. Together these two works provide a nearly photographic image of the physical reality of New Amsterdam in the summer of 1660. Our knowledge of the city at this time is further filled in by a surviving census called the Nicasius de Sille List, compiled in July 1660; it enumerates every structure in the city at the time and its occupants. It is

therefore possible to identify all 342 dwellings and buildings on the Castello Plan as well as their occupants over several years. Even the selling prices and minute physical details of some houses are known.

The Castello Plan is the earliest street plan of New Amsterdam. It is at once evident that the city was not carefully planned in its early years, which accounts for the mazelike arrangement of streets in lower Manhattan today. Streets were often the result of practical exigencies, such as cattle paths or shortcuts between important locations. As a result, they had no regularity of length or width. Also irregular in size, if not in shape, were the individual lots. As can be seen from the plan, most were long rectangles modeled after Dutch farms, which were so designed to aid drainage in the flood-plagued homeland.

Two of Manhattan's most famous thoroughfares, Broadway and Wall Street, can be seen on the plan in nascent form. Broadway, the widest horizontal street at the top part of the plan, was originally called Wagen Wegh and then later Brede

Wegh. Its original purpose was to connect the fort with the gardens and orchards in the upper right area of the plan that belonged to the Dutch West India Company. Wall Street got its name from the wall that stretches from river to river just inside the right-hand margin of the plan. It was constructed in 1653 when England and the Netherlands were at war. Word reached New Amsterdam that New Englanders were planning to invade the city. A sizable invasion fleet had assembled in Boston ready to sail for New Amsterdam, which would have been an easy target for the vastly superior English forces. Instead, just before the attack was to be launched, the Dutch and English signed a peace treaty, thereby allowing New Amsterdam another ten years of existence.

Today's Broad Street was originally a canal; it is the first north-south street east of Broadway on the plan. The canal, empty of water at low tide, would fill as the tide came in, thus allowing easy entry of cargo from ships into the city. There were three bridges for crossing the canal, which can be

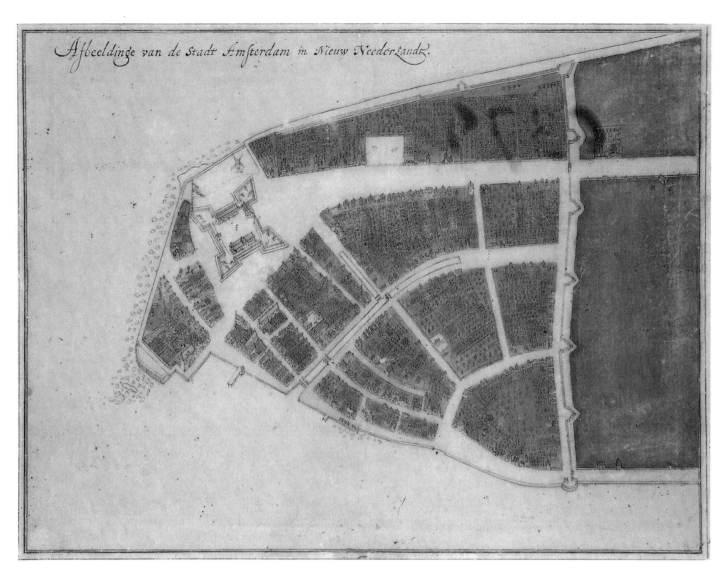

Afbeeldinge van de Stadt Amsterdam in Nieuw Neederlandt.

seen on the plan. The offshoot of the canal is present-day Beaver Street. The plan also shows Bowling Green in its original form as a recreational area; it is the small grassy area (on the Stokes reconstruction) just north of the fort at the foot of Broadway. Another important thoroughfare was Pearl Street, which had the same name then as now. It was the city's easternmost street in 1660 and the site of some of its better residences and of the warehouses of its most successful merchants.

The central structure in New Amsterdam in 1660 was still the fort, which contained several buildings, including the church, the governor's house, a barracks, a prison, and a structure that was either a storehouse or officers' quarters. The other major municipal structure was the Stadt

Huys, or City Hall, which was the center for public assembly as well as of administration. This building had been the City Tavern until 1653. On the plan it is the large building, the only one that has a wharf in front of it, located along the strand a block east of the canal, in the area of present-day Hall Place.

New Amsterdam had long been in need of an official survey, which would legally determine the size of each colonist's lot and settle questions of title. As early as 1647, it was clear that the real-estate situation in Manhattan was out of control, contributing to the near collapse of the colony. The conditions are vividly described in a public ordinance of that year:

As we have seen and remarked the disorderly manner . . . in building

and erecting houses, in extending lots far beyond their boundaries, in placing pig pens and privies on the public roads and streets, in neglecting the cultivation of granted lots, the Director General Petrus Stuyvesant and Council have deemed it advisable to decide upon the appointment of three Surveyors . . . whom we hereby authorize and empower, to condemn all improper and disorderly buildings, fences, palisades, posts, rails, etc. . . .

There is no evidence that the "three Surveyors" ever produced anything or were in fact even appointed. The earliest known official survey of the city was finally completed by Captain Frederick de Koningh in 1656. By the end of the 1650s, the number of inhabitants had nearly doubled to fifteen hundred. With such a rapid influx of new settlers, it was imperative that the demarcations between lots be precisely known, so that new ones could be apportioned. Another factor necessitating a survey was that a municipal form of government took effect in New Amsterdam in 1653. This meant that local authorities now had the power to issue land grants, make decisions regarding land use, and oversee the transference of property.

De Koningh's survey was followed by four by Jacques Cortelyou in 1657, 1658, 1660, and 1661. The Castello Plan is a copy of the third of these. Peter Stuyvesant, the director general at the time, sent Cortelyou's 1660 survey back to the directors of the West India Company in Amsterdam, who commented that too much land was given over to gardens and orchards and not enough to dwellings, indicating a greater concern for planning on the part of the company. Another sign of this was that Cortelyou had the official title of surveyor general of New Netherlands.

The Adams-Stokes version of the Castello Plan reveals that most of the dwellings in New Amsterdam were simple, two-story wooden structures. Gone were the primitive straw-roofed shacks, which were extreme fire hazards. Also, several large brick homes with fine ornamental gardens and orchards can be seen, evidence that New Amsterdam had survived the crises of the 1640s and early 1650s to prosper. In fact, visitors of the day often remarked how attractive the town was; one described homes made of "Bricks . . . of divers Coullers [colors] and laid in checks, being glazed."

In one respect, the Castello Plan is unintentionally misleading. Although New Amsterdam may look like a cozy Dutch village of charming homes and ornamental gardens on the plan, records suggest it was hardly that. It was a place driven by the pursuit of quick wealth and an already quite cosmopolitan place where eighteen languages were spoken. Violence was common, as was litigation; criminal justice was

erratic, if not barbaric. Alcohol was an ever-present fact of life; the preferred occupations in New Amsterdam were tavern owner or innkeeper and brewer. In fact, in 1657 there were twenty-one taverns, tap rooms, and grogshops in the city, the most popular of which was the Blue Dove on Pearl Street.

What Peter Stuyvesant had actually sent back to Amsterdam was most likely a more detailed prototype of the Castello Plan. It accompanied a letter by Stuyvesant dated October 1660, in which he states: "After closing our letter the Burgomasters [of New Amsterdam] have shown us the plan of this city, which we did not think would be ready before the sailing of this ship." That a plan was received by the directors is clear from their reply of December 24 of that year:

> We have been pleased to receive the map of the city of New Amsterdam: we noticed that according to our opinion too great spaces are as yet without buildings, as for instance between Smee Street and Princes Gracht or between Prince Street and Tuyn Street, also between Heeren Street and Bevers Gracht, where the houses apparently are surrounded by excessively large lots and gardens; . . .

These comments indicate that the plan the directors saw contained street names that were not on the Castello Plan, thus indicating that the latter was probably a somewhat rough copy of the original survey.

The Castello Plan is named after the villa in Florence where it was discovered at the beginning of this century. Recent research has answered the intriguing question of how this unique record of Manhattan's past found its way to Italy. The Florentine prince Cosimo de' Medici III, well-acquainted with the cartographic talent of the Dutch, visited in December 1667 the greatest Dutch mapmaker of the period, Jan Blaeu. From Blaeu, he purchased the so-called *Atlas Vingboons*, which contained numerous hand-drawn maps and plans of towns, harbors, and forts. Included in the atlas was this copy of the Cortelyou survey and a copy of the Manatus Map (see p. 14).

27

THE FALL OF NEW AMSTERDAM
THE DUKE'S PLAN

TITLE: A Description. of The Towne. Of.
Mannados : Or. New. Amsterdam : as it was
in September 1661 . . . Anno : Domini. 1664
DATE DEPICTED: 1661
DATE DRAWN: 1664
CARTOGRAPHER: JACQUES CORTELYOU(?)
Watercolor on vellum heightened with gold,
21¾ x 27¼ inches
British Library, London

We, your Honours' loyal, sorrowful, and desolate subjects, cannot neglect nor keep from relating the event [the fall of New Amsterdam], which thro' God's pleasure thus unexpectedly happened to us in consequence of your Honours neglect and forgetfulness. . . . Done in Jorck [York], heretofore named Amsterdam in New Netherland.
—The burgomasters of the former New Amsterdam reporting to the directors of the West India Company, September 1664

The exquisite, illuminated manuscript known as the Duke's Plan, the most beautiful of all the early maps of the city, can be viewed as a kind of trophy of the English conquest of Manhattan in 1664. It was most likely intended to provide James, the duke of York (hence the Duke's Plan), a suitably embellished portrait of his new acquisition. The duke had been given New Amsterdam and a considerable portion of the Northeast by his royal brother, the then recently restored Charles II. The fact that the plan is dated 1664 and depicts English flags flying from the fort and from several warships clearly indicate that it was drawn after the English takeover. However, the map's title goes on to state that it depicts the city as it was in 1661, during the Dutch Period. It was, therefore, most likely copied from a 1661 survey by Jacques Cortelyou, the surveyor general of New Netherlands and the author of the original of the Castello Plan (see p. 24).

Neither the source, draftsman, nor circumstances of the creation of the Duke's Plan is positively known. The most intriguing speculation suggests that it was prepared by an English spy investigating the city's defenses for an invasion the English were planning in 1661 but never carried out. This supposition is based on the existence of a manuscript description of the city that is also dated 1661 and which has nearly the identical title as the map. The description, which notes in detail the city's defenses,

corresponds in most particulars to the map. Therefore, some theorize that the map was drawn to illustrate the description as part of the spy's report. However, the map's fine draftsmanship suggests something fit for presentation to nobility rather than the sketches of a spy. In fact, its lavish style is that of the so-called Thames school, a group of English draftsmen who produced highly wrought manuscript maps, often for nobility. Therefore, it is very possible that a copy of Cortelyou's survey was sent to England to be rerendered by a nameless practitioner of the Thames school for presentation to the duke.

Fortunately for its citizens, New Amsterdam ended with a whimper. Never having turned a profit for the Dutch West India Company, which was having troubles on many fronts, New Amsterdam was written off as a bad investment and therefore never adequately defended. In this vacuum, not only did growing English towns surround the city, but also the English began to assume important roles in New Amsterdam itself. In addition, the English as a nation welcomed any opportunity to take advantage of the Dutch, who had been their primary (and usually more successful) commercial rivals as well as, occasionally, opponents in war. Such was English contempt for Dutch claims to Manhattan and the Northeast that, in March 1664, Charles II simply bequeathed the areas to his brother, James. In addition to New Amsterdam,

the king's largesse included the land between the Connecticut River and Delaware Bay, all of the Hudson River, Long Island, Martha's Vineyard, Nantucket, and part of Maine.

The Duke of York immediately organized an invasion fleet of four warships under the command of Colonel Richard Nicolls. Arriving in New York Harbor on August 26, Nicolls demanded the town in the name of his king. Stuyvesant, the Dutch director general, who was a proud man with wide military experience, temporized with written arguments reviewing Dutch claims, hoping still to mount a defense. Spurning polemics, Nicolls simply informed the Dutch that they had two days to surrender or he would invade. He also promised generous terms. Once this was learned by the general populace, they urged Stuyvesant to surrender, who did so reluctantly. The surrender was officially signed on September 8. Nicolls became the first English governor of New York and lived up to his promise of merciful terms by allowing his Dutch subjects to retain their property and to worship as they chose.

As is the custom with conquerors, Nicolls set about renaming things. The city, of course, became New York. Although this was effected immediately as indicated by a letter Nicolls sent just after the seizure, the new name, curiously, does not appear on the Duke's Plan. Also peculiar is that the English renamed the Hudson River (called

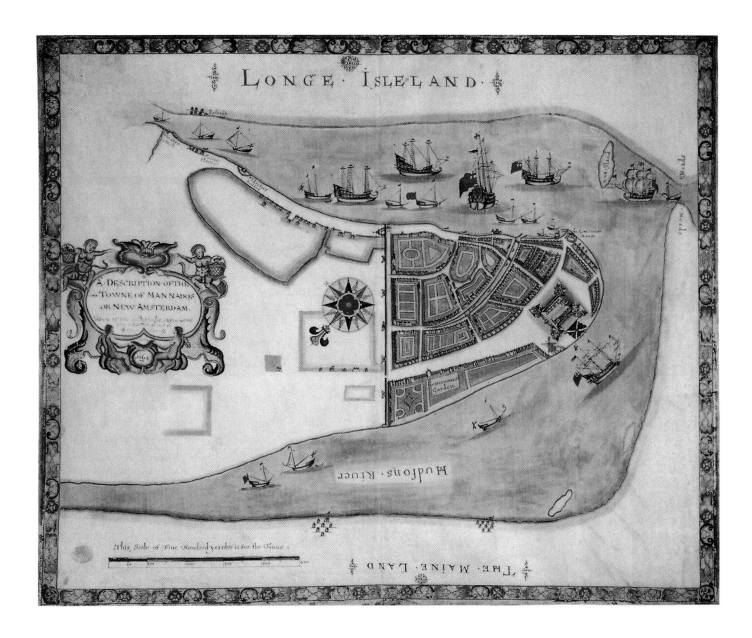

the North River by the Dutch) after the explorer who had discovered it in behalf of the *Dutch*. The new name is on the plan. (The name for the river would soon revert to North and not become the Hudson until early in the nineteenth century.) In other changes, Fort Amsterdam became Fort James, also after the duke, and the Company's Farm, the lands which belonged to the West India Company, became the Duke's Farm. (These last changes are not on the plan.)

The Duke's Plan shows new development north of the wall that was not on the Castello Plan. In fact, this area can be considered the city's first suburban develop-

ment. (Harlem was a separate settlement, hence not a suburb of New Amsterdam.) The large, irregularly shaped area north of the wall along the East River was called Smith's Fly but was referred to simply as the Voorstadt, meaning suburb. The road or passage dividing its two sections is in the area of present-day Maiden Lane. At the northern end of this area is a fairly large structure called Alderton's Building, which was probably a warehouse. To the north of this along the river is Passage Place, the embarkation point for the ferry to Brooklyn. Still farther to the north is the water mill at the end of a stream that would have emerged from the Fresh Water,

the large lake that existed in Manhattan just to the north of the area shown on the plan. The location of the mill is the intersection of present-day Pearl and James streets. The other squares north of the wall are areas that had been recently granted to various citizens, with the exception of the northernmost plot along the Hudson River, which is open to the north. It was most likely the Company's Farm, later called the Duke's Farm.

The Duke's Plan was rediscovered in 1858 by George H. Moore, librarian of the New-York Historical Society, after lying unobserved for nearly two centuries in the British Museum. He also named it.

THE ENGLISH SURVEY THEIR PRIZE
THE NICOLLS MAP

TITLE: Main map untitled. Inset: The Towne
of New-York
DATE DEPICTED: c. 1664–68
DATE DRAWN: c. 1664–68
Pen and ink on paper, 18 x 54 inches
British Library, London

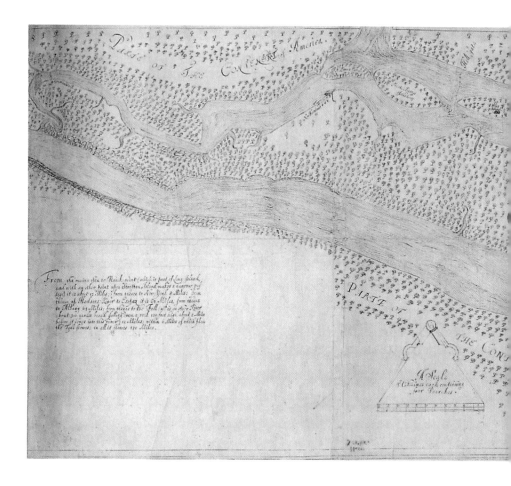

Both the Nicolls Map and the Duke's Plan
(see p. 28) were drawn soon after the
British capture of Manhattan for the duke
of York and his colonial administrators.
While the Duke's Plan was an ornamental
representation of a captured prize, this
more sober document was most likely
made to aid colonial officials in administer-
ing the new possession. It is named after
the first English governor of New York and
was probably ordered by him. It was the
first map of Manhattan based on a survey
actually conducted by the English.

When the English acquired Manhattan
along with most of the Northeast, they
were ill-prepared to manage and defend this
vast territory. To be feared were the French
and Spanish, who had been long
entrenched in America, and, of course, the
Dutch. By early 1665, the English and
Dutch were again officially at war, no doubt
heightening English concern for their
recently gained territory. Events would
prove that the English in New York had not
heard the last of the Dutch. Thus the inset
plan of the town in the upper right-hand
area of the map emphasizes its defenses. The
key on the plan notes the locations of batteries along the wall and East River, and
there is also an illustration of the fort.

The provenance of the map also suggests that it was intended for official use
with a particular emphasis on military matters. The map was part of a collection of
fortification plans made for Charles I and
Charles II and their advisors. Charles II

gave New York to his brother, James, the
duke of York, and was king when the
Nicolls Map was made. Before coming to
the British Library, this collection was in
Forde Abbey, the family home of the
Gwyns. (Eleanor Gwyn, an actress, was the
mistress of Charles II.) Recent research has
shown that the Gwyn papers were part of a
state archive, hence establishing the official
stature of this collection of plans.

That the Nicolls Plan was intended for
distant colonial administrators is implied by
some very basic information that would
not have been needed by a user closer at
hand. Calling the New Jersey side of the
Hudson River "Parte of the Continente of
America" suggests that the intended viewer

of the map required the most rudimentary
geographic information. Similar information is found in the note on the left-hand
side of the map; it places New York in its
geographic context by listing the distances
between it and various key points, such as
the entrance of the harbor and Albany.
While somewhat crude in its detail, the
survey provides an excellent overview of
Manhattan and the extent of its development, which would have been of chief
interest to administrators. For the first time,
a map allows one to see just how little of
the island was actually settled in the early
stages of its development.

The Nicolls Map is also the first to
show the other early, and for a time,

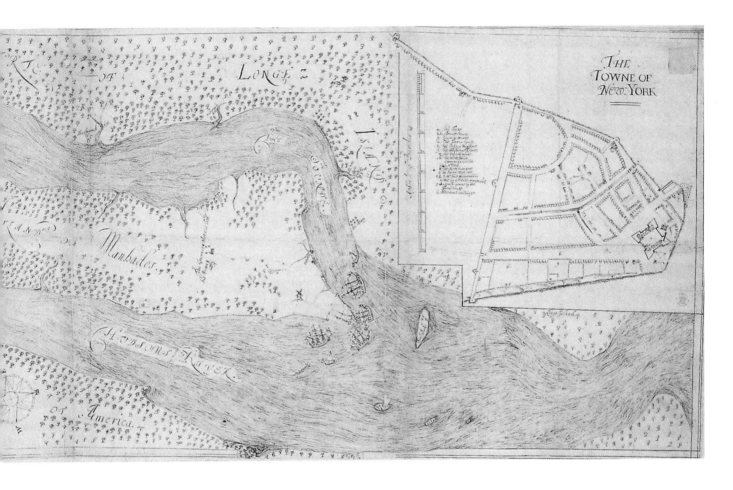

independent settlement that existed on Manhattan at the time: New Harlem, which was founded in 1659. In 1665, Governor Nicolls declared that New York would consist of the entire island of Manhattan, thereby incorporating Harlem into the city. The general map also delineates the longer roads (as opposed to streets) on the island, which are indicated by dotted lines. All of the town's streets and roads were still unpaved at the time. There is no indication on the map of the Wagen Wegh (Wagon Way), the road that would connect New York and Harlem and would become part of Broadway, which was ordered by Governor Lovelace in February 1669. (Even when this road was

completed, it was still a three-hour journey from New York to Harlem.) The absence of the Wagon Way on the map helps to place its date within Nicolls's administration, 1664–68.

The inset plan in the upper right corner, entitled "The Towne of New-York," is the earliest instance of the use of the new name on a map. Although less detailed than the earlier Duke's and Castello plans, it shows an area of new development just to the northeast of the quay, the constructed promontory at the southeast tip of the island that was used for the loading and unloading of ships. There appears to be additional landfill in this area, on which a new row of houses has been built, demon-

strating again how early the process of expanding Manhattan with landfill was used. Also on the plan, Broadway (labeled b) is called Broad Street, well on its way to its eventual name.

Of interest on the general map is the prominent notice given to Peter Stuyvesant's farm, or bouwery, with the note reading: "The Governers that was last his Bowry." Also on the general map is a large representation of the windmill that was erected in 1663 and lasted until the early 1720s. Also preserved on the map are numerous deep inlets on both sides of the island that had never been completely shown on earlier maps. All of them were filled in as the city developed.

DUTCH AGAIN
THE ALLARD MAP

TITLE: Totius Neobelgii Nova Et Accuratissima Tabula
DATE DEPICTED: 1673
CARTOGRAPHER: AUGUSTINE HERMANN(?)
PUBLISHED: *Separately,* CAROLUS ALLARD, AMSTERDAM, 1674?
Hand-colored copperplate engraving,
18 ⅛ x 21 inches
Private collection

Just as the Duke's Plan (see p. 28) celebrated the English conquest of New Amsterdam, the Allard Map memorialized its startling recapture by the Dutch on August 7, 1673. In fact, the view inset along the bottom right of the engraving depicts the event in progress, showing Dutch soldiers marching along the quay and a cannon firing from the fort. It has been called the Restitutio View, referring to the restitution of Dutch power. The Dutch would hold Manhattan for just little more than a year. Yet maps with the view commemorating this fleeting triumph would appear in several editions as late as about 1760.

By the time Allard's map appeared, Dutch overseas power had been waning, particularly in America. Continual wars with England as well as with Continental foes had ground down the once-wealthy nation. Allard's map, with its long publishing life, can therefore be seen as a symptom of the decline of Dutch influence. Its grandiose presentation of a momentary triumph played to the need for some affirmation of Dutch power in the face of overwhelming evidence to the contrary.

The sight of a fleet of heavily armed Dutch ships (illustrated on the map along the southern shore of Long Island) entering New York Harbor in early August 1673 must have been a shock to the town's residents. All accounts of the period indicate that New York at the time was thriving under the benevolent administration of Nicolls and his successor, Francis Lovelace.

New roads and ferries were being built, and the paving of streets had been ordered. Most citizens now lived in attractive and comfortable stone houses. Although the invasion force was not unwelcomed by the town's Dutch residents, its arrival was not prompted by an internal rebellion. Instead, it was more of a sideshow in yet another Anglo-Dutch war, which began in April 1672.

In the course of this conflict, Dutch land forces had been rendered impotent, but at sea they remained formidable. In December 1672, a small fleet of four warships was sent to America to harass or capture anything English. Under the command of Admiral Cornelis Evertsen the Younger, one of the most capable Dutch naval leaders, the fleet joined forces with another group of four vessels under Jacob Binckes. Emboldened by their added size, which included a force of six hundred soldiers, they decided to go after the most alluring English prize in North America—New York. To their good fortune, they found New York much in the same situation as the English invasion force had found it nine years earlier—badly defended. To make matters even more favorable for the Dutch, the English governor, Lovelace, was away at the time. With the same arrogance displayed by the English earlier, Evertsen simply demanded the city. This time, however, shots were actually fired, as the Dutch ships laid salvos on the fort. The English attempted to return fire, but many of the fort's rusted guns failed. Captain Antony

Colve then landed six hundred troops behind the governor's garden at Trinity Church, marched them up Broadway, and eventually took the fort. The view erroneously shows the soldiers landing along the east side of Manhattan.

Colve became governor and immediately renamed Manhattan as New Orange and Albany as Willemstad, both after the prince of Orange. Neither name found its way onto this map. With considerable support in Manhattan, Colve reinstated the Dutch political system and attempted to consolidate his position by repairing the city's defenses. Although the English in Manhattan and throughout the Northeast were outraged by the Dutch seizure of the city, their own factionalism prevented a coordinated effort to dislodge the Dutch.

Despite the advantages the Dutch had, their resurgence was doomed to be short-lived. There was no desire in the beleaguered homeland to support a new colony. In addition, Colve quickly became unpopular due to harsh taxes and a nasty disposition, so that even the Dutch citizens of New Orange began to long for the more enlightened style of the English governors. Therefore, in February 1674, when the English and Dutch were negotiating peace terms concluding their hostilities, the Dutch almost eagerly offered Manhattan in exchange for English recognition of Surinam, the last Dutch stronghold in the Western Hemisphere. Formal surrender would not come for several months, when Colve gave over the city to the new English governor, Major Edmond Andros, on October 11, 1674. The Dutch restoration proved to be merely an interruption.

The general map used by Allard here is the Jansson-Visscher Map (see p. 18) with modifications. Ironically, even though the map's *raison d'être* was the celebration of the Dutch reconquest of Manhattan, much of

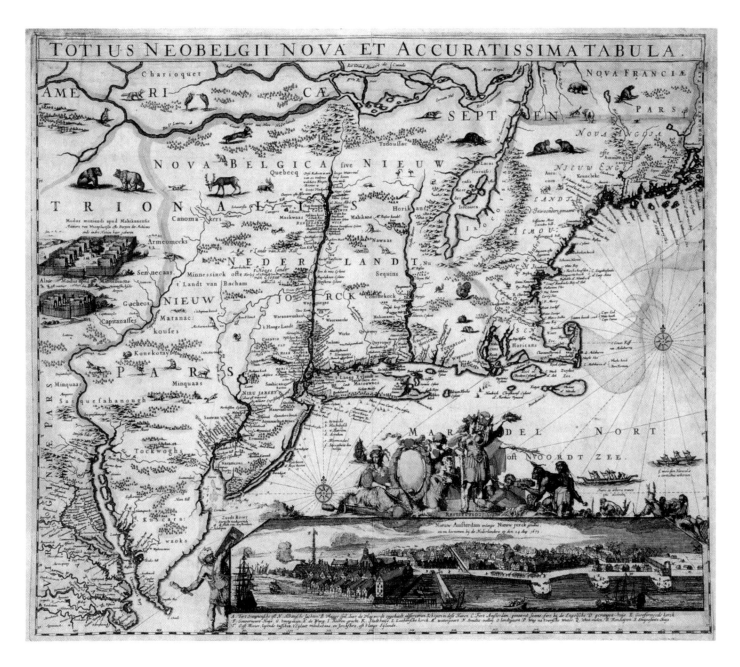

the new information added to the general map reflects the Anglicization that had occurred in the previous nine years under English rule. Several of the new English place-names appear, including New Jersey, Albany ("Nova Albania"), and Yorkshire ("Iorck-shire"), the English name for the area that included Long Island. Newer English towns that did not appear on the earlier states of the map are shown here: Milfort (in New Jersey), Bergen, Gamoenipa, and Iamaica.

The Restitutio View, which depicts the town as seen directly from the east, enables one to visualize some of its features that were only schematically showed on earlier maps. On the right-hand side of the view is part of the wall that became Wall Street with its guardhouse and gate. To the right of the wall are the new settlements north of the wall that were indicated on the three previous maps. Also in this area is a faint representation of the Fresh Water or Collect Pond (indicated by *P*), called the aquam dulcem (sweet water) in the key. Along the quay are the three roundouts fortified with cannon that are also represented on the three earlier maps. To the left of these in the center of the view is the canal (*I*) that cut into the city from the harbor, shown here for the first time in its completed state with its walls fully sheathed. An interesting feature to the left of the canal, at the head of the pier, is the watergate that was roughly represented on the Duke's Plan. The view has several errors, such as the disproportionately large roundouts, that suggest it was not based on a drawing done on the spot but worked up from sketches or verbal reports or both in the Netherlands. In all, thirteen editions of the map appeared.

THE ENGLISH DOMAIN
THE THORNTON-MORDEN-LEA MAP

TITLE: A New Map of New England : New York : New Jersey : Pensilvania : Maryland and Virginia
DATE DEPICTED: c. 1685
CARTOGRAPHERS: JOHN THORNTON, ROBERT MORDEN, AND PHILIP LEA
PUBLISHED: *Separately,* LONDON, c. 1685
Hand-colored copperplate engraving, 17½ x 21⅜ inches
Private collection

An English citizen of the late seventeenth century contemplating emigration to America might well have consulted the Thornton-Morden-Lea Map. It contained the latest geographic information from America and was available in separate sheets in the shops of John Thornton, Robert Morden, and Philip Lea at a time when English colonization of North America began to accelerate. The English had at the time just become masters of the entire area stretching from Maine to the Carolinas. To the ambitious person, the map would have presented an enticing vista: it displays a loose federation of colonies, between and beyond which there appears to be ample unclaimed land. It creates an image of an area comfortably linked by civilization but still containing much open territory. The trees liberally sprinkled throughout the map and the occasional animals give the impression of more free land than most likely existed at the time. These minor but meaningful distortions must have acted as a lure to emigration, as did many early maps.

The potential colonist would have been further heartened by the small chart of New York Harbor tucked into the bottom right-hand corner of this map. Here the complex entrance to one of the centers of British America is precisely laid out and arrayed with familiar English place-names. Surprisingly, this modest inset map was the earliest *printed* chart of New York Harbor.

Although complex and challenging to the navigator, New York Harbor had been fairly well surveyed well before the publication of this map. Even as early as 1524, Verrazano had sketched its general outlines, as can be seen from the Gastaldi Map (p. 4), and later in 1609, Henry Hudson, as seen on the Velasco Map (p. 7), delineated the harbor in some detail. Further, the Block map and Minuit Chart (pp. 8 and 10) demonstrate that the Dutch had good knowledge of the harbor early on. One reason that a printed chart of the harbor did not appear until this one is that ship pilots relied on hand-drafted charts and so did not require a printed one. Also, since New York was a potential target of invasion throughout most of its history, first by the English, then by the French, it might have been deemed unwise to publicize knowledge of the harbor through printed charts.

As a piece of mapmaking, the little chart is quite well done. It is the clearest presentation of any map seen thus far of just how difficult the entry is into the Lower Bay of the harbor. The chart clearly shows the shallow waters that block virtually its entire entrance. It is no wonder that even today local pilots must guide larger vessels through the harbor. Once in the Lower Bay, one encounters another large area of shoals in the western part of it, leaving again a narrow channel through the Narrows into the Upper Bay. Depth readings are given throughout. The island of Manhattan is quite accurately shaped on the chart, but other land masses, such as Staten Island, are more crudely rendered.

An unusual bit of nomenclature is the East River shown as the York River on the chart. This could have been the mapmakers' tribute to James, the duke of York, who became King James II about the time the map was published.

It is significant that the mapmakers chose to feature an inset map relating to New York City on a work that also includes Boston. Already at work at the time the map was published were the forces that would propel New York past Boston in size and prosperity. New York was beginning to take the lead in trade with the other colonies, and in 1684 it was declared the sole port of entry in the area. (This was especially detrimental to Southhampton on eastern Long Island, which had been rising as a port town.) Further, the stature of New York was raised when James, the duke of York, the proprietor of the colony, ascended the throne in 1685. It is possible that this event even prompted the inclusion of the New York inset on the map. Whatever the reason for the inclusion, it is clear that it was the result of a last-minute decision and was added *after* the general map had already been engraved. The top border of the inset cuts into one of the ornamental ships on the map, and rhumb lines from the general map can be seen to continue lightly through the inset.

The general map provides a comprehensive picture of the considerable territory gained by the English from the Dutch in 1674 along with the original English colonies: New England, New York, East and West Jersey, Pennsylvania, Maryland, and Virginia. Borderlines can be discerned between some of them, several of which would eventually become state boundaries.

As England was gaining political strength in North America, mapmaking in England began to come of age. The Thornton-Morden-Lea Map was an

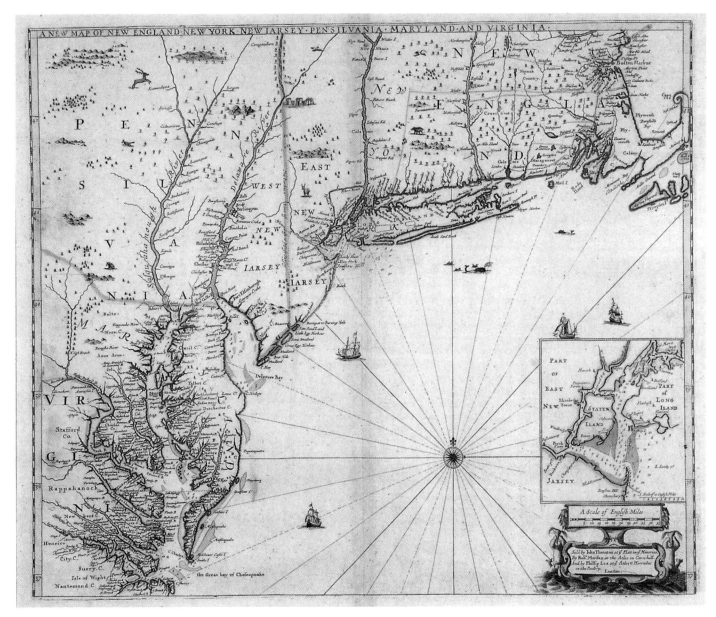

important part of this trend, as it was one of the first English maps relating to America that relied nearly completely on English as opposed to Dutch sources. The publication of the map was a collaborative venture of three prominent English map publishers. That a single map required the combined efforts and resources of the three is a measure of the still-modest proportions of the English map-publishing trade of the day. John Thornton was the most important of the three men involved in this map and was himself a proficient chartmaker, an unusual skill among map publishers at that time. He published with John Seller, in 1689, *The English Coast Pilot*, a nautical atlas

that remained in publication for over a century. While lesser lights, both Robert Morden and Philip Lea were involved in the production of other important maps of the English colonies in America.

Since the Thornton-Morden-Lea Map was separately published, very few examples have survived. The ones that have were most likely bound into composite, personalized atlases after having been acquired as separates. Despite the map's scarcity, four or possibly five states of it have been identified. The long publishing life of the map is another indication of the undeveloped state of the English map trade at the time. English map publishers sought to

squeeze commercial life out of a map long after it had become outdated, as was the case with this map. Pictured here is the earliest known state. It seems that an earlier or at least proof state existed and is now lost, as there are signs of the several plate alterations on the impression pictured here.

The dating of the map is based on internal evidence. The presence of Philadelphia dictates that the map must have been published later than 1682, when the city was settled. Another piece of evidence narrowing the date is that Philip Lea did business at the address listed on the map (". . . at the Atlas and Hercules in the Poultry") between 1683 and 1686.

CARTOGRAPHIC ILLUSION: FORTRESS NEW YORK
THE FRANQUELIN PLAN

TITLE: Ville de Manathe ou Nouvelle-Yorc
DATE DEPICTED: c. 1693
DATE DRAWN: 1693
CARTOGRAPHER: JEAN-BAPTISTE-LOUIS FRANQUELIN
PUBLISHED: JACQUES-NICHOLAS BELLIN, *Le Petit Atlas Maritime*, PARIS, 1763/1764
Hand-colored copperplate engraving, 8½ x 6⅜ inches
Private collection

Fear of attack by the French cast a chilling shadow on life in New York throughout most of the entire colonial period. It was not until their final defeat in the French and Indian War in 1763 that the threat was truly lifted. The plan pictured here is a printed version of an inset found on a hand-drawn map by J. B. L. Franquelin in 1693. When the original map was made, France and England had been at war for four years. The struggling but strategically located colony of New York would have been an inviting target for the French. Control of it and of the Hudson River could have resulted in the strangulation of the English settlements in the Northeast and the almost complete elimination of the English from North America. Evidence of how great the fear of the French was in New York is the fact that the first book published in the city, which appeared the year this map was drawn, was a condemnation of the French attempt to conquer the Mohawk Indians, allies of the English. Similarly, many of the earliest documents printed in the city were broadsides calling for the improvement of the city's defenses.

In 1693, attack seemed imminent. Governor Fletcher was even informed by England that a French fleet was on its way to invade the city. New York's militia was put on alert; fire beacons were set up; and in August, guns were mounted on Sandy Hook, the narrow peninsula at the entrance to the harbor. Earlier in the year Fletcher had ordered a new battery to be built near the fort; this might be represented on the plan by the semicircle to the left of the fort.

It is possible that in its original form this very plan was consulted in the contemplated invasion of the city by the French. Its crude, schematic look suggests something prepared quickly, perhaps even surreptitiously by a spy. Further, it emphasizes militarily pertinent detail, such as defenses, the location of the powder magazine, and gun emplacements. Moreover, Franquelin's original map could very well have been the result of a reconnaissance of possible targets of invasion, as many documents of the period discuss the planning of an attack on New York.

The ultimate source for the plan of New York is not known, as Franquelin merely compiled the map from various sources. However, a shadowy character named John Reaux is a possibility. He was a French privateer of uncommon audacity, who nevertheless was naturalized as a citizen of New York in 1692. He promptly sank a vessel he was the master of and absconded with several thousand pounds sterling. If early records can be believed, he was captured, then escaped, fled to France, returned to New York claiming to have a commission from the French king, stole two boats, was recaptured and finally imprisoned. In his confession, Reaux said that he had been interviewed by French naval authorities as to the feasibility of an attack on the city. Reaux claimed to have discouraged the invasion, arguing that the city was strongly defended with a large fort, that the harbor was difficult to negotiate, and that the population of the surrounding region was considerable.

While one would certainly be skeptical of any utterance of an individual in Reaux's situation, this plan does bear him out in one respect. As depicted here, New York is a veritable fortress. The fort itself occupies a considerable area of the town, which is shown as nearly completely enclosed by walls or ditches. In fact, the city appears here as kind of a citadel, with hilly shoreline indicated along both the east and west sides. The wharf at the very southern portion of the island is enclosed by what appears to be a stout constructed enclosure that has only a narrow entrance. The impression is given that the town is not otherwise approachable from the water. Several batteries are shown along the walls, and another one is indicated to the right of the dock area. Overall, the plan presents New York as a much more strongly defended place than it actually was. In reality, the fort and northern wall were often not in a good state of repair, and there were wharfs along the east side of the city by 1693 that would have offered easier access than the plan suggests. Therefore, even if it was not Reaux himself that dissuaded the French from attacking the city, it is quite possible that this plan, portraying a stout fortresslike town, played a role in this decision.

The version of the map reproduced here is a nearly exact, printed reduction of

the original manuscript, published some seventy-one years later. It appeared in Jacques-Nicholas Bellin's five-volume *Petit Atlas Maritime* in 1764. Another state of the map appeared a year earlier in Bellin's *Petit Atlas Francois*. The 1764 state can be distinguished by the presence of the inscription "Tome I, No. 33" in the upper right above the image. It is quite surprising that this highly regarded French chartmaker and atlas publisher would have chosen to include this already very outdated plan in works that presented themselves as collections of up-to-date maps and plans. The remarkable fact is that Bellin or any other map publisher of the day simply did not have a more recent model to draw upon. One can see in the succeeding pages of this book that there were indeed some maps of the city produced between 1693 and 1764. However, they were either manuscripts that were produced in single examples or maps that were printed in New York itself and had very limited circulation. There is little chance that any of these would have been available to Bellin. Bellin's work, published some 240 years after the founding of the first European colony on Manhattan, is therefore the earliest printed plan of the city acquirable by the collector today (excluding the fictional plan of the city published by Jollain in 1672, depicted on p. 20).

Jacques-Nicholas Bellin (1703–1772), in addition to being a commercial map publisher, held official status as both royal

hydrographer and ingénieur géographe de la marine et du Dépot des Cartes et Plans. In the latter position, he was responsible for compiling atlases of sailing charts for military and official use as well as for commercial publication. His two great collections of charts were the *Neptune Française* (1753) and the *Hydrographie Francaise* (1756–65).

Jean-Baptiste-Louis Franquelin (1653–c. 1725) played a unique and crucial role among early mapmakers. At the time when the French were making their historic explorations of the the western Great Lakes

and Mississippi River and valley, Franquelin worked as a kind of one-man cartographic clearinghouse. Employed by various governors in Quebec, Franquelin was the first to receive new cartographic intelligence from explorers such as Jacques Marquette, Louis Jolliet, and Rene-Robert Cavalier de La Salle. His surviving maps, all of which are in manuscript, like the original on which this one is based, often represent the earliest attempts to integrate new discoveries with existing knowledge.

EXPANSION UNDER ENGLISH RULE
THE MILLER PLAN

TITLE: New Yorke
DATE DEPICTED: 1695
DATE DRAWN: c. 1696
CARTOGRAPHER: JOHN MILLER
Pen and ink on paper, 9⅞ x 14⅛ inches
British Library, London

The Miller Plan was accompanied by a richly detailed description of the city, *New York Considered and Improved,* based on Miller's three-years residence there from 1692 to 1695. As an idealistic and somewhat inflexible Episcopal chaplain of the king's troops at Fort William Henry, Miller attempted to minister, often in vain, to a population for most of whom religion was not a primary concern. While railing against the liberal use of profanity by New Yorkers, Miller points out that they so relished its use that each attempted to outdo the other in the richness of their vulgarity. Miller, however, provided a surprisingly accurate record of newly added streets and structures, of the condition of the fort and its armament, and generally, a good sense of the physical reality of the town. This is all the more remarkable since he drew his map entirely from memory. In July 1695 on the return voyage to England, Miller's ship was seized by a French privateer, at which time Miller threw all his notes and drawings overboard. This was a wise thing to do from the point of view of both national and personal security, because his maps and drawings detailed the city's defenses. Miller was then imprisoned in France, probably at St. Malo, where he recreated his maps, drawings, and account of the city. By some means, he was able to send all of this material from prison to the bishop of London. These documents surfaced in 1842, were sold at auction, and then published in 1843. They were finally acquired by the British

Museum in 1845, where they now reside.

When Miller drew his fine plan of the city, thirty years had passed since the beginning of English rule and since the last extant English plan of the city was made, The Nicolls Map (see p. 30). In that time, the size of the city had nearly doubled, and its population increased from about two thousand to five thousand over this period. As can be seen on the map, the developed territory above the wall nearly equaled that below it, although there were still certainly more streets in the southern portion. New at the time were Pine, Cedar, Crown (later Liberty), and John streets, which were all laid out in 1692. Also in 1692, the parcel of land along the East River bordered by Wall, Pearl, and Fulton streets was sold off to several buyers. Each owner was required as a condition of purchase to erect wharfs adjoining their lots, which can be seen in completed form on the map. The then most recent street shown on the plan is the easternmost one in the northern section of town, called Queen Street, laid out in 1694. The northernmost completed east-west street on the map is Maiden Lane, this being the first instance of the use of that name for the street, which was in the area favored by women for washing clothes because of the creek that passed there.

An important part of the city's religious history is recorded on the map. It was the first to show the location of what was not only New York's, but also North America's, earliest synagogue, indicated by the number 14. (The legend that identified the numbers on the plan is within Miller's text, not on the plan itself.) Begun around 1691, it was located on the south side of present-day Beaver Street, in the middle of the block between Broadway and Broad Street. It was actually a private home that was used as a place of worship, a fact reflecting the status of Jews in early New York. During the

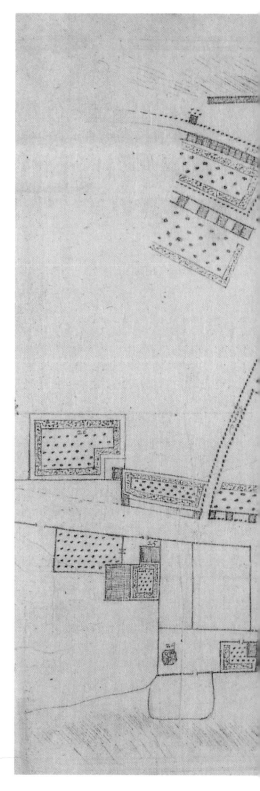

Dutch period, there was an enforced toleration of Jews. Because Dutch Jews were among the investors in the Dutch West India Company, they were allowed to settle in New Amsterdam and enjoy some freedom, despite some colonists' contrary

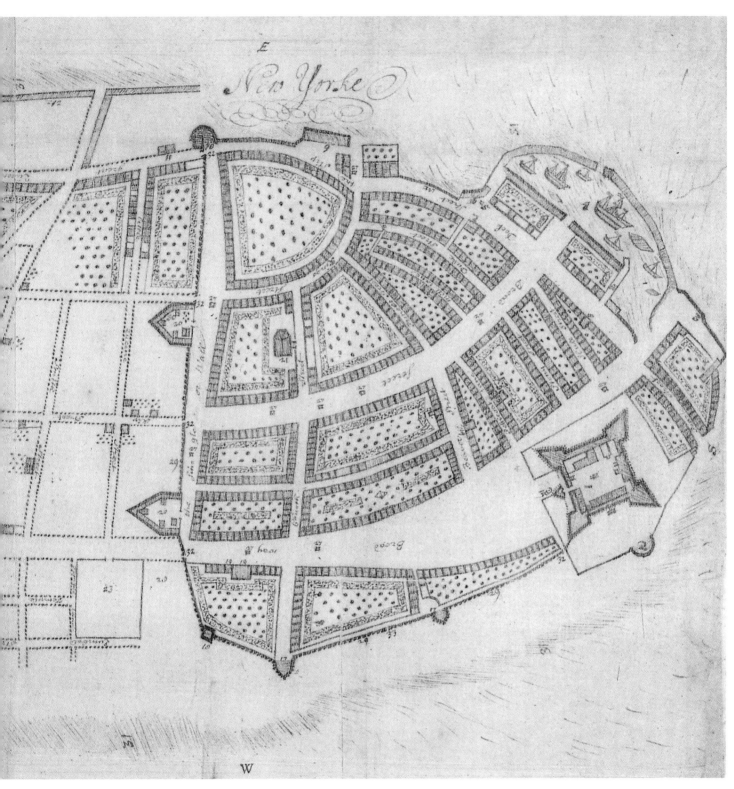

opinions of these policies. By the early British period, Jews seemed to be a more accepted part of society in New York. However, a synagogue housed in its own building was not built until 1729–30 (see the Lyne-Bradford Plan, p. 40).

Both Miller's plan of the city and the small, inset plan of the fort reflect the fact that England and France were at war from 1689 to 1697 and that the threat of French invasion from Canada was a constant worry during the period. New York as depicted

here was a much more heavily fortified place than previously shown. There were now thirty-six cannons in the fort, and gun emplacements had recently been added below the fort, near number 2, and in the southeastern parts of the town, near numbers 3 and 6.

FROM TOWN TO CITY
THE LYNE-BRADFORD PLAN

TITLE: A Plan of the City of New York from an actual Survey Made by Iames Lyne
DATE DEPICTED: 1730
CARTOGRAPHER: JAMES LYNE
PUBLISHED: *Separately,* WILLIAM BRADFORD, NEW YORK, 1731
Uncolored copperplate engraving, 18 x 20¼ *inches*
The New York Public Library

After the Miller Plan of 1695 (see p. 38), there is another remarkable cartographic drought of several decades until the next surviving map of the city, the Lyne-Bradford Plan. During this period, New York changed fundamentally from a struggling town to a small but commercially important city. Both its look and even sound changed. In 1695 most of the city's structures were two stories high, reflecting the fact that people often lived and worked in the same building. With commercial development, nascent industry, and greater concentration of wealth came the beginning of vertical growth. Also, the clatter of carriages, just coming into general use in 1731, could be heard along the city's streets, many of which were now paved with cobblestones. The increase of trade with far-away places, especially the West Indies, made New York a more cosmopolitan place. A quick glance at the legend of important structures in the city in the upper left-hand portion of the Bradford Plan conveys the city's growing commercialism. Added to the usual list of churches, one now finds markets for various commodities, suggesting a greater organization of trade. The presence of these markets also shows that New Yorkers for the most part no longer gathered their own food, but had become dependent on outside sources. Noted also in the legend is Byards Sugar House, the city's first sugar refinery, which was built in 1728. It along with shipbuilding and the processing of tobacco into snuff

were some of the important industries that sprang up in the city since the beginning of the century.

The growth of New York as a port city is especially evident on the map in the new piers on the west side. Also not seen on previous maps is the network of docks along the east side above Wall Street. The city's image of itself as a port is further brought home by the several illustrations of ships and boats decorating the map.

Not only is the Lyne-Bradford Plan the first map of New York printed in the city itself, but, remarkably, it is the very first printed plan of New York to have been published anywhere (if one excludes the fictitious Jollain View). The map's publisher, William Bradford, was the city's first printer, having set up its first press in 1693; he also began the city's earliest newspaper, the *New-York Gazette,* in 1725. The surveyor James Lyne, on whose work the plan is based, is a more obscure figure, who held some minor posts and advertised his services as a tutor. Despite Bradford's prominence, the circumstances of the publication of the map are not known. Its commercial sale was not actively promoted; Bradford advertised it just once in his newspaper, in the issue of August 30 to September 6, 1731. (This allows a firm dating of the undated map.) Furthermore, only three copies of the map survive today, which suggests a very limited publication run.

With the seal of the city and arms of the Crown decorating the map, along with

its dedication to the governor, the plan has the look of an official document, which it very well could have been. It appeared just after the issue of Montgomerie's Charter, which both reorganized the city's existing six wards and added a new seventh one. A Mr. Du Simitiere, writing in 1769, observed: "The boundaries of every ward are described in the charter, but they can not easily be understood without the help of the plan publish'd at that time by Wm Bradford. . . ." Since the charter also reaffirmed the city's right to sell or lease land as it saw fit, it would have been important at the time to see just what land was already occupied and what was not and therefore still under the city's control. An indication of this function of the map is that streets are darkly shaded in areas that were most likely occupied by houses or other structures and unshaded where unoccupied. Whether officially commissioned or not, it appears that the Lyne-Bradford Plan was published to make known the city's municipal reorganization as well as show the real estate controlled by the city.

The Lyne-Bradford Plan was the first to show the city divided into that distinctive urban unit, the ward (even though New York was first divided into wards, six of them, in 1683). The new seventh ward, call Montgomerie's Ward after Thomas Montgomerie, the governor at the time, can be seen in the northern section of the map. In this area, it is evident that development had begun to force its way through,

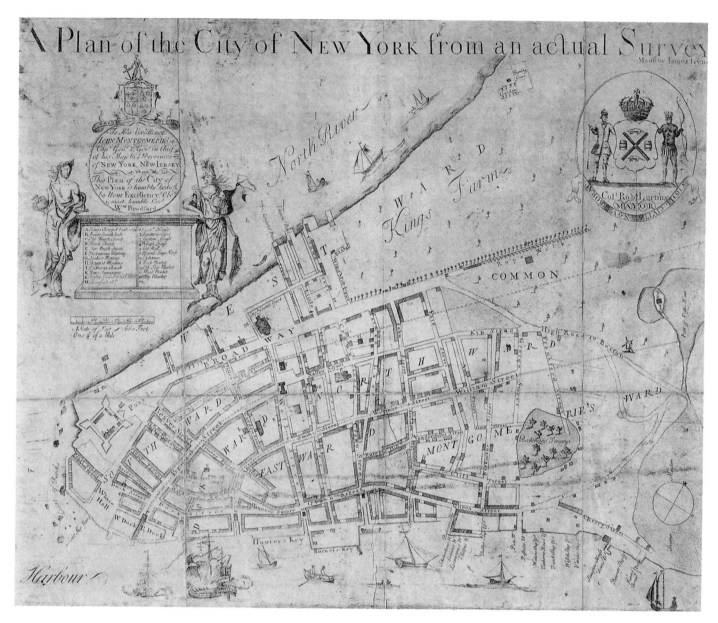

rather than around, natural obstacles. Note the road penetrating Beekman's Swamp, and another one closing in on the very large Swamp Meadow. This tendency to obliterate natural topography in the course of development can be observed throughout the city's growth. It was, in fact, about the time the map was issued that the first attempt to drain the large lake in lower Manhattan, called the Fresh Water or Collect Pond, was made. (Only part of this large, ten-acre body of water is shown on the map in the city's northernmost area.) Also shown on the map in the northern area of the city is the "High Road to Boston," the only road leading out of the

city at the time and the original Post Road.

Although the city was developing, most visitors of the day still described it as an attractive place, which retained many of its original, colorful Dutch-style residences. The Lyne-Bradford Plan suggests that Broadway was a wide, tree-lined thoroughfare of considerable charm. One visitor, in fact, described a walk through the city during the summer at this time as very much like a walk through a garden. And although New Yorkers of the day were often described as commercially minded to the extreme, they were just as often noted for their fondness for good living. The personal effects of the map's dedicatee, Governor

Montgomerie, that were advertised for auction at his death reveal an especially well-stocked wine and liquor cellar and a great deal of finery in both apparel and furnishings. While evidence of extremes of wealth and poverty did begin to appear by 1731, polarization was not yet a glaring feature of the city. In fact, New York's poor at the time were able to subsist on oysters, which abounded in the harbor, particularly between Staten Island and Manhattan.

In the time between the Miller and Lyne-Bradford maps, New York enjoyed its first period of sustained growth, beginning with the conclusion of Queen Anne's War with France in 1713 and lasting for the next two decades. Since 1695 the city's population had roughly doubled, reaching about 8,600 in 1731. Despite this spurt, New York was still very much a small city, especially considering that by this time it was already a century old. Boston and Philadelphia were at the time larger. One need only view the extent of settlement shown on the Lyne-Bradford Plan superimposed on a map of the entire island of Manhattan to see how relatively little of it had been developed. Just north of the settled area on the map, which was still below present Canal Street, was still real wilderness where cattle could get lost. If one follows Broadway north on the map, it soon becomes a "Rope Walk," that is, a mere path through the woods guided by a kind of rope railing. Nevertheless, the Lyne-Bradford Plan clearly shows that the developed area of the city above Wall Street began to exceed in size the area below it. (As of 1699 Wall Street no longer had a wall running along it and soon after became one of the city's most fashionable residential streets.) However, most of the city's population still lived below Wall Street. The northernmost development shown on the map extends to approximately the location of today's City Hall. Cherry Street, along the extreme east side, extends a little farther north to about the area of the Manhattan Bridge.

The irregular arrangement of the new streets seen in the northern section of the map suggests that there was still very little

in the way of street planning. The expansion of the city with landfill, which was first depicted on the c. 1664–68 Nicolls Map, had clearly increased in the early part of the eighteenth century, as can be seen from the Lyne-Bradford Plan. All of the area east of Queen Street, the long north-south street along the east side, consisted of landfill that had been created since the Nicolls Map. An indication of the commitment to the use of landfill is that as early as 1723 Greenwich and Washington streets along the Hudson River were proposed and a year later surveyed while they were still under water. They are not shown on the map because the landfill had not been completed by the time the map was published. However, it is possible that the two small rectangles in the Hudson River at about the north end of the fort delimit the landfill for the proposed streets. This means of expanding the city has continued throughout its history to the current day, with the massive, recently completed Battery Park City project being an extension of the landfill begun in 1723.

Surprisingly, most of the streets in the northern section of the map have survived with their original names, including even small ones like Gold, Cliff, Ann, and Frankfort (misspelled on the map) streets. Those that did not survive, such as George Street, were associated with English monarchs and were thus changed during the American Revolution. Along the upper east side shoreline can be seen the names of the

owners of the wharfs, piers, and slips shown there. Among them are those of many of New York's important early families, who were beginning to build their fortunes at the time of the map: Beekman, Livingstone, Schermerhorn, and Roosevelt.

Since the time of the Miller Plan, a number of important structures had arisen in the city that are indicated on the Lyne-Bradford Plan. A new City Hall (number 5 in the legend), a fine Tuscan-style structure, was built in 1700 on Wall Street. Just completed in 1729 or 1730 was the city's first synagogue (*K*), the Shearith Israel, or Remnant of Israel, which was located on Mill Street, east of Broad Street between Prince and Milk streets. Other structures, all churches, completed since the Miller Plan and their dates of completion are the Anglican Trinity Church, 1696 (*B*); the Quakers' Meeting House, 1703 (*G*); the French Church, 1704 (*D*); the Presbyterian Meeting House, 1719 (*F*); the Baptist Meeting House, 1724 (*H*); and the New or Middle Dutch Church, 1729 (*E*). The Trinity Church shown on the map was the first of three by that name; the still existing one was completed in 1839. Added in manuscript at the bottom of the legend are references to the English and Dutch Free Schools, evidence of New York's first attempts at public education.

ALL BUT LOST
THE CARWITHAM PLAN AND CHART

TITLE: On Single Sheet: (p. 58) A Plan of the City of New York.
(p. 59) A Plan of the Harbour of New York
DATE DEPICTED: C. 1730
DATE PRINTED: C. 1740
ENGRAVER: JOHN CARWITHAM
Uncolored copperplate engraving, 12 x 17 inches
Holkham Hall, Norfolk, England

This well executed double image of New York City and Harbor, known in only two surviving impressions, was printed in London but never commercially published. Based largely on the accurate Lyne-Bradford Plan (see p. 40), it should have been the work that provided Europeans with an up-to-date delineation of New York in the middle decades of the eighteenth century. Curiously, this never happened, leaving the period between 1730 and 1763 without the publication of a single plan of New York. In fact, so nearly lost was this work that the impression of it illustrated here was not discovered until 1991, when Helen Wallis, the late map librarian of the British Library, came upon it in the English manor house, Holkham Hall, in Norfolk. Moreover, the other known impression, which is in the print department of the Bibliothèque Nationale in Paris, was not brought to light until early in this century.

The Carwitham Plan provides some updating of its model, the Lyne-Bradford Plan, and is also a neater, more legible engraving. It covers more territory to the north, and more houses are shown shaded in along the streets. Also, the Carwitham Plan is made richer by several small illustrations of important buildings, such as the Synagogue on Mill Street, the Dutch Church on Garden Street, and the First Presbyterian Church on Wall Street. Perhaps the most interesting change that is found on both the plan and chart is that

both "North" and "Hudson" are offered as possible names for the river, with the latter being a new development. The river's nomenclature is one of the curiosities of New York history: the English long insisted on calling it the North River even though Hudson, the first European to navigate the river, was an Englishman. The problem for the English arose from the fact that Hudson had been in the employ of the Dutch when he journeyed up the river, and the use of his name for the river would have lent support to Dutch territorial claims. However, by the time this map was drafted, the Dutch had long been in eclipse, and so the English evidently felt secure enough to give Hudson his due.

Another curiosity that appears on the chart, and which is not seen on any other map, is a place called Cuckold Town on Staten Island. We have not found a reference to such a place elsewhere. Another rarely seen peculiarity of nomenclature on the chart is that York Island is offered as an alternative name for Manhattan. The chart also indicates the area in the harbor— around Liberty and Ellis Islands—where oysters were the most plentiful. I. N. Phelps Stokes in *The Iconography of Manhattan* points out that many place-names are misspelled on the plan and chart, suggesting that its draftsman or engraver was unfamiliar with the area and was possibly copying another work.

The only thing that is known for certain about the production of this work is

that it was engraved by John Carwitham, whose name appears below the title of the harbor chart. He was an engraver of bookplates and prints who worked in London from about 1723 to 1741. Wallis discovered the Holkham Hall impression of the plan and chart in a composite atlas that was compiled as a kind of hobby by John Innys (1695–1778), who, along with his brother, William, had been a prominent London printer and publisher. The impression in the Innys atlas was most likely a trial proof of an illustration for a book that was planned but never published. Wallis further found that this aborted publishing project most likely had its genesis with William Byrd II (1674–1744), a Virginia plantation owner, colonial official, and amateur naturalist. It is known that Byrd had been gathering images—including several maps—for a historical work on Virginia. (At the time, this place-name could still encompass much of the eastern United States, including New York.) It appears that some time after 1737 Byrd sent the images he had gathered to Peter Collinson, a London merchant and associate of Byrd. Collinson was to arrange for their engraving and publication in London and must have engaged one or both of the Innys brothers for this project. The plates were then engraved, but since Byrd died shortly after, the text he was to furnish to accompany the plates was never completed. Thus, only a few trial impressions must have been pulled. The plates themselves still survive in the Bodleian Library at Oxford, with the exception of the one for the New York plan and chart, which is lost.

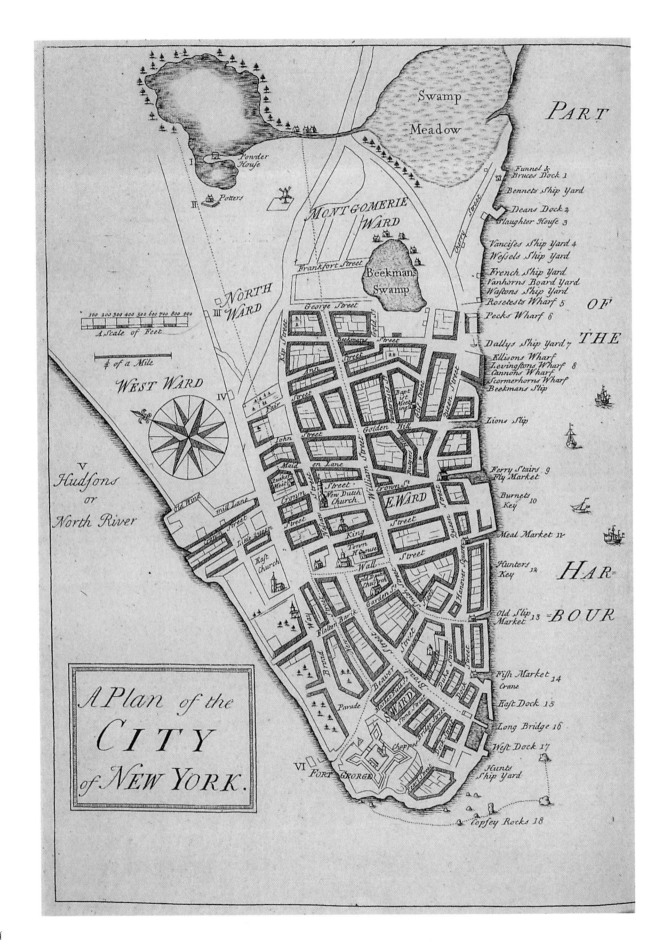

A Plan of the
CITY
of NEW YORK.

Swamp
Meadow

PART

Powder House
I
II Potters
MONTGOMERIE WARD
Frankfort Street
Beekmans Swamp
NORTH WARD
III
George Street
Beekmans Street
Kip Street
Fair Street
WEST WARD
IV
John Street
Maiden Lane
Quaker Meet
Cromn Street
Mill Lane
Old Wind
Golden Hill
William Street
Baptist Meeting
Crown St
Queen Street
E. WARD
Little Queen
Kast church
Fish Bank
Flatten Barrik
King Town House
Wall Street
Old Dutch Church
Garden St
Hanover Square
V
Hudsons
or
North River
Beaver Street
Parade
Duke Street
Dock Street
S WARD
Stone Street
Bridge Lane
VI FORT GEORGE
Chappel Street

Funnel & Bruces Dock 1
Bennets Ship Yard
Deans Dock 2
Slaughter House 3
Vancises Ship Yard 4
Wessels Ship Yard
French Ship Yard
Vanhorns Board Yard
Wastons Ship Yard
Rosetests Wharf 5
Pecks Wharf 6
Dallys Ship Yard 7
Ellisons Wharf
Levingstons Wharf 8
Cannons Wharf
Scormerhorns Wharf
Beekmans Slip
Lions Slip
Ferry Stairs 9
Fly Market
Burnets Key 10
Meal Market 11
Hunters Key 12
Old Slip Market 13
Fish Market 14
Crane
Kast Dock 15
Long Bridge 16
West Dock 17
Hunts Ship Yard
Topsey Rocks 18

OF
THE
HAR=
BOUR

100 200 300 400 500 600 700 800 900
A Scale of Feet

¼ of a Mile

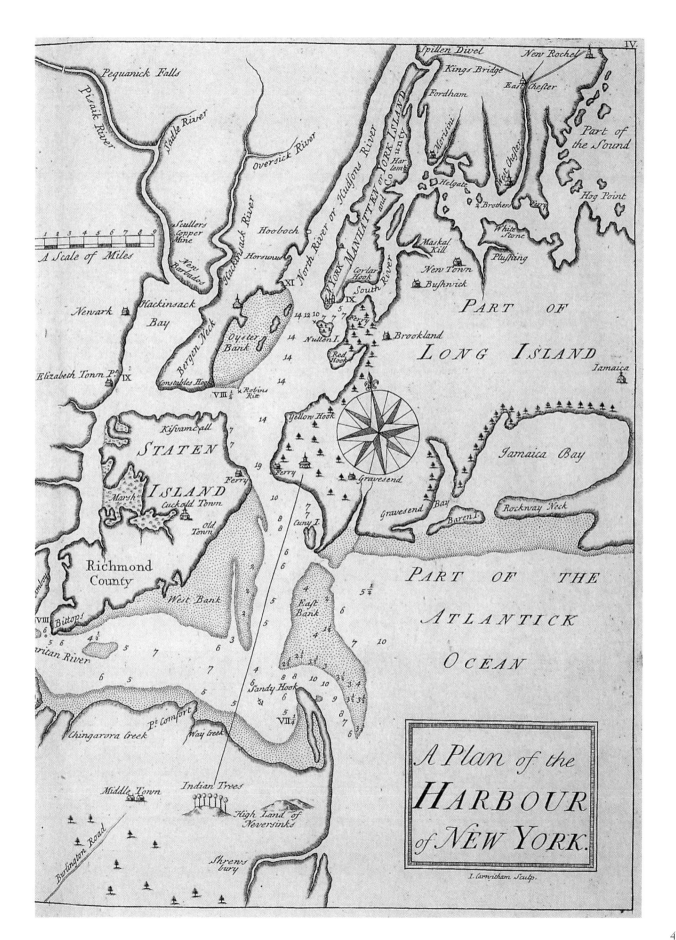

A Plan of the HARBOUR of NEW YORK.

I. Carwitham Sculp.

A CITIZEN'S MAP
MRS. BUCHNERD'S PLAN

TITLE: Plan of the City of New York In the Year 1735
DATE DEPICTED: c. 1732–35
DATE DRAWN: 1735
CARTOGRAPHER: MRS. BUCHNERD (?)
Pen and ink on paper mounted on linen, 15¼ x 18½ inches
The New York Public Library, I.N. Phelps Stokes Collection

One quickly sees that Mrs. Buchnerd's Plan is much less polished than the carefully prepared, if not professional, works previously illustrated. Its homespun quality is further revealed in the tortured spelling found on it: tavrin for tavern, est for east, boding for bowling, and gardin for garden. Also, the map shows more social, cultural and leisure-related locations than any other early map; places such as taverns, inns, gardens, recreation areas, and even a theater. This suggests that the map was originally an informal, personalized guide to the city made by an ordinary citizen.

Nothing is known of the circumstances of the map's creation, although the name of a "Mrs. Buchnerd" appears on it in the upper right corner. While some think that she was most likely an owner of the map rather than its author, the handwriting for her name appears to match the hand of the other written material on the map. If the map was indeed her work, this would certainly be the earliest extant map of New York by a woman. Traces of folds on the paper on which the map was drawn indicate that it was at one time folded down to letter size. It is therefore possible that the map was intended as a sketch of the city to accompany a personal letter.

An important development in the city seen for the first time on the map is the existence of a large recreational area just outside of the settled part of the city. It was located along the western extreme of the city just north of the settled area and would have

been in the vicinity of number 22 on the map, which refers to the Bowling Green Garden (identified as Bolding Green in the legend below the map). (It is not to be confused with the area now bearing that name, which was the location of a parade ground and later a fine park just north of the fort.) This area is in the vicinity of today's Greenwich and Warren streets. Built in 1733–34, the area developed into a fashionable resort that offered dancing, strolls through dimly lit groves, and dining, all in a sylvan setting. It later was called Vauxhall Garden after the one in London. Nearby three other resort or recreational centers are shown; one called Spring Garden, at present-day Park Row and Broadway is indicated by the number 21, and another, the "John Ell. Gardin," is shown farther to the north on Broadway. The third, just below the Spring Garden, is called the winyerd; it may have been a vineyard at one time but was an ornamental garden at the time of the map. Also located in the area of the Bowling Green Garden are two drinking establishments called Meed houses on the plan, belonging to Shairman(?) and Van Denberger (actually Van Denber). These recreational areas were precursors of the city's park system and were an early response to increasing congestion. They filled a need for open space necessitated by the elimination of large gardens on private property in the city and of space between buildings.

Also on the map are signs of a related trend toward large country estates owned

by the city's wealthy residents. In a few decades, Manhattan north of its developed area would be interspersed with sprawling manors. The locations of farms owned by the prominent Stuyvesant, Rutgers, and De Lancey families can be seen on the map.

A center for conviviality in New York at the time was William Street, where several taverns were located. The most popular was probably the Horse and Cart, number 16 on the map. Another important social center shown on the map is a coffeehouse, which was in the commercial district near Dock Street.

Because the area covered by this map extends farther north than the Lyne-Bradford and Miller plans, it is interesting to see what else was located in what would have been the countryside at the time. Two tanneries can be seen on either side of Beekman's Swamp, which is shown as a kind of oval cloud on the east side just above the city. These would have been relegated to this area because of the noxious odors they produced. Likewise, the Powder House, which manufactured gunpowder, was located a safe distance from town; it is the structure between the bodies of water labeled the "Fresh Water" and "Swamp." Reflective of the inferior status of Jews and blacks, their burying grounds were forlornly situated near swamps. A detail on the map suggesting the charms of old New York countryside are the two little ponds seen on either side of the northernmost part of Bowre Layn, original route of today's

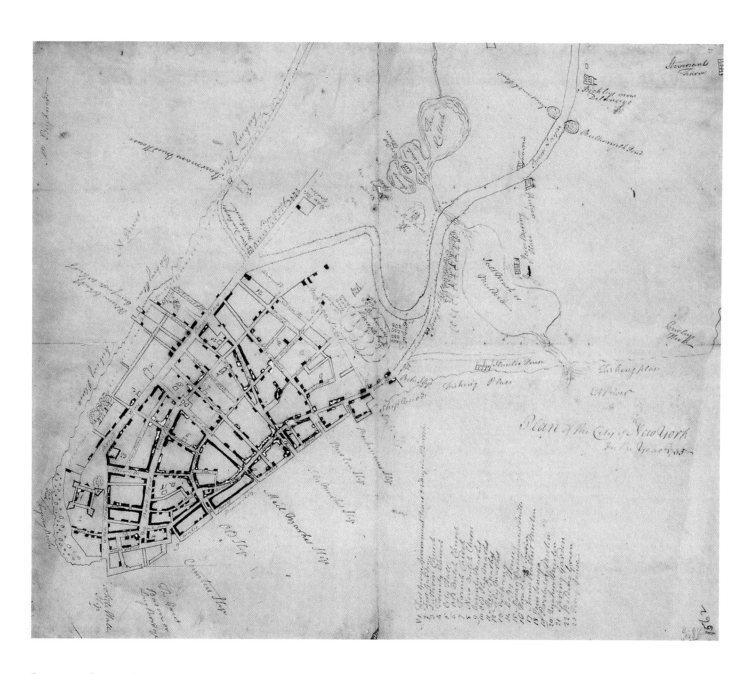

Bowery. Only one other early map even shows the two ponds; this one also thankfully preserved their idyllic names, Buttermilk and Sweetmilk. A reminder of one of New York's once rich natural resources is the notation "Fishing Place," appearing numerous times along both its western shoreline and along part of the busier eastern shore, north of the docks and piers.

An important structure for New York's cultural history, its earliest theater, is shown for the first time on this map; it was first mentioned in historical records in 1732. Appropriately, it was located at the base of Broadway just above Beaver Street.

Even though this manuscript appeared just five years after the Lyne-Bradford Plan (see p. 40), it reveals that some important

expansion had occurred in the city in the meantime. Water Street, which is shown completed and named for the first time, had become the easternmost thoroughfare of the city. Also seen for the first time on a map is Cortlandt Street, which was laid out and named in 1733. A relic of New York street nomenclature on the map is Elbow Street, the old name for Cliff Street.

MAPPING FROM MEMORY
THE GRIM PLAN

TITLE: A Plan of the City and Environs of New York as they were in the years 1742 1743 & 1744
DATE DEPICTED: C. 1742–44
DATE DRAWN: AUGUST 1813
CARTOGRAPHER: DAVID GRIM
Pen and ink with watercolor on paper, mounted on paper, 22⅛ x 21⅞ inches
New-York Historical Society

Remarkably, the richly detailed Grim Plan was drawn from memory by a seventy-six-year-old man recalling the city he knew as a young boy some seventy years earlier. It was completed in 1813, but as its title states, it depicts the city as it was in the years 1742, 1743, and 1744. A fact that dates the map at the time that Grim claims is that it does not include the streets in Montgomerie's Ward in the northeastern part of the city, which were just being surveyed and laid out at the time the map is supposed to represent. Another detail specific to the time claimed for the map is the presence of the palisade, a kind of a second Wall Street built across the width of Manhattan in 1745, when an attack by the French was thought imminent. It began at Cherry Street on the east side and ran to the Hudson River at about the location of Franklin Street, not far to the south of present-day Canal Street.

In a note on the back of the map (now covered over by the paper on which the map is mounted), Grim claims to recall each of the city's streets as they were in his boyhood, which he says numbered about thirty, and also where there were structures and where vacant lots. It is possible that Grim's memory was aided by studying the Lyne-Bradford Plan (see p. 40). The number and arrangement of streets on his plan compare very closely with those on that map.

Among the plans of New York of the first half of the eighteenth century, Grim's is unique in the kind of visual detail it provides. In particular, it offers an excellent representation of Manhattan north of the developed part of the city, an area for which very little visual record exists. Much of this area had been wilderness and swamp at the beginning of the century, but from the Grim Plan, we can see that it had largely come under cultivation. There are a number of sprawling farms interconnected by country roads in the area. Many of them would evolve during the course of the century into the country estates of the city's wealthy. There is evidence of this process on the map in the several patterned, ornamental gardens that can be seen amid the fields and orchards. Also, seen clearly for the first time on this map is the course of the stream emanating from the Collect Pond and emptying into the East River. Present-day Canal Street runs along part of the route of the stream. Also important on the Grim Plan are the drawings of important structures along the top border. Some of them are the only surviving visual records of the buildings they depict, notably the ones of the synagogue, poorhouse, and the Baptist and Quaker meetinghouses.

An episode that had been scalded into Grim's memory and which was one of the most shameful and harrowing in the city's history is the so-called Negro plot of 1741. Even in Grim's 1813 recollections recorded in the note on the back of the map, the events are still fresh in his mind and spoken of with emotion. The plan shows the locations (numbers 55–57 in the legend) of the brutal executions by burning and hanging that were part of the episode. Gallows with hanging men and a burning stake can be seen at these sites, which are just north of the thickly settled part of the city. Such an impression was left by these events that the

area of the gallows on the East River (number 57) was for a long time called Hughson Point, after the name of the supposed leader of the "plot," who was hanged there.

The events of 1741 were not the first uprising of New York's slaves, who had been a substantial part of the city's population (about one-sixth) since early in the century. For a good deal of the eighteenth century, New York was the largest slave-holding area by percentage north of the Chesapeake Bay. One result was that white New Yorkers at the time seemed to live in continual fear of slave revolt. This was exacerbated by Manhattan's geography, where wilderness was adjacent to its developed area. It was thus not that difficult for slaves to escape and hide, which is borne out by the numerous ads in newspapers concerning runaway slaves. To control slaves, there was severe punishment for even minor infractions and absolutely harrowing punishment, usually burning at the stake, for anything serious. Rebellion by slaves, such as the one of 1712, met with even more severe reprisals with twenty-one slaves being executed at the time. In the events of 1741, a series of fires in the city was believed by the white populace to be the beginning of a plot by slaves to take over the city. Rumor galvanized into conviction as witnesses, both white and black, emerged to corroborate the plot. The witnesses were eventually found to be unreliable, most having been already in prison on other charges. Nevertheless, 154 slaves were imprisoned, 31 executed, and 71 deported; even 21 whites were arrested and four executed as ring leaders. Even more disturbing was that the prosecutions were carried out by the city's leading citizens, who felt that they had done a great service. Even Grim, leaving no mistake about his sympathies, refers to the events as the "horrid plot."

The growth of commerce and industry

in the city at the time is reflected in several details on the plan. Six different markets for various products are indicated (numbers 18–23), and four tanneries (numbers 37–40) and two potteries (numbers 43 and 44) also appear. It is also clear from the plan that New Yorkers had not lost their thirst for alcoholic beverages, as four breweries (numbers 33–36) are shown, a significant

number for the population of no more than ten thousand.

In David Grim's long life (1737–1826), he worked in a number of capacities that follow a career pattern typical of many successful New Yorkers of the time. In his early days, he served aboard a merchant ship for two years in the West Indies, a key trading area for New Yorkers. Next he worked as an

innkeeper and then tavern owner, lines of work that were very popular throughout the city's early history. He then became a successful merchant and held several offices. In his later years, for his own amusement, he took to making drawings and maps such as this one that recreated the city's earlier days. He presented this plan to the New-York Historical Society, where it still resides.

EARLY PLANNED GROWTH
THE MAERSCHALCK PLAN

TITLE: A Plan of the City of New York from an actual Survey Anno Domini—M, DCC, IV
DATE DEPICTED: 1754
CARTOGRAPHER: FRANCIS MAERSCHALCK
PUBLISHED: GERARDUS DUYCKINCK, NEW YORK, 1755
Uncolored copperplate engraving, 17⅝ x 33¼ inches
New-York Historical Society

A dramatic change occurred in the way New York expanded in the mid-eighteenth century, and the nature of this change is clearly revealed on the Maerschalck Plan. There are three distinct areas of new growth on the plan that are marked by a regularity of design not seen before. One is located in the upper west side in the area labeled King's Farm; this is just north of the area where the World Trade Center now is. Another new section is to the northeast of the Fresh Water or Collect Pond (in the area of today's Little Italy, just to the north of Canal Street). The third is to the south and east of the former along the East River. These three areas represent the beginnings of more structured growth in the city.

While the first of the three areas belonged to Trinity Church, the latter two were privately owned, being parts of much larger holdings of the prosperous Bayard and Rutgers families, respectively. It is most likely that the development of streets on the properties belonging to the two families was a privately directed enterprise. These two areas of new growth, therefore, are the earliest instances of the systematic development of land in New York for profit. This indicates that land was becoming a serious income-producing commodity in the city. This trend would influence the way streets were laid out and have consequences that can be felt even today in the city.

Seen for the first time on the Maerschalck Plan is the use of the street grid, the pattern which would eventually be imposed on most of Manhattan. The grid scheme has the virtue of simplicity, as its use ignores often complex issues raised by the land's natural topography or other challenges of design. Perhaps the greatest advantage of the grid is to the owner of the land; it allows for the maximum number of streets and lots to be arrayed on a piece of land. Another reason for the use of a street pattern that maximized the number of lots is simply that Manhattan had only one direction in which to expand—north. It did not have the luxury of radiating at a measured pace from a central area. Even when there were acres of undeveloped land on Manhattan, it was still important to create as many lots as close as possible to the city, because it had just the one direction in which it could grow. If the city had originated in the middle of the island instead of at the southern tip, it would certainly look and feel differently today.

The effects of the street grid on day-to-day life are abundantly clear to anyone who has spent any time at all in New York. It forces traffic to meet frequently at numerous intersections, making movement inevitably a stop-and-go affair. On the other hand, because of the density enforced by the grid, distances to services are shorter, thus allowing New Yorkers to conduct a good deal of life's business on foot. Also, again because of the numerous intersections inherent in a grid pattern, there is an enforced frequency of contact among both pedestrians and vehicles. The consequence is a continual jostling of people and vehicles, which no doubt has influenced the personality of the city. Lastly, as mentioned above, a strict grid pattern results in the near eradication, or at least, segregation of the natural world from the urban landscape.

The many new streets that are seen for the first time on the Maerschalck Plan were laid out over about a ten-year period beginning in the mid 1740s. The names of many of them as they appear on the plan were later changed. Some of their original and current names are (moving west to east on the plan): Partition, now Fulton Street; Robinson, now Park Place; Kip, now Nassau Street; Chapel Street, now West Broadway; Skinner's (fittingly, in the tannery district), now Cliff Street; Winne, now part of Mott Street; Ryndert, now Center Street; Judith, now Grand Street; Hevins, now Broome Street; Nicholas, now Walker Street; Olive, now Lafayette Street; and others. Ironically, the name of Rutgers Street, running through the heart of the Rutgers property in the northeastern part of the city, was changed; it is now called Monroe Street. (There is another Rutgers Street in the city that was laid out later in a different location.) Among the more familiar streets that appear on this plan for the first time and whose names have *not* been changed are Mott, Mulberry, Hester, Bayard, Church, Vesey, and Dey.

The newly developed area shown on the plan in the upper west side was owned and developed by Trinity Church, the city's Anglican house of worship. Here was the original location of Columbia University, then called King's College, which was founded in 1754, a year before the map was published. It is possible that the structures indicated but not named on the plan in this area are those of the college.

If the Maerschalck Plan looks very much like the Lyne-Bradford Plan (see p.(see p.

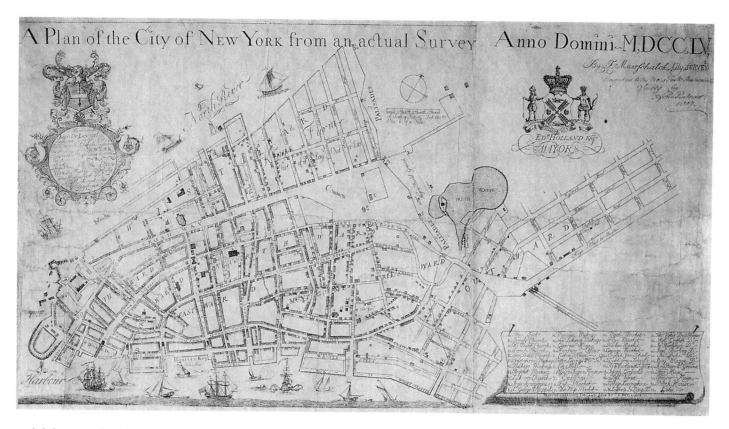

40), it is no accident. Maerschalck actually used the same copperplate from which the Lyne-Bradford Plan had been printed; he simply added a new section to it and altered the original with new information. The joint separating the new and old parts of the plate can be easily made out on the plan; it runs along a vertical line passing through the middle of the Fresh Water or Collect Pond. However, the original area of the plate to the left of this line was so extensively reworked by Maerschalck that one wonders why he did not engrave a wholly new plan. On the other hand, it is not difficult to alter a copperplate; since it is a relatively soft metal, an engraved area could simply be hammered flat and then newly engraved over.

To the original part of the plan, Maerschalck added entirely new sections of streets in the King's Farm and Rutgers property areas. Also, the dedication and its highly ornamental cartouche and all of the decorative sailing vessels have been completely changed. Several important alterations were also made to the lower part of the city by Maerschalck. Along the lower west side, it is clear that progress had been

made with the landfill that had begun in the mid 1720s; parts of present-day Greenwich and Washington streets can be seen. A number of the piers along the east side are more extended here than on the Lyne-Bradford Plan. Maerschalck also added the many new streets that had been laid out in Montgomerie's Ward, to the immediate southeast of the Fresh Water. These were, in fact, surveyed by Maerschalck himself in 1744. Also, the fortifications built in 1745, including the palisade running across the entire city and the new batteries added near the fort, are seen here. The Maerschalck Plan denotes structures that had been built since the Lyne-Bradford Plan by means of shaded areas along the streets.

Little is known about Gerardus Duyckinck, whose name appears on the plan as its publisher. The publication and selling of this map seems to have been merely one of several commercial activities he engaged in, as he was not a professional publisher. He advertised the availability of the map in the March 3, 1755, issue of the *New-York Gazette*; there is nothing in the advertisement to suggest that the publica-

tion of the map was anything more than an individual commercial venture. In any case, the map was not a best-seller, since fewer than five copies of it are extant. Only this example from the Library of Congress has the ornamental border.

Francis Maerschalck (d. 1776) had a long and productive career as the city surveyor of New York beginning in 1733. He personally surveyed many of the new streets that appear on the plan. Among his other achievements was the surveying of the Bloomingdale Road in 1760, which ran from about Twenty-third Street to Harlem along the west side. (*Bloomingdale*, from a Dutch word for vale of flowers, originally referred to much of the west side of Manhattan, which had large, flowering fields.) In 1749, he surveyed the boundary between Harlem and the rest of the city. Yet, remarkably, this is his only original printed work that has survived, and only a few of his manuscript surveys are extant. There is a later, 1763 edition of this map that was reengraved in reduced and simplified form. It is part of a rare collection of thirty plans of American forts issued by Mary Ann Rocque.

THE TIDDEMAN CHART

TITLE: A Draught of New York from the Hook to New York Town
DATE DEPICTED: c. 1730
CARTOGRAPHER: MARK TIDDEMAN
PUBLISHED: *The English Pilot,* BOOK 4, LONDON, c. 1732–80
Hand-colored copperplate engraving, 18 x 21½ inches
Richard B. Arkway, Inc.

THE DESBARRES RECOGNITION VIEWS

TITLE: A View of the Highland of Neversunk . . . / The South Shore of Long Island . . . /
New York, with the Entrance of the North and East Rivers / The Light House on Sandy
Hook, S.E. One Mile. / The Narrows, . . .
DATE DEPICTED: c. 1773
CARTOGRAPHER: J. F. W. DESBARRES
PUBLISHED: J. F. W. DESBARRES, *The Atlantic Neptune,* LONDON, OCTOBER 4, 1777
Hand-colored aquatints, 29¼ x 21¼ inches
Private collection

THE DESBARRES CHART

TITLE: A Chart of New York Harbour . . . for the Use of Pilotage
DATE DEPICTED: c. 1776
CARTOGRAPHER: J. F. W. DESBARRES
PUBLISHED: J. F. W. DESBARRES, *The Atlantic Neptune,* LONDON, 1779
Hand-colored copperplate engraving, 31⅜ x 23⅞ inches
Private collection

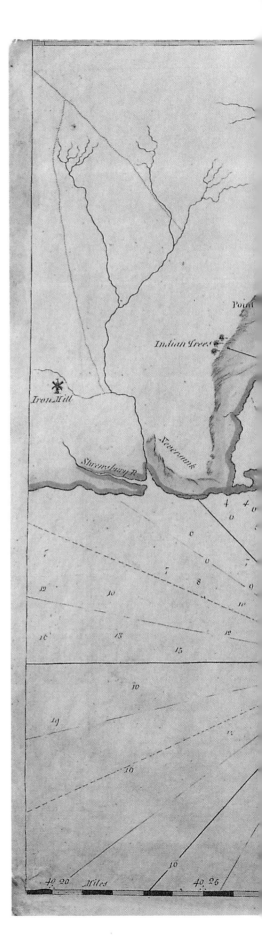

Nautical charting took an unprecedented leap toward greater precision and graphic sophistication with the publication of DesBarres's *Atlantic Neptune.* Its charts covered the American coastline from the Canadian Maritime Provinces to the Mississippi River. The *Neptune* provided the first generally accurate charts of many areas, and it was relied upon well into the nineteenth century. DesBarres also standardized many of the symbols, such as for navigational hazards, that are found on nautical charts to this day.

As can be seen from the Tiddeman Chart, the works that preceded DesBarres appear to be altogether of a different era. In fact, their inaccuracy was blamed for the loss of scores of British and American ships. Although the Tiddeman Chart is not nearly as poor as others of the day, it, for example, makes the entrance to the Lower Bay of New York Harbor appear to be less of a challenge than it really is. The poor quality of these earlier charts was compounded by their having been published over long periods of time with little or no corrections. Remarkably, the Tiddeman Chart was in publication for forty-eight years, from 1732 to 1780, and was even available after the DesBarres Chart appeared. Tiddeman's work was published in *The English Pilot,* Book 4, which was the only printed chart

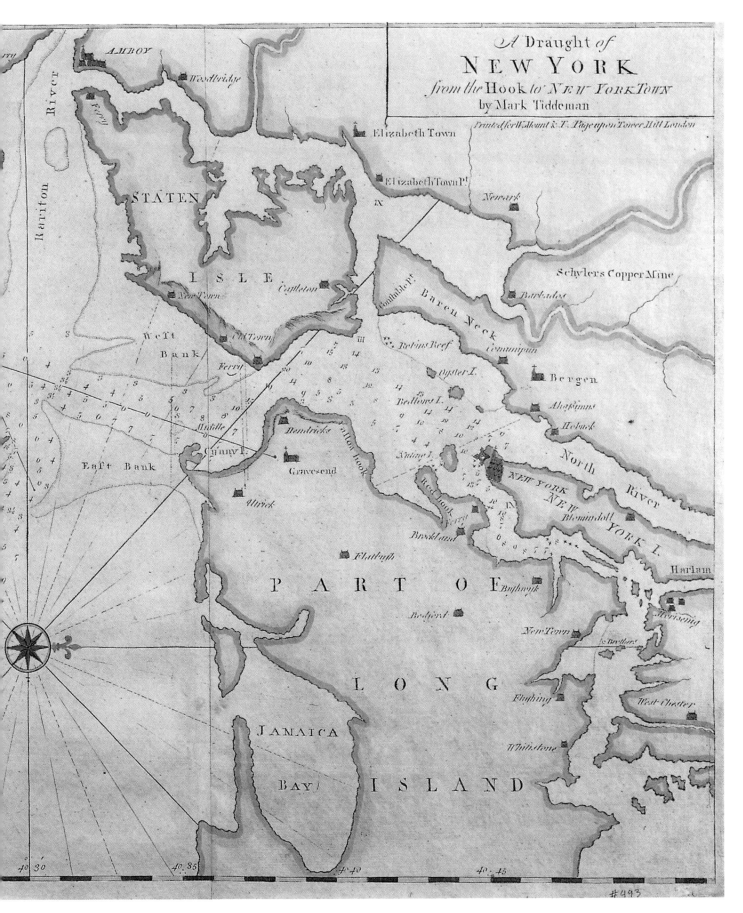

A Draught of
NEW YORK
from the Hook to NEW YORK TOWN
by Mark Tiddeman

Printed for W. Mount & T. Page upon Tower Hill London

AMBOY

Woodbridge

Ferry

Elizabeth Town

STATEN

Elizabeth Town Pt.

Newark

ISLE

Castleton

New Town

Conitable pt.

Baren Neck

Schylers Copper Mine

Barbadoes

WeSt

Bank

Old Town

Ferry

St. Petins Reef

Comunipun

Oyster I.

Bergen

Middle

Bedlows I.

Ahasimus

Hebuck

EaSt Bank

Gunny I.

Hendricks

Gratton hook

States I.

NEW YORK

North

River

Red hook

Gravesend

Ferry

Ulrick

Brockland

Blomindoll

YORK I.

Harlam

Flatbush

PART OF

Bushwyk

Morisenia

Bedford

New Town

2 Brothers

Flushing

WeSt Chester

JAMAICA

LONG

Whitstone

BAY

ISLAND

Rariton River

40. 30   40. 35   40. 40   40. 45

#493

53

book of the American coastline available in England from the end of the seventeenth century until the publication of the *Neptune* nearly a century later.

Not only were DesBarres's charts technically superior to earlier works, but they were also objects of fine printing and possessed an artistry that transcended their utilitarian purpose. Moreover, this was achieved on works that were often breathtakingly large in scale, with some charts measuring over ten feet in length. In all, 257 plates, most of them elephant folio in size, were produced for the *Neptune*. Among the artistically finest charts are those that include insets of delicately rendered views of the coastline, called recognition views, as is the case with the one of New York. These views were provided literally to show the navigator what he could expect to see from a given position. For important harbors, such as New York, DesBarres provided a series of views on a single sheet. The five of New York, which are subtly accented with hand color, afford us the opportunity to see what an eighteenth-century sailor saw as he approached New York City. Unfortunately, they are not arranged in the correct order on the sheet. Their proper sequence would be, first, the view (second from the top) showing the south shore of Long Island; second, the view (top) showing in the distance the Navesink Highlands, an elevation that served as a landmark for the entrance of the Lower Bay; third, the view (second from the bottom) showing the lighthouse on Sandy Hook at the entrance of the Lower Bay; fourth, the view (bottom) of the Narrows between the Upper and Lower bays; and finally the view (middle) on which one sights in the distance the already dense skyline of New York City and its ship-filled harbor. So skillfully executed are these works that they appear to be fine pen-and-ink drawings that were freshly done on the

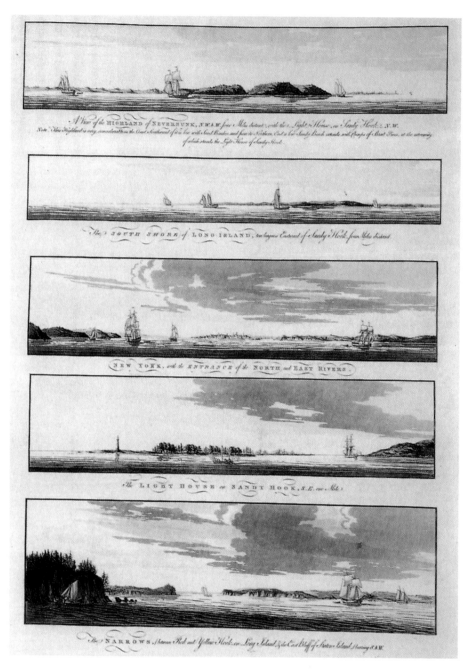

spot. Most of the views in the *Neptune* were, in fact, produced by the aquatint process, which can achieve more subtle gradations of shading than ordinary line engraving. DesBarres was the first in England to make extensive use of the process.

While aesthetically pleasing, the recognition views often served a vital navigational purpose, which is the case with the two on the New York Harbor chart. A text sheet entitled "Nautical Directions to Sail into the Harbour of New-York" accompanied the chart in the atlas and explained

how these views functioned. The view to the right shows how a group of landmarks, namely a lighthouse, the peak of an elevated area, and a group of cedar trees, are to align in relation to one another when seen from a particular point at the entrance near the Lower Bay off Sandy Hook. When the navigator sees exactly what the view shows, he knows that at that point he can set a particular course (given in the printed instructions) to get him safely through the very narrow entrance of the Lower Bay. One line on the chart beginning at the entrance of the Lower Bay shows the direction the navigator would look to sight what the view shows, while another line intersecting with this one shows the course he is to follow. The view on the left similarly cues the navigator when to head north once he is in the Lower Bay. Thus the views together with the text offer elegant solutions to difficult navigational problems in an age when a navigator could not determine his exact position.

Most of the surveys on which the charts of the *Neptune* were based were conducted between 1763 and 1773. DesBarres was then commissioned to assemble these surveys, which included his own fine work in Nova Scotia, prepare their engraving, and have them bound into a usable format. Surveys of the New York and New England areas were carried out by various officers under the command of Major Samuel Holland, one of the most capable of all colonial cartographers. He was most likely the maker of the fine military survey the Holland Map (see p. 68). In some but not all cases, DesBarres provided the names of the actual surveyors on the charts, as he did in the case of the one of New York Harbor. Lieutenants John Knight and John Hunter are cited. Hunter had been assigned to the *Eagle*, the flagship of the English naval commander Lord Howe. He later became governor of New South Wales, Australia, and was instrumental in the exploration and mapping of that continent. Less is known of Knight, though he was later knighted. No sources are given for the series of five recognition views, although it is possible they were the work of the same officers.

When war with the American colonies broke out, the need for good charts of American waters became imperative, and in the years prior to the war, DesBarres's project was given high priority. Between 1776 and 1779, DesBarres and his more than

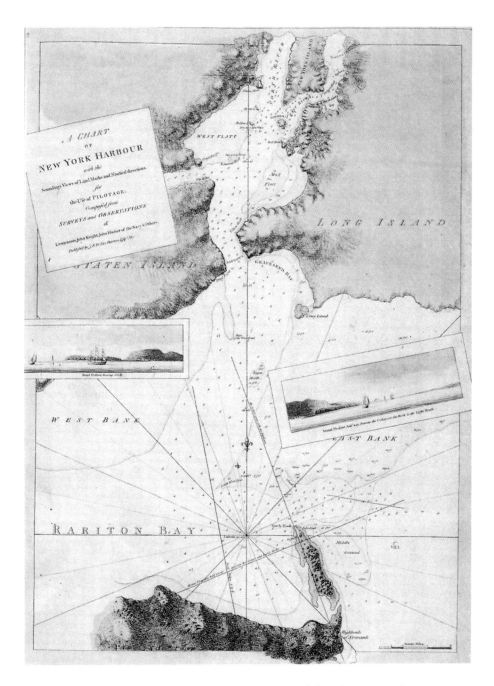

twenty assistants had taken over two London townhouses to complete the *Neptune*. Individual charts were sent out to British naval commanders in America as early as 1774, some three years before the first publication of the complete atlas. However, it is unlikely that the New York chart was used in the New York campaigns of 1776, since the first known issue of the chart has a 1779 date. Given Hunter's position on Howe's flagship, it is more likely that the chart was made during the campaign and perhaps used in manuscript form.

Nevertheless, the New York area was given very thorough treatment in the *Neptune*. In addition to the two works illustrated here, the atlas also contained an excellent bird's-eye view of the city, a general map of Manhattan and the surrounding region giving the military situation, another chart that contained an inset of upper Manhattan and Hell Gate, and a dramatic view of American fireships launched toward the British ships the *Phoenix* and Rose on the Hudson River above Manhattan.

CLANDESTINE CARTOGRAPHY
THE MONTRESOR PLAN

TITLE: A Plan of the City of New-York & its Environs to Greenwich
on the North or Hudsons River, . . . survey'd in the Winter, 1766
DATE DEPICTED: 1766
CARTOGRAPHER: JOHN MONTRESOR
ENGRAVER: P. ANDREWS
PUBLISHED: MARY ANN ROCQUE, LONDON, 1767
Hand-colored copperplate engraving, 20⅝ x 25⅜ inches
Private collection

While Boston and Philadelphia are usually associated with the key early events of the American Revolution, the initial spasms of the war were actually felt more keenly in New York. In fact, in 1765, just two years after the French and Indian War and the year the Montresor Plan was begun, New York had already become a dangerous place. So much so that this work, which was based on a survey by a British military engineer, was marred by the hostile conditions under which it was made.

At the conclusion of the French and Indian War (1763), England attempted a stern revision of its colonial policy. The colonies, which had grown prosperous, would be compelled by the enforcement of the Navigation Acts and other legal devices to produce revenue for the Crown and pay for their own defense. Virtually all trade would be forced to flow through England and be carried on English ships. These measures particularly affected New York merchants, who had developed trading relations with a great number of nations. When these measures did not produce enough revenue, the odious Stamp Act was passed in 1765, which required the use of a stamp on all legal documents. Again, New York, with its great number of lawyers and merchants, would be especially put upon by this law. The Quartering Act, which forced colonials to house British troops, was also particularly onerous to New Yorkers, since the city was the headquarters for the British army in America. Also, during this

period there was continual friction between the often arrogant British soldiers and the city's common citizens, many of whom were unemployed at the time and therefore primed for revolt.

Fearing that Manhattan would soon become a battleground and needing to know the city's layout, General Thomas Gage, the commander-in-chief of British forces, summoned to his office his best engineer, Lieutenant John Montresor, on December 7, 1765. At this time, Gage asked Montresor simply to "procure" a map of the city and its surroundings. Not finding one, Montresor was ordered to, as he noted in his journal, "Sketch him [Gage] a Plan of this Place on a large Scale. . . ." Montresor worked on the plan at a time of violent hostility toward British officials and soldiers. Rioting in response to the arrival of the hated stamps had nearly plunged the city into chaos. In the midst of the turmoil, Montresor conducted the surveys for this plan in secret because, as he noted, if he were detected, it "might endanger ones house and effects if not ones life." The following passage from Montresor's journal evokes his perilous working conditions at the height of the riots:

This night about 8 o'clock the Effigies of Lord Colville Mr Grenville and General Murray were paraded several times through the streets amidst a large concourse of people who halted first where the Governor was in company and gave

3 Huzzas, they were carried to the Common and there burnt. Their numerous attendants the Mob were furnished all with Candles which they forced from the Houses as they went along, threatening to set them on fire if Refused. I continued on the General's Draught [map] and daily taking the Bearings & distances & Sketching in the country about this place.

The effects of making the plan under these circumstances can readily be seen, as only a few streets on it are identified, and their lengths are imprecisely plotted. Very few structures are represented, and there is relatively little detail of any kind in the settled area. Some of these shortcomings, however, are due to the original intent of the plan as a military survey, which would focus more on topography and key installations. Nevertheless, other errors, such as the omission of the small pond that was part of the Collect or Fresh Water, as well as of the docks along the East River, were certainly the result of the trying circumstances under which the mapmaker worked. Moreover, although the Montresor Plan was made over ten years later than the Maerschalck Plan (see p. 50), the Montresor has only one group of streets not appearing on the earlier work. It is the small grid to the east of Bowery Lane. In fact, the Maerschalck Plan provides a more complete picture of the city's streets in the upper west portion of town.

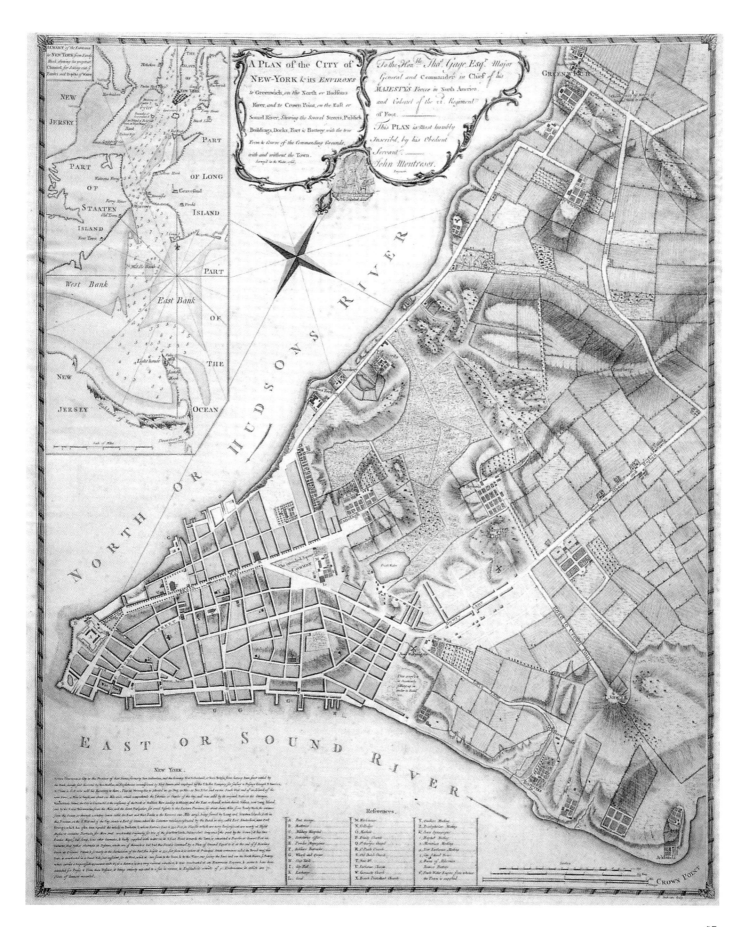

Of great significance, however, is that the Montresor Plan is the first map of New York to provide a detailed glimpse of Manhattan beyond the city itself and thus give an idea of the island's predevelopment topography. The northernmost area on the plan is present-day Greenwich Village, which was actually Manhattan's earliest settlement. (The Indians who lived in the area of Greenwich Village prior to the arrival of the Dutch called it Sapokanican. Throughout the city's early history it remained a separate settlement and grew considerably in the early nineteenth century, when plague forced many to relocate away from the main part of town. Because of its long history as a separate settlement, its irregular streets were already in place when a grid street design was adopted for much of Manhattan at the beginning of the nineteenth century.) Many sprawling manors with geometric gardens built by the city's wealthy can be seen north of the city, including the properties of the De Lancey, Rutgers, Warren, Lispenard, Bayard, and Mortier families. Elsewhere in the northern area, the Montresor Plan delicately displays both cultivated and wooded areas and other topographic details, such as elevated areas that have since been leveled. One such area is even called *Mount* Pleasant (near the Bayard property). Also, the plan shows the network of roads to the north of the city; it is the first to sketch the entire length of the road from Greenwich Village to the city proper.

In the city itself, the Montresor Plan shows for the first time King's, later Columbia, College (*N* in the references), which appears as an attractive and spacious campus set among gardens. Number 6 in the references indicates the location of a "Fresh Water Engine from whence the Town is supplied." The existence of this central water supply implies that at least some private wells had by this time been polluted or pumped dry. A number of the other items in the references are military in nature, such as powder magazines and bat-

teries. Fourteen churches and meetinghouses are listed. The note in the lower left corner provides a brief history of the city and a very critical description of the condition of the fort as seen by the stern eyes of a military engineer.

On September 1, 1766, Gage ordered Montresor to survey New York Harbor and its islands. The chart in the upper left corner of this engraving is no doubt based on this survey. On it, Ellis Island is given two names: Brown's or Oyster, the latter because this area was the best source for oysters in the harbor. Liberty Island also receives two names: Kennedy's or Corporation. A note near it says that it is made of rock and not visible at high tide.

Surprisingly, just a year after Montresor completed this military survey for the eyes of his commander, the very same work was commercially published in London. That is what is illustrated here. This was in fact not an unusual occurrence, as many of the maps of America made by English military surveyors and engineers were eventually published. It must have been a perquisite of service that allowed officers to find publishers for surveys made in the line of duty and profit by it. A recent study by Mary Pedley in *Imago Mundi*, vol. 48 showed that even after war broke out there was an unregulated trade in maps of America between map publishers in England and France, the ally of the United States. In this way, much of the fine work done prior to the war by English military engineers found its way into the hands of American commanders.

On February 18, 1766, Montresor reduced his original survey to a size of about two by three feet and presented it to Gage. (This original manuscript survives and hangs on a wall at Firle Place, the ancestral home of the Gage family.) On October 30 of the same year, Montresor sailed home with drafts of several maps. In London, his New York plan was engraved by P. Andrews at the shop of Mary Ann Rocque, widow of John Rocque. In May of

the following year, Montresor received a proof of it from the engraver, on which he found thirty-one errors that were presumably corrected. (A proof of the map survives in the Stokes Collection at the New York Public Library.) As can be seen, the map was transformed into a handsome, commercial production complete with an ornamental border and cartouches enclosing the title and dedication to Gage. It was not a success in its initial printing in 1766, however, as only a few examples of this edition have survived. A 1775 edition published after the war began seems to have been much more successful, since a number of examples of it are extant; this edition was also bound into William Faden's *North American Atlas* of military plans. In a disingenuous effort to market the map, the publisher states on it that it was "Survey'd in the Winter, 1775," in order to make it seem fresher than it was. This edition can also be distinguished from the earlier one by the imprint of the publisher, A. Dury. The two editions are otherwise identical. Still later, in 1777, a French edition was published by Le Rouge.

John Montresor (1736–1788?) was one of the most active and wide-ranging military engineers operating in America in the period spanned by the French and Indian War and the American Revolution. He was also one of the most highly regarded, having been appointed chief engineer in December 1775. Also indicative of his stature is the compelling portrait of him by John Singleton Copley, now at the Detroit Institute of Arts. During the Revolution, he was attached to two leading British commanders besides Gage—Sir William Howe and Sir Henry Clinton. Among his projects were surveys of Bunker's Hill (1775) and Philadelphia (1777), and a general map of the Province of New York (1775). During the war, Montresor returned to New York City and bought Randalls Island in the East River and lived there with his family, during which time it was known as Montresor Island.

A MILITARY SURVEY BECOMES A MASTERPIECE

THE RATZEN PLAN

TITLE: To His Excellency Sr. Henry Moore. Bart. . . . This Plan of the City of New York, Is Most Humbly Inscribed . . .
DATE DEPICTED: 1766–67
CARTOGRAPHER: BERNARD RATZER
PUBLISHED: FADEN AND JEFFERYS, LONDON, JANUARY 12, 1776
Hand-colored copperplate engraving, 23 x 33 inches
Private collection

THE RATZER MAP

TITLE: Plan of the City of New York, in North America : Surveyed in the Years 1766 & 1767
DATE DEPICTED: 1766–67
CARTOGRAPHER: BERNARD RATZER
PUBLISHED: FADEN AND JEFFERYS, LONDON, JANUARY 12, 1776
Hand-colored copperplate engraving, 47⅜ x 35 inches (joined)
Private collection

John Montresor's flawed plan (see p. 56) was extended and refined in two phases by Bernard Ratzer into perhaps the finest map of an American city and its environs produced in the eighteenth century. In its final form, its geographic precision combined with highly artistic engraving was unsurpassed in the urban cartography of its day. It affords a rare and vivid picture of New York as a small, charming city set in a richly variegated landscape.

In the latter part of 1766 and early 1767, Lieutenant Bernard Ratzer continued the surveying of Manhattan begun by Montresor. In 1767, he completed the Ratzen Plan, so called because the mapmaker's name was thusly misspelled. It is a larger and more finished work than the Montresor Plan and covers a somewhat larger area, especially on the east side, which extends north to present-day Fourteenth Street. It provides much detail that was absent from the Montresor Plan, such as street names, newly laid out streets, and wards. An elegant cartouche encloses the map's dedication to Sir Henry Moore, its title, and a table of important structures. There were two editions of the Ratzer Map, one undated, but most likely issued in 1770, and the other, illustrated here, that is

dated 1776 and has the imprint of Faden and Jefferys. Both plans by Ratzer have the same dedication and nearly the same titles and were published just a year apart in 1769 and 1770. To make matters even more confusing, both are most often seen in their 1776 editions, which appeared on the very same day, January 12.

Later in 1767, Ratzer made further surveys of both Manhattan and the surrounding area. As a result, the second of these two works, the Ratzer Map, extends the coverage of Manhattan north to about present-day Fiftieth Street. No earlier map provided such a detailed view of the predevelopment topography of Manhattan. Moreover, it is complemented by an accurate and finely engraved view of the city as seen from Governors Island. Also, for the first time, an early map includes a detailed rendering of the then agrarian landscape of Brooklyn and Queens and a small portion of New Jersey.

The Ratzer Map evokes a halcyon period in the history of Manhattan, at least in regard to its physical reality. The city at the time was a small but vibrant place with a population of about twenty-five thousand, for whom the countryside was a short carriage ride away. Also readily at hand were

the recreational delights as well as economic advantages of the sea. As can be seen from the map, most of the island was still a very attractive combination of cultivated fields, forest, and salt meadows, interspersed with large estates possessing fine, geometric gardens. The three manors belonging to the Stuyvesant family, which would develop into a separate village, can be seen about halfway up the east side. Another cluster of estates that would become Greenwich Village is visible about three-quarters of the way up the west side. Farther up along the west side is the country seat of Captain Thomas Clarke, which he named Chelsea in memory of the English home for invalid soldiers. The neighborhood presently between Fourteenth and Twenty-third streets in this area still bears the name of the estate.

All the major roads north of the city are shown and named for the first time on the map, and even country lanes and estate roads are indicated, often with the trees that lined them. All the rivers, streams, and inlets that once existed in this area of Manhattan are also clearly delineated. The Ratzer Map shows that the process of the eradication of the Fresh Water, the sizable lake in the area of present-day Canal Street, was well under

way at the time. Apparently, the lower portion of the lake had already been filled in, since only its outline is shown on the map, and there are signs that even part of the large upper segment seems to have been filled in as well.

The new streets shown on the plan are mainly located just outside of town to the northeast, around what is called "De Lancey Square." The area just to the south of this section was occupied by a swamp on the Montresor Plan with the notation "This overflow is constantly filling up to Build on." Apparently by the time Ratzer finished his map, the "filling up" had been completed because a network of streets can now be seen over the outline of the swamp on it. Also, Division Street, so named because it was the dividing line between the Rutgers and De Lancey properties, is seen completed for the first time here. In addition, the streets along the upper west side of the developed part of town, especially those in the vicinity of King's College, are more fully shown here than on the Montresor Plan.

Like the map itself, the view at the bottom of the engraving is a masterful work. Although the city is depicted at a considerable distance (from Governors Island), the details of its skyline, dominated by church spires, can be clearly made out. The area of the city seen in the view extends from the Battery to Corlear's Hook, also called Crown Point on the map. The artist seems to flaunt his command of realistic detail and perspective by showing in the foreground, at various distances, two gentlemen in conversation and two others fishing, with a woman holding a parasol nearby. The smoke that can be seen rising from the center of the city was at one time offered as evidence that the map was not originally published until 1776, the year a great fire swept the city. One can see, however, that the smoke issues from an area along the east side of the city, while the fire occurred in the city's west side. A closer look reveals the smoke is coming from the area of a careened ship and therefore most likely originated from the boiling tar that was used for the caulking of ships. The source for the view surfaced only in the mid-1980s, when the view was bought at auction by a private collector. It is a large, well executed watercolor by an English officer, Captain-Lieutenant Thomas Davies, and is dated 1760.

The 1770 date given for the undated first issue of the Ratzer Map is based on an advertisement for its sale by publisher Thomas Kitchin in the October 15, 1770, issue of the New-York Gazette. Like the Montresor Plan, the original issue of the Ratzer map was not a success. Only two examples of it are known to have survived, one that belonged to King George III (presently at the British Library) and another in the collection of the New-York Historical Society. Although reissued in 1776 by the commercial map publishers Faden and Jefferys, the map was generally not found in their atlases. Only occasionally is it found in William Faden's *North American Atlas* (1777), as in the copy in the Library of Congress. Therefore, the map is rarely seen on the market.

Bernard Ratzer was one of a number of very skilled military engineers who were recruited by the British and sent to America during the French and Indian War. Most, like Ratzer, served in the Sixtieth or Royal American Regiment. The work of these men, who included Samuel Holland, J. F. W. DesBarres, C. J. Sauthier, De Brahm, Blaskowitz, Brasier, John Montresor, and others, brought a professionalism to the mapping of many parts of North America that had been lacking. Ratzer reached the rank of captain in 1773, and his earliest recorded work is a chart of Passamaquoddy Bay between Maine and New Brunswick drawn in 1756, known only in manuscript. It was followed by several unpublished surveys of forts and frontier areas done in the early 1760s. He collaborated with Sauthier on a map of both New York and New Jersey published in 1776. Also, in 1769, Sir Henry Moore, the governor of New York, gave Ratzer the important commission of surveying the border between New York and New Jersey. It was most likely in gratitude for this commission that Ratzer also dedicated this map to the governor.

VICTORY IN RETREAT
THE FADEN CAMPAIGN MAP

TITLE: A Plan of New York Island, with part of Long Island, Staten Island & East New Jersey, . . .
PERIOD DEPICTED: AUGUST 22–SEPTEMBER 16, 1776
PUBLISHED: WILLIAM FADEN, *The North American Atlas*, LONDON, DATED OCTOBER 19, 1776 (BUT LIKELY EARLY 1777 [STATE 5])
Hand-colored copperplate engraving, 30 x 18¼ inches (including text)
Martayan Lan, Inc., New York

The American Revolution could have easily ended in New York in the late summer of 1776, soon after it had begun. The Continental Congress had played into the hands of the British by ordering Washington to defend the city. By August, 10,500 troops of a total American fighting force of 18,000 had been assembled for the defense of the city. This would have given the British the opportunity they had hoped for: the chance to deliver a crushing blow to the patriot army in a decisive battle and thereby extinguish the Revolution. The story of how this did not come about is told on the Faden Campaign Map.

Remarkably, Faden's map was published just weeks after the events depicted on it. It was most likely prepared by a member of the staff of Sir William Howe, the British commander, and delineates the military events in and around Manhattan from August 27 to September 15, 1776. When it was originally issued on October 19 of 1776, only seven weeks had passed since the latest event shown on it. Since a packet ship took four to six weeks to cross the Atlantic at the time, this was astonishing quickness for publishing a map. In this way, Faden's map was the eighteenth-century equivalent of today's satellite transmission from the scene of a news event. It would have provided the public with its first opportunity to learn in detail of the contest for New York. In fact, many copies of the map were published as broadsides, that is, separately printed sheets that were sold in the streets

of London as news bulletins. Copies were also later bound into Faden's *North American Atlas* (1777) and his *Atlas of the Battles of the American Revolution* (1793).

New York City was vital to the British because their grand strategy at the outset of the war was to gain control of the Hudson River with forces originating from the north at Quebec and from the south in New York and thereby cut off the Northeast. Moreover, after their humiliation at Bunker Hill and subsequent evacuation from Boston at the end of the previous year, the British desired an early, decisive battle. In fact, converging on New York in August of 1776 was the largest military force ever gathered in one place in English history up to that time. It consisted of thirty-two thousand troops, ten thousand seamen, seventy-three warships, and four hundred transports under the joint command of the Howe brothers, with Sir William leading the land forces and Lord Richard ("Black Dick") the naval.

The Faden Campaign Map and its text must be seen for what they are: a general's presentation of a recently concluded campaign meant for the public eye. While the map is very precise and detailed as to Howe's tactics and the progress of events, it at best blurs some important facts of the campaign. For example, by looking at the map to get an idea of the relative sizes of the American forces shown in blue versus the British shown in red, one would never know the latter enjoyed a decisive numeri-

cal superiority. Most significantly, never alluded to is the all-important fact that there were several instances where the British had the chance to wipe out what would have been the majority of the entire American fighting force.

As can be seen from the map, the first encounters in the New York campaign were fought in Brooklyn, which the Americans had been fortifying since February 1776. On August 22, Howe landed about fifteen thousand troops at Gravesend Bay in the southeastern portion of Brooklyn; a smaller force landed somewhat to the north just inside the Narrows. Meanwhile, Washington had moved about ten thousand men on to Brooklyn, with a strongly fortified position in Brooklyn Heights just across from Manhattan, and a more tenuous one farther south in the area called The Woody Heights of Guana on the map. This was a long wooded area with elevations of from forty to eighty feet that ran through most of Brooklyn and a good part of Queens. As can be seen from the plan, the adroitly deployed British forces hit the Americans at three points on August 27. The result of this, the first pitched battle of the Revolution, was a rout of the American forces. While engaging two British forces, the Americans were surprised by a third, which had maneuvered far to the American left to reach the high ground the Americans were holding. The patriot army was eventually overwhelmed after a stand of about four hours; some soldiers retreating in panic

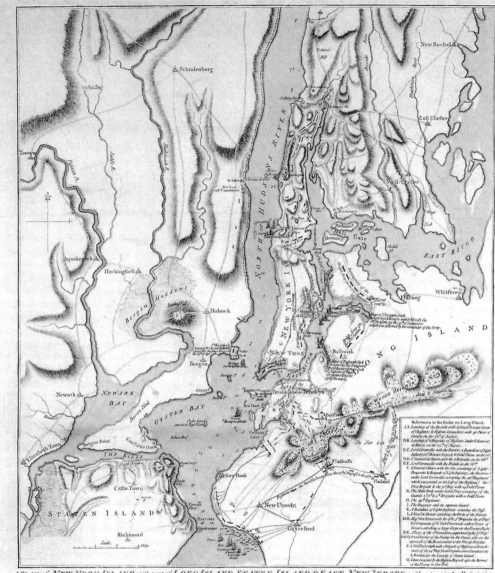

A PLAN of NEW YORK ISLAND, with part of LONG ISLAND, STATEN ISLAND & EAST NEW JERSEY, with a particular Description of the ENGAGEMENT on the Woody Heights of Long Island, between FLATBUSH and BROOKLYN, on the 27th of August 1776, between HIS MAJESTY'S FORCES Commanded by General HOWE and the AMERICANS under Major General PUTNAM, Shewing also the Landing of the BRITISH ARMY on New-York Island, and the Taking of the CITY of NEW YORK &c. on the 15th of September following, with the Subsequent Disposition of Both the Armies.

An ACCOUNT of the Proceedings of His Majesty's Forces at the Attack of the Rebels Works on LONG ISLAND, on the 27th of August, 1776.

Taken from Gen. HOWE's Letter to Lord GEORGE GERMAINE, principal Secretary of State for the American Department.

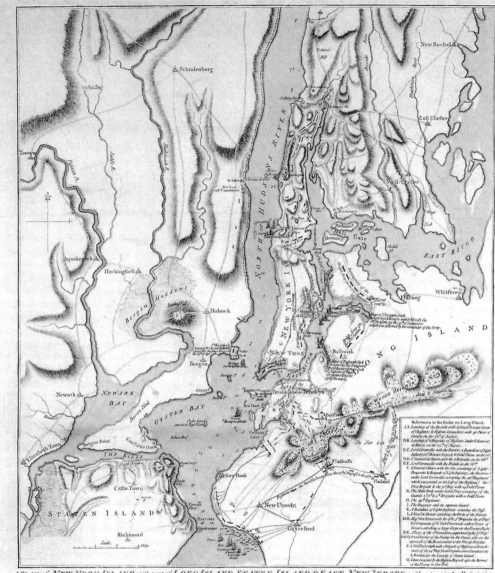

drowned in the swamp seen on the plan near the American position at Brooklyn Heights. Although two American generals were captured and hundreds of prisoners taken, most of the force returned safely to their stronger position at Brooklyn Heights.

The American army, with their backs to the harbor, were still vulnerable here. Despite this, Howe never followed up his advantage, nor were the Americans ever cut off by the British navy, which controlled the waters unopposed. Bad weather might have stalled British efforts at this point. However, the British could have also bypassed this cornered American force and attacked the now lightly defended city. Instead, in heavy fog on the night of August 29, the entire American force, in a Dunkirk-like operation, was silently ferried back to Manhattan in small boats with muffled oars. Washington himself supervised the operation, which was one of the great logistical feats of the Revolution. This episode, of course, is only mentioned in passing in Howe's text on the map.

Despite this escape, Howe still had the chance to bottle up Washington's army in lower Manhattan. However, well over two weeks would pass before he would attack Manhattan itself. It is not clear what caused his delay; the passage of so much time is not even alluded to in the text. Apparently, Howe kept busy by arraying his forces into five separate encampments in Queens. He finally attacked Manhattan on September 15 at Kips Bay at present-day Thirty-fourth Street on the east side. This move was presaged by an intense artillery barrage from his fleet and a number of diversionary manueuvers. The offensive scattered the Americans defending the area, and the English had an easy entry into the city, so much so that Howe felt sufficiently relaxed to pause with his staff for a lavish luncheon at the home of Robert Murray in the Murray Hill section of the city. It was during this respite that an American force of 3,500 men still caught in lower Manhattan was able to escape at the moment when they could have been easily cut off. Their path of escape, which was led by Aaron Burr, is shown on the plan. Thus, it seems that it was New York's legendary propensity for lavish hospitality that saved the day.

The chronology of the Faden Campaign Map concludes with Washington's army lodged in a strong defensive position in the heights above Harlem with the British forces situated just to the south. Manhattan as a whole (as opposed to just the city itself) would not be in the hands of the British until two months later, on November 16, when Fort Washington, in the area of what is now called Washington Heights, was taken by the British. However, by this time, most of the American army had left the city for Westchester. For the next seven years, until the peace was signed in November 1783, New York City would remain in British hands.

A possible explanation for the series of opportunites missed by the British in New York might lie in Howe's experience at the Battle of Bunker Hill, where he was in command. At Bunker Hill, he uncharacteristically ordered a frontal attack and doggedly persisted in it, which resulted in astonishing losses: his entire personal staff was killed, and 40 percent of his army was either killed or wounded. Not surprisingly, therefore, the New York campaign was all maneuver, subtle deployment, careful preparation, and ample use of naval artillery. It is also not surprising to notice in Howe's account on the map an inordinate concern with the casualty ratio. In every case, British losses are minimized and American ones exaggerated. For example, Howe claims that 3,300 Americans were killed, wounded, or imprisoned in the battle in Brooklyn, whereas Washington in a letter accounted a total loss of eight hundred men, three quarters of whom were prisoners.

Howe's presentation of the New York campaign has chilling echoes of the American military reporting of the Vietnam War, a struggle with certain military analogies to the Revolution. The Faden map and Howe's text can be seen as part of a public relations war. Like the military reporting of the Vietnam War, it was a war fought with casualty statistics, lists of captured matériel, subtly misleading graphic presentation, and the omission of key facts. As a result, a series of events like the taking of New York is presented as a clear victory, as were many of the battles of the Vietnam War, when, in fact, they were episodes in a larger pattern of defeat.

In all, five different issues, or states, of the map were published, some of which update the action to particular points in time, while others make less important alterations. (A detailed analysis of the five states can be found in "Comparative Cartography" by Henry Stevens and Roland Tree, and in I. N. Phelps Stokes's *Iconography of Manhattan Island*, vol. 1.) The example reproduced here is the final state, which provides the most complete picture of the engagements. As is the case here, the map is sometimes accompanied by a printed text below it. There are two editions of the text, one describing events up to September 3, and the other narrating the actual taking of the city between September 3 and 21. Inexplicably, the earlier edition of the text accompanies the map reproduced here. Both editions are purportedly excerpts taken from letters by Howe to the colonial secretary, George Germain, who along with Howe planned British strategy during the war. A list of sixteen references, primarily describing British troop movements, appears to the right of the map.

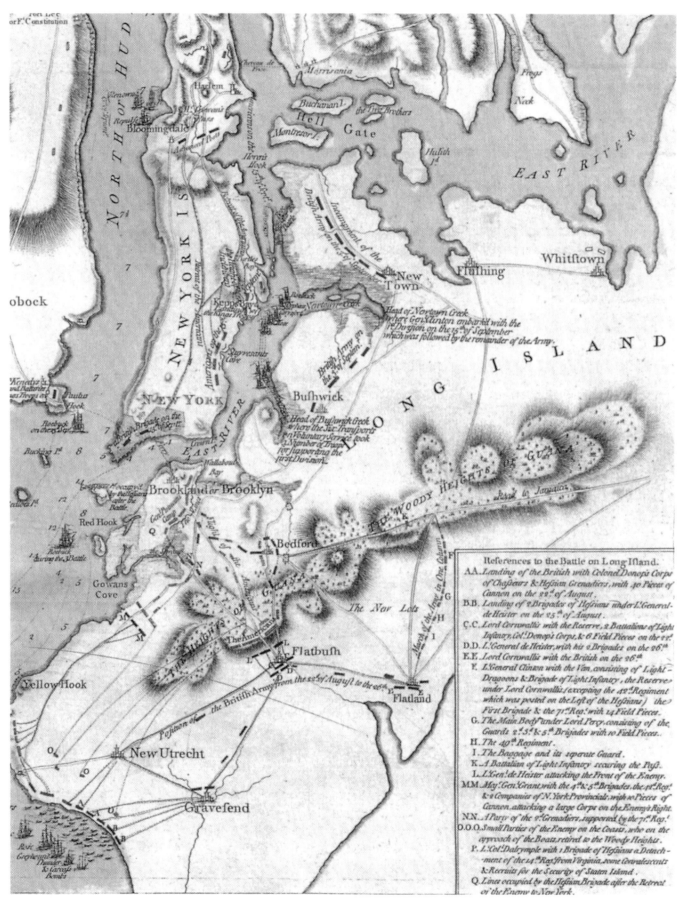

References to the Battle on Long Island.

AA. Landing of the British with Colonel Donop's Corps of Chasseurs & Hessian Grenadiers, with 40 Pieces of Cannon on the 22d of August.

BB. Landing of 2 Brigades of Hessians under Lt General de Heister on the 25 of August.

CC. Lord Cornwallis with the Reserve, 2 Battalions of Light Infantry, Col: Donop's Corps, & 6 Field Pieces on the 22d

DD. Lt General de Heister, with his 2 Brigades on the 26th

EE. Lord Cornwallis with the British on the 26th

F. Lt General Clinton with the Van, consisting of Light Dragoons & Brigade of Light Infantry, the Reserve under Lord Cornwallis (excepting the 42d Regiment which was posted on the Left of the Hessians) the First Brigade & the 71st Regt with 14 Field Pieces.

G. The Main Body under Lord Percy, consisting of the Guards 2d 5th & 6th Brigades with 10 Field Pieces.

H. The 49th Regiment.

I. The Baggage and its separate Guard.

K. A Battalion of Light Infantry securing the Pass.

L. Lt Gen: de Heister attacking the Front of the Enemy.

MM. Maj: Gen: Grant with the 4th & 5th Brigades, the 1st Regt & 2 Companies of N. York Provincials with 10 Pieces of Cannon attacking a large Corps on the Enemy's Right.

NN. A Party of the 2d Grenadiers supported by the 71st Regt

OOO. Small Parties of the Enemy on the Coasts, who on the approach of the Boats retired to the Woody Heights.

P. Lt Col: Dalrymple with 1 Brigade of Hessians a Detachment of the 14th Regt from Virginia, some Convalescents & Recruits for the Security of Staten Island.

Q. Lines occupied by the Hessian Brigade after the Retreat of the Enemy to New York.

CONFLAGRATION
THE HOLLAND MAP

Untitled

DATE DEPICTED: 1776

DATE DRAWN: C. 1776–77

CARTOGRAPHER: SAMUEL HOLLAND

Pen and ink with watercolor on paper,
51½ x 29½ inches
New York State Library, Albany

New York City, which the British captured on September 15, 1776, had been shockingly transformed from the charming place that some British officers might have known from previous duty there. The British reported a population of merely three thousand when they entered the city, by far its lowest total for the century. Prorevolutionists, or Whigs, who had comprised the majority of New Yorkers, had fled the city when the British takeover appeared inevitable. Moreover, earlier in the year, most of the Tory population had likewise fled when the American army held the city. Physically, the city had been brutalized: it was crisscrossed by a network of defensive works; streets were blockaded; most trees had been cut down; fine structures had been converted to military purposes, and much of value had been carted away.

The careful, hand-drawn Holland Map was prepared by an English military surveyor just after the British capture of the city. Unlike the Faden Campaign Map (see p.64), which was a public relations piece showing the campaigns in the area, this was a professional military document. The information it gives has been distilled down to primarily what was of military value, such as fortifications, defensive emplacements, and topography. It was no doubt made to aid the British command in the defense of what would be the center of their military operations for the duration of the war.

The map also displays the results of one of the most traumatic events in the colonial history of the city. Just six days after the British capture of the city, a horrible fire transformed a sizable part of New York into a ghastly shell. The fire broke out at about midnight of September 20 in what is believed to have been a bordello frequented by British sailors in Whitehall Slip, just on the eastern side of the southern tip of the island. Everything seemed to conspire to make the fire particularly deadly and destructive. The wind had been blowing stiffly from the south-southeast, driving the fire, at least initially, across the densest part of the town. Most church and alarm bells had been taken from the city by patriots to be converted into ammunition, resulting in a great number of deaths among women and children in particular. Likewise, most of the firefighters were supporters of the patriot cause and had fled the city. Further, many of the city's houses were still made of wood, and nearly all had cedar shingles.

Clearly marked off in yellow on the map is the path followed by the fire and the extensive damage it did. Over a quarter of the city, including 493 houses, was destroyed. One of the city's most conspicuous religious structures, Trinity Church, was very badly burned; it stood as a charred skeleton for several years until finally being demolished in 1788. One can see from the map the starting point of the fire in the lower eastern tip of the city and its path to the northwest.

As if the fire was not horrible enough, the early morning of September 21 turned truly hellish, as British soldiers and sailors who were sent to fight the fire attacked citizens in the midst of the flames and looted homes. The British soldiery had been utterly convinced that patriot sympathizers would torch the city if taken by the British. Therefore, anyone remotely suspected of spreading the fire or interfering with putting it out was ruthlessly set upon.

Despite this barbarous rampage, it was finally the efforts of British sailors and soldiers that prevented the fire from being much worse than it was.

The fire made the early years of the British occupation grim in many respects. With the loss of so much living space, the quartering of troops became a particular problem. The lives of the thousands of American prisoners held by the British in the city were often unspeakably harsh, as many were incarcerated year-round on ships. It is believed that as many as twelve thousand died on the prison ships in Wallabout Bay in Brooklyn. Many of the city's public buildings and churches, such as King's College, were converted to hospitals or put to some military use. Many had been looted; even the books from the library in City Hall were stolen by British officers. The damage done to the city by the fire was compounded in 1778 by another major but not nearly as destructive fire. Nevertheless, sixty-four dwellings were lost in the area of Dock and Little Dock streets near the wharfs. The extent of this fire is not shown on the map.

The fire of 1776 was the first of four great fires that New York suffered, the other three occurring in 1811, 1835, and 1845. In addition to causing enormous damage, each altered the city's very identity in profound ways. In the case of this first fire, perhaps the most poignant loss it inflicted was the virtual obliteration of the city's connection to its early days as a Dutch village, since most of the structures that dated from this period were lost in the fire. With them perished some of New York's special charm, for it was these delightful structures that had allowed the city to retain some of the feeling of village life in the midst of urbanization.

The Holland Map inventories the numerous bulwarks, redoubts, and fortifications left by the retreating

Americans that clogged the city at the time of the British takeover. In this way, the plan supplies visual verification of extant written descriptions of the defenses erected by the Americans. A long wall can be seen stretching along most of the southern tip of the island. A particularly dense network of emplacements is depicted in the area of the Rutgers property in the upper east area shown on the map. Also, many details relevant to battles fought in Brooklyn are shown. It also shows the embarkation point of the dramatic escape of the patriot army to Manhattan.

The street plan shown on the map is modeled after the so-called Ratzen Plan (see p. 59). In addition to the military information that is obviously not present on the Ratzen Plan, the present work also redrew the wharfs along the east side. In addition, it seems to correct the Ratzen Plan by marking some streets in the upper east side of town with dotted lines to indicate that they were not completely laid out. They are delineated with solid lines on the Ratzen Plan. The Holland Map also shows the city's drainage system, which does not appear on earlier maps.

The Holland Map has neither the name of its maker nor a date inscribed on it. However, in his essay in *Imago Mundi*, vol. 31, William P. Cumming persuasively showed that Major Samuel Holland was most likely the map's author. He had been surveyor general of the Northern District of the British colonies in North America since 1765 and was one of the most productive cartographers of the period. Further, it is known that Holland surveyed the area of the battle at its conclusion, which is reflected on the map. Also, the map was found among Holland's papers, which were owned by the Holland family until 1930. Therefore, if Holland did not himself draw the map, he must have at least supervised its

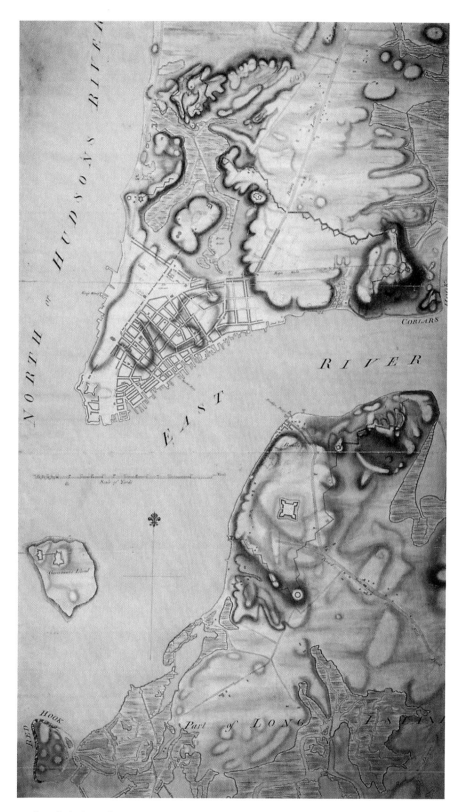

preparation. A dating of 1776 or possibly early 1777 is most likely for the map because a survey with the kind of information it contains would have been needed immediately after the British capture of the

city. Further, the fortifications on it are considerably less extensive than those shown on the Hills Plan (see p. 74), which delineates the city in 1782.

MANHATTAN'S ORIGINAL TOPOGRAPHY PRESERVED ON PAPER

THE BRITISH HEADQUARTERS MAP

Untitled

DATE DEPICTED: 1782(?)
DATE DRAWN: 1782(?)
Pen and ink with watercolor on paper, 37½ x 125 inches
Public Records Office, London

Despite the hardships caused by the fire of 1776 and by the American Revolution, New York under British occupation returned to some degree of normalcy. In fact, a strangely festive atmosphere pervaded the city at times, while in the background hundreds of patriot prisoners suffered horrifying conditions and the area destroyed by the fire had become a canvas-tent shantytown. An activity for which there was ample time during the occupation was surveying and mapping. The cream of English cartographic talent worked at one time or another in New York during the war. This is borne out by the scores of maps and plans of the city done during the war that still survive in archives throughout the world. The major collections can be found at the Library of Congress, the Clements Library at the University of Michigan, and the Public Records Office and the British Library in London. As a result of the presence of these surveyors and engineers in the city through the war, New York, which was one of the most poorly mapped American cities before the war, became by its end the most thoroughly mapped urban area of the United States.

The British mapping of the city culminated in this extraordinary, large-scale depiction of the entire island, called the British Headquarters Map. It most likely hung in the command room of British forces and was used to plan the defense of the city. The map is certainly interesting as a military document that comprehensively

catalogs the extensive defensive works in the city at the time. However, it is for another reason that it is one of the most precious and uniquely informative historical records of Manhattan of any kind. It is the only surviving, virtually complete record of the topography of the island. Drawn on an exceptionally large scale (6½ inches = 1 mile), the map delineates every stream, pond, swamp, marsh, elevation, and contour of shoreline of Manhattan. Needless to say, nearly every detail of the island's original landscape has since been either obliterated or drastically altered. Therefore, it is only through this map that we are able to visualize the entire island of Manhattan in something near to its natural state. Although earlier maps like the Manatus (see p. 14) and Nicolls maps (see p. 30) showed the entire island, neither did so with anything approaching the detail of this one. Moreover, the early maps that did show detail comparable to this one, such as the Ratzer Map (see p. 59), only did so for a relatively small portion of the island. In addition to providing topographic detail, the British Headquarters Map is the only surviving early document fully to display the roads, lanes, structures, estates, and villages that once existed on Manhattan north of the town itself.

Viewing this map, one realizes what a rich and varied visual experience a carriage ride through Manhattan would have been in the late eighteenth century. Journeying north out of town along Bowery Lane, the

widest of the north-south roads seen on the map, one would pass changing vistas of spacious, manicured estates; patchworks of cultivated fields; and salt meadows along with noisome swamps and bogs. Heading toward the east above Turtle Bay or the low Fifties on today's map, one would encounter a craggy, glacially carved landscape. Remnants of this rugged terrain can still be seen in Central Park. The Upper East Side, between the Sixties and Nineties, would have been one of the most sparsely settled parts of the island at the time of the map and consisted of forest and cultivated fields. Moving north along the east side, at about Hell Gate, the landscape would turn into marshy wetlands interlaced with streams. At about the area of present-day One-hundredth Street, the southern rim of Harlem, one would cross a sizable stream called Pension's Creek on the map. This no-longer-existing rivulet wended through about two-thirds of the width of the island. The remaining landscape of the northern part of Manhattan provided a dramatic topographic contrast. Much of Harlem was the largest stretch of flatland on Manhattan and is, in fact, called the Harlem Plains on the map. This gave way in the north to the highest elevations found on the island. These rugged highlands at the northern tip were the favored area for fox hunting by British officers during the war. A part of the area, now occupied by Fort Tryon and Inwood Hill parks, remains in pretty much its natural state today.

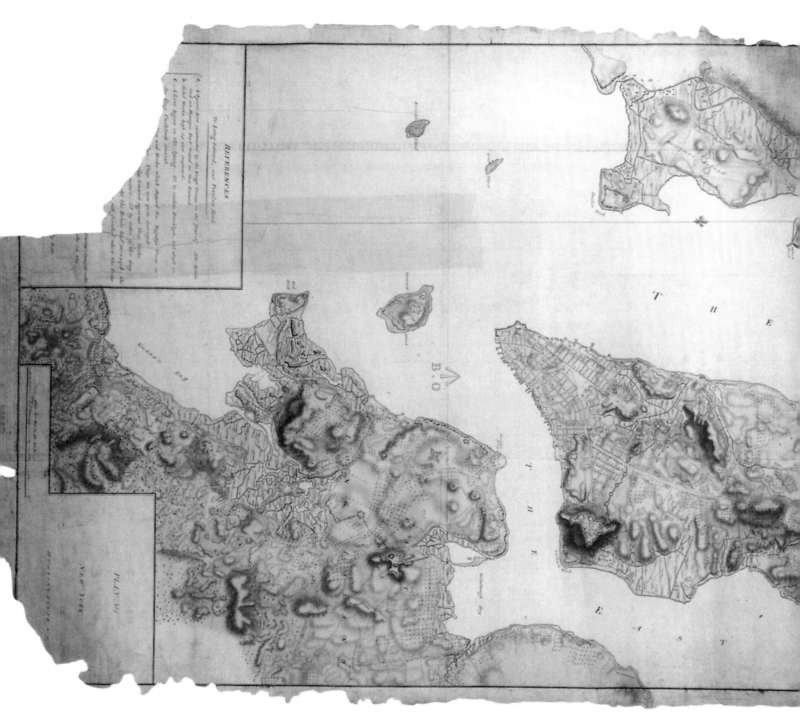

The same topographic variety can also be observed along the west side of the city, much of it interspersed with flowering fields that moved the Dutch to call a large part of the Upper West Side, Bloomingdale. Seen along the lower west side is the Minetta Brook, also called Bestaver's Rivulet. An important waterway used for transporting goods, it began at about Twenty-first Street and Fifth Avenue, worked its way to the southwest, passed through Washington Square, then through the west portion of Greenwich Village, and ended near the Hudson River at the southern extreme of Greenwich Village. The waters of some of these long-filled streams still run underground today and must be taken into account when cables are laid or foundations dug.

While the map shows that much of Manhattan still consisted of rugged, partially cultivated terrain, it was, nevertheless, surprisingly well-serviced by a network of roads. However, most of these in the northern part of the island were probably unpaved country lanes. The map further reveals that there were pockets of settlement (houses are shown in red) north of the main town, other than well-documented ones like Harlem and Greenwich Village. A sizable settlement can be seen just north of Turtle Bay along the east side. Also shown on the map is the elaborate system of

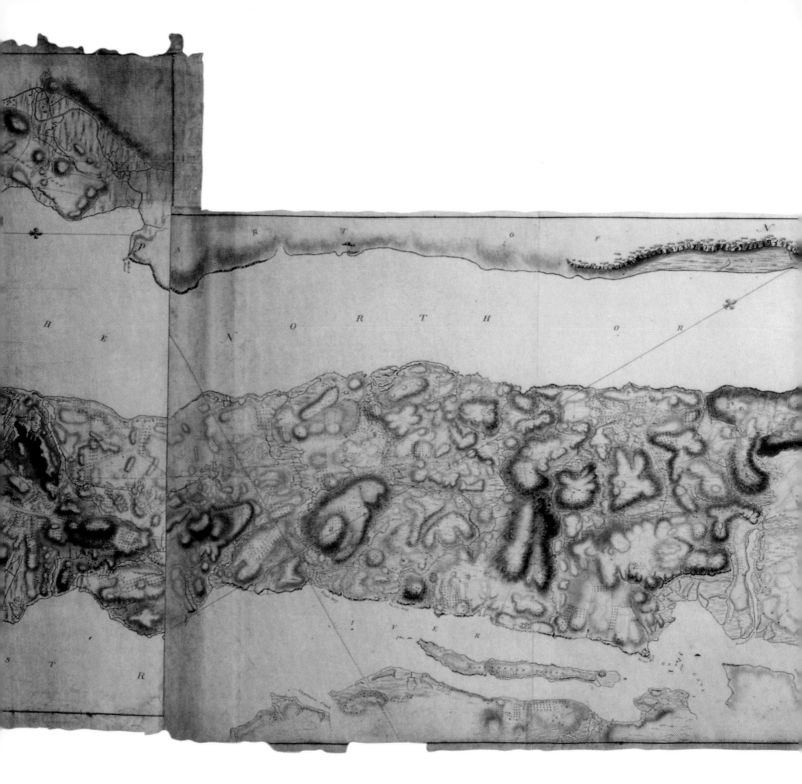

drainage and irrigation ditches, which connect at some points with wetland areas.

As mentioned earlier, the map also provides the most complete cartographic record of the fortifications erected in Manhattan during the American Revolution. It reveals that virtually every part of the island had one form of defensive emplacement or other on it. The highlands of the northern tip, obviously

considered a vulnerable point for a land assault, were especially well-defended. There was Fort Washington, here called Knyphausen after the Hessian general who commanded its capture. Two other forts can be seen in the area: George, facing the east, and Tryon, the northernmost. Just south of the forts are three lines of barricades further protecting against entry from the north. The list of references on the map

describes the major fortifications in both Manhattan and Brooklyn, noting if they had been built by the British or Americans. One must wonder at the physical effort and resources squandered by the British in erecting and bracing these elaborate defenses that were never used during the war.

Nothing is known about the map's authorship or exactly how and when it was compiled. It appears that it was most likely

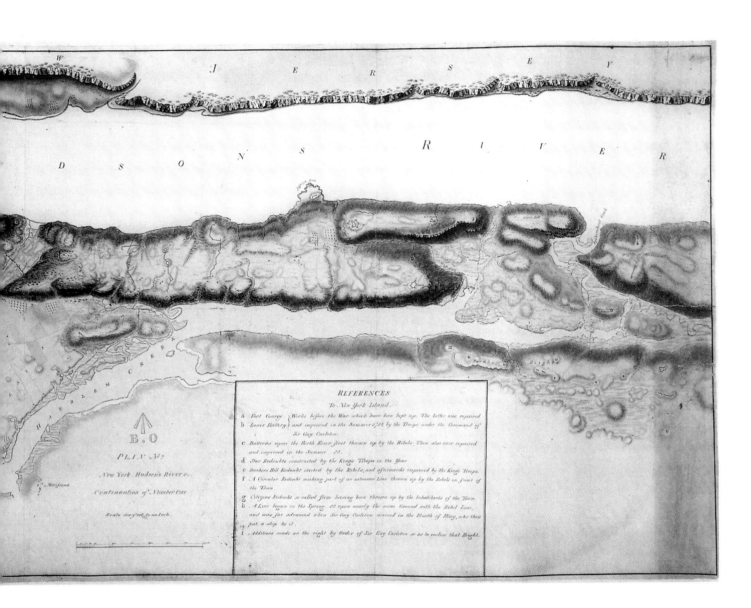

the final product of an ongoing project, judging from the fact that there are two other maps very much like it in existence, but in less finished form. In style, it is most reminiscent of the work of C. J. Sauthier, who produced several manuscript maps of the city during the war and one focusing on northern Manhattan that was printed. However, a project of this scale must have been a collaborative effort of the many surveyors and engineers that were stationed in Manhattan during the war.

Unfortunately, it appears that this superb map was never put to any use after the war in the planning or development of the city. Perhaps if this fine portrait of Manhattan's topographic variety had been available, it could have suggested schemes of development in greater harmony with the area's natural characteristics than the rigid grid plan that was adopted. The map had been housed at the War Office in London earlier in the century but is now at the Public Records Office, also in London. In 1900, B. F. Stevens published an excellent full-scale facsimile of the map printed on twenty-four sheets. This is the first time that the map itself has been reproduced in a book.

DIMINISHED BY WAR
THE HILLS PLAN

DATE DEPICTED: 1782
DATE DRAWN: 1785
SURVEYOR/DRAFTSMAN: JOHN HILLS
Pen and ink with watercolor (faded) on paper mounted on linen, 65¼ x 58¼ inches
New-York Historical Society

Based on a survey made in the final year of the British occupation of New York, John Hills's precisely drawn plan reveals a city that had contracted over the course of the revolutionary war into a veritable fortress. Showing Manhattan as far north as present-day Twenty-third Street, it reveals a place ensnarled by fortifications of every variety. Virtually every elevated area is crowned with a battery, if not an actual fort. So elaborate were the defensive emplacements on the northern rim of the city (roughly along present-day Delancey and Spring streets) that they nearly constituted a northern wall of the kind that had protected New Amsterdam in the previous century. Also quite daunting to potential invaders were the elaborate defenses at the southern tip of the island. Even inhospitable terrain, such as the swampy region to the west of the Fresh Water or Collect Pond, merited some manner of fortification.

Hills's inventory of the city's "works," as they were called, is remarkably thorough and rendered with professional exactitude. They have even been color coded so that the viewer of the map can distinguish those that were installed by the American army in 1776 (in yellow), those of the Americans that had been repaired by the British (in orange), and those erected solely by the British after their capture of the city (in green). As testimony to the efficiency of American engineers, the map reveals that the majority of the works in the city were the ones erected by the Americans during the early part of 1776.

When compared with the Ratzer Map (see p. 59), drawn some fourteen years earlier, this one shows that in the intervening period the city had actually become smaller. Due to the devastation of the fires of 1776 and 1778, this would surely have been the case in regard to the number of structures in the city. Regarding streets, there are several that had appeared on the Ratzer Map that can no longer be found on Hills's work. In the northeastern extreme of the developed part of the city, Bullock, Ann, and Grand streets, which had been on the Ratzer Map, have been effaced by fortifications on the Hills Plan. Arundel and Suffolk streets, which were the easternmost streets on the Ratzer Map, were evidently also obliterated. Likewise, on the west side, the northernmost street there was Reade, and much less of it appears on Hills's plan than on Ratzer's work.

Only Broadway is seen on Hills's plan as more developed than it was on Ratzer's. It now reaches as far north as present-day Houston Street, where it meets Monument Lane, the road that led to the northern part of what was Greenwich Village at the time. Also, in the list of thirty-seven structures in the references in the bottom right-hand corner are a few that had been added since the late 1760s, in particular the Lutheran, Scotch Presbyterian, and Methodist churches. Also, of note among the references are three prisons, which held the large population of American prisoners-of-war in the city at the time.

Hills's was the last map of the city on which street names relating to English royalty appeared. In 1794, the names of streets such as King George, Orange, King, Little Queen, and Queen were changed. In some cases, the alteration was to something more appropriately patriotic, such as changing Crown to Liberty. Likewise, in 1784 King's College was given the thoroughly American name of Columbia.

The city was diminished in another, instantly visible way in the course of the war. It is said that much of Manhattan was denuded of trees by the end of the war, giving it a starkly ravaged look. Although this cannot be seen on the Hills Plan, the plan nevertheless suggests one reason for it. The miles of elaborate defensive works seen here required tremendous amounts of timber. Another drain on wood was caused by the greater than usual demand for firewood due to abnormally cold winters during the British occupation.

One might initially wonder at the sheer quantity of the city's defensive works on the plan, given the fact that New York stayed securely in British hands from November 1776 until November 1783. Although Americans made several minor forays into the city toward the end of the war, it was never subject to an actual invasion. Nevertheless, invasions were contemplated, especially after the French entry into the Revolution in 1778. Fear of American attack was at its greatest in the winter of 1780 when the Hudson River froze over, which would have allowed an army to simply march across the river and enter the city at any point.

John Hills, like Samuel Holland, Bernard Ratzer, and John Montresor discussed earlier, was one of the many talented military surveyors in the British army during the Revolution. Hills, however, was unique among his colleagues in that he remained in

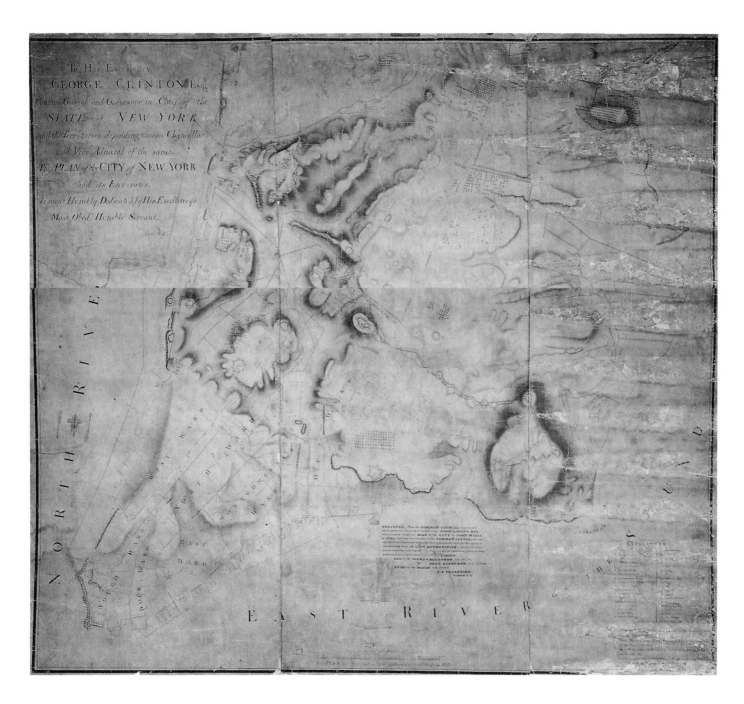

America after the war, where he worked as a surveyor, land accessor, engineer, and mapmaker. However, in 1785, when this map was actually drawn, Hills seems to have been struggling to establish himself in business, listing addresses at 200 Water Street in New York and in Princeton, New Jersey. In drafting this map, Hills was likely attempting to follow the tradition established by other military surveyors like Ratzer and Montresor in trying to transform a work that had been done for military purposes

(the original surveys for it being performed in 1782) into a commercial product. Hills had, in fact, supplied several plans of specific battle sites to the London publisher William Faden, who had also published work by Montresor and Ratzer. This work, however, was never published except much later in reduced form in scholarly works and guidebooks. In addition to his military mapmaking, Hills is best known for a handsome atlas of twenty manuscript maps of parts of New Jersey prepared between 1778 and 1782 for

Sir Henry Clinton, the British commander-in-chief after Sir William Howe. He also produced in 1796 and 1808 two important engraved plans of Philadelphia, where he eventually settled.

In 1847, the Hills Plan was given to the city by John Lozier and was deposited at the New-York Historical Society, where it can be found today. Lozier's gift is memorialized with an appreciative inscription penned onto the map itself and endorsed by the mayor and other dignitaries.

CAPITAL RECOVERY
THE DIRECTORY PLAN OF 1789

DATE DEPICTED: 1789
CARTOGRAPHER: JOHN MCCOMB, JR.
ENGRAVER: CORNELIUS TIEBOUT
PUBLISHED: *The New-York Directory and Register for the Year 1789*
(NEW YORK: HODGE, ALLEN, AND CAMPBELL, 1789)
Uncolored copperplate engraving, 8⅞ x 14⅜ inches
New-York Historical Society

One measure of a city's growth is the need for a directory of its residents, which would occur when its citizens no longer knew each other on a face-to-face basis. Early directories were precursors of today's telephone book; in fact, they were published annually in New York from the end of the eighteenth century until superseded by the telephone book early in the twentieth century. A great variety of other kinds of information can be provided by early directories, such as currency values, coach schedules, the names of officials, and organizations and societies with their meeting times and rosters of membership. Generally speaking, a directory, as opposed to a guidebook, was primarily intended to aid the residents of a city in the conduct of everyday life and business. It was only a few years after the Revolution, as New York began to rebuild, that its first directory was published in 1786 by David C. Franks. Philadelphia was the only American city that had a directory earlier; two were issued there in 1785. New York's first directory was prompted not only by the city's expansion, but also by the fact that New York was at the time the seat of the federal government. The volume served as a kind of primer for the recently formed national government. One is reminded that simply comprehending the structure of the government of the newly born nation must have been a challenge for the average citizen at the time.

A city plan is a natural accompaniment of a directory, but one was not included until New York's third directory was published in 1789. It was the first directory map published for any city in the United States. Its presence in the volume is prominently advertised on the title page as an "accurate and elegant Plan of the City." While hardly the latter, it is nevertheless an important record of the city in the years just after the Revolution. It is all the more important because a good, large-scale plan of the city would not appear again until the Taylor-Roberts Plan of 1797 (see p. 80). A 1795 edition of the Directory Plan of 1789 did provide some updating and a transition to the Taylor-Roberts Plan.

The Directory Plan of 1789 was the only map of the city published in the brief period that New York was the capital of the country: from March 4, 1789, when Congress first met there under the new Constitution, to August 30, 1790, when President Washington left the city. The capitol of the federal government, Federal Hall (number 1 in the references on the map) was located on Wall Street between Broad (now Nassau) and William streets. Formerly the city's second city hall, its refurbishment was directed by Pierre L'Enfant, who would later design the street plan for Washington, D.C. On April 9, 1789, Washington was elected president by Congress at Federal Hall and then was inaugurated on its balcony on April 30.

The Directory Plan of 1789 reveals that a few important areas, which had been long in developing, were finally completed in the years after the revolutionary war. However, the vigorous growth of the city that would happen before the end of the century is not yet in evidence. Greenwich Street, the westernmost thoroughfare on the Directory Plan of 1789, is seen for the first time in completed form. The fifty-year-long project to complete the street was the first of many such excruciatingly long development schemes in the city's history. When initially laid out in 1739, the area for the street was entirely under the waters of the Hudson River and was to be gradually filled in over the years. This process was apparently accelerated after the war, as the street was resurveyed and extended in 1784, and then regulated in 1785 to extend from the Battery to Cortlandt Street. What must have helped the process along was the dismantling of the numerous fortifications and earthworks erected during the war. Much of the material that resulted from this process served as landfill. It is known, for example, that the fort that stood since the early Dutch period began to be torn down by the time this map was published; the dirt and refuse from it was used to extend the Battery and Broadway. (The fort is, nevertheless, shown intact on the plan, this being its final appearance on a map of the city.)

As discussed in the essay on the Maerschalck Plan (see p. 50), the development of the Rutgers family property was the first example of both planning and the use of a grid in the city's history. A new, important segment of it is shown laid out in streets for the first time on the Directory Plan of 1789 in the northeasternmost part of the city. On today's map it is the area bounded by Catherine, South, and Governeur streets and East Broadway and is the site of large public housing projects. This area, like Greenwich Street, had also been long in developing, having been surveyed by Francis Maerschalck before the war on July 16, 1775. However, the streets were evidently not completed until after the war, as none of the maps prepared during the war show them. Among the new streets in this area were Harman (East Broadway today), named after one of the patriarchs of the Rutgers family; George (Market Street today); and Charlotte (Pike Street today). Other streets in the area shown on the plan appear without names.

Another important street making its first appearance on this plan was Front, in the city's fabled waterfront area in the southeastern section. Regulated in 1787, Front became the easternmost street in the city's busiest commercial area and was a sure sign of the city's recovery after the war. The city's northward development increased slightly as well with the extended Byard Lane (later Broome Street) being the northernmost east-west street for the first time.

A most important street that had undergone significant change was Broadway. This may have been the only case of street improvement in the city made by the British during the occupation. It is seen here extending much farther north than it had before the revolutionary war (compare with the Ratzer Map, p. 59). On the Directory Plan of 1789, Broadway is called Great George Street above Ann Street, but this appellation would last only until 1794.

The Directory Plan of 1789 indicates that the streets destroyed by the Great Fire of 1776 were rebuilt soon after the war. Also, there is evidence of new streets in the upper west portion of the city, but they are unnamed on the plan. They are today's Chambers, Reade, and Duane streets. While the above represented some important strides in the city's growth, the overall size of the city had not increased significantly. In fact, the Directory Plan still shows the city as consisting of the same seven wards that were mandated by the Montgomerie Charter of 1730. The city's wards would not be reorganized until 1791.

A number of key structures are noted for the first time on the Directory Plan of 1789. One of these is the Bridewell (number 30 in the references), the first city prison. The city's first Catholic church, St. Peter's (number 9), is shown here for the first time on a map. Its cornerstone was laid in October 1785 at Church and Barclay streets. Also on the plan is New York Hospital (number 33), begun in 1773 and designed by John McComb, the father of the man who drew this plan.

Although the name of the draftsman of the plan is given on it as "I. M. Comb Junr.," this is in all probability an archaic spelling of the name of John McComb, Junior (1763–1853). He is listed in the 1787 directory of the city as a surveyor, but like his father became an architect of considerable stature. He is best known for the grandly detailed City Hall, begun in 1802 and designed with Joseph F. Mangin. He also designed three lighthouses, including the one at Montauk that still stands.

The Directory Plan of 1789 was also an early project of its engraver, Cornelius Tiebout (1777–1832), and if his reported date of birth can be believed, an extremely early one; he would have been only twelve years of age when the map was published. This is possible given the scarcity of engraving talent in America at the time. In fact, authorities describe Tiebout himself as the first American-born engraver to produce high-quality work. As would have been typical at the time, Tiebout learned copperplate engraving from his apprenticeship in an allied field, gold or silver smithing. Aware of his inadequacies in engraving for printing, he traveled to England in 1793 to refine his skills and returned to New York in 1796. Included in his output were some of the maps in the America's first road atlas, Christopher Colles's *Survey of the Roads of the United States*, published the same year as the Directory Plan of 1789 and very similar to it in style. Tiebout also engraved an updated, second edition of this plan in 1795. He was especially skilled at portrait work, and his 1795 engraving of John Jay is considered the finest early American work of this kind. He also produced views of Columbia College, Wall Street, City Hall, and Trinity Church before relocating to Philadelphia in 1799.

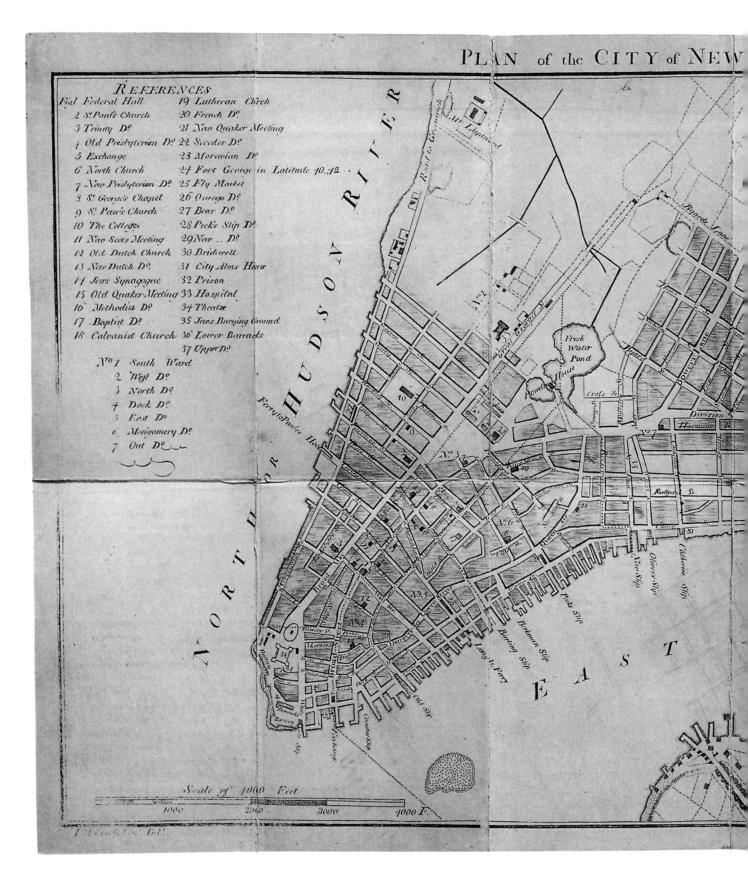

REFERENCES

Fial Federal Hall	19 Lutheran Chrch
2 St Pauls Church	20 French Dº
3 Trinity Dº	21 New Quaker Meeting
4 Old Presbyterian Dº	22 Seeder Dº
5 Exchange	23 Moravian Dº
6 North Church	24 Fort George in Latitude 40.42
7 New Presbyterian Dº	25 Fly Market
8 St George's Chapel	26 Oswego Dº
9 St Peter's Church	27 Bear Dº
10 The College	28 Peck's Slip Dº
11 New Scots Meeting	29 New Dº
12 Old Dutch Church	30 Bridewell
13 New Dutch Dº	31 City Alms House
14 Jews Synagogue	32 Prison
15 Old Quaker Meeting	33 Hospital
16 Methodist Dº	34 Theatre
17 Baptist Dº	35 Jews Burying Ground
18 Calvanist Church	36 Lower Barracks
	37 Upper Dº

Nº 1 South Ward
2 West Dº
3 North Dº
4 Dock Dº
5 East Dº
6 Montgomery Dº
7 Out Dº

NORTH OR HUDSON RIVER

EAST

Scale of 1000 Feet

1000   2000   3000   4000 F.

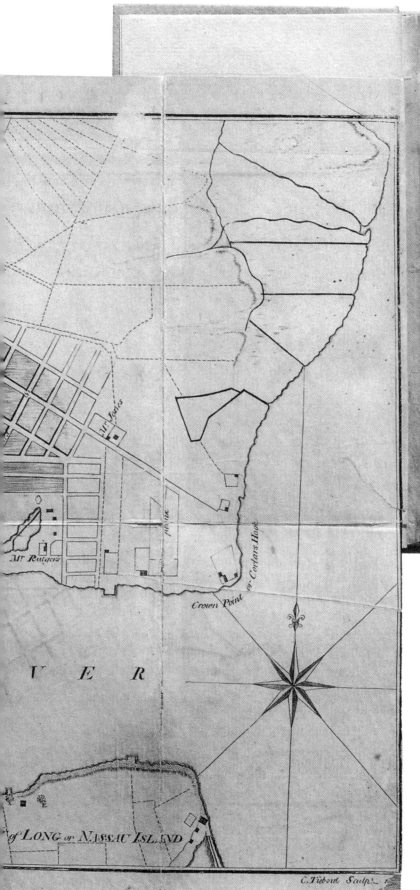

THE

NEW-YORK DIRECTORY,

AND

REGISTER,

FOR THE YEAR 1789.

Illustrated with an accurate and elegant PLAN of the CITY of NEW-YORK, and part of LONG-ISLAND, including the SUBURBS, with all the STREETS, LANES, PUBLIC BUILDINGS, WHARVES, &c. exactly laid down,

FROM THE LATEST SURVEY.

CONTAINING,

An alphabetical List of the Names, Occupations, and Places of abode of the Citizens,
A Register of the Congress of the United States,
Foreign Ministers,
Governors of different States,
Officers of the State of New-York,
Officers in Chancery,
Assembly,
Senate,
Officers of City and County,
Chamber of Commerce,
Marine Society,
Assurance Company,

Ministers of the Gospel,
Medical Society,
The other Societies in City,
Roll of Attornies of Supreme Court,
Columbia College,
Library Society,
Militia Officers,
Masonic Lodges,
Post Days, Stages, and &c. Rates,
Impost Law.
Extracts from sundry Laws for the regulation of Trade, &c.

PRICE—3s. 6d. WITH THE PLAN OF THE CITY.

NEW-YORK, PRINTED
FOR HODGE, ALLEN, AND CAMPBELL, AND SOLD
AT THEIR RESPECTIVE STORES.
M,DCCLXXXIX.

A PRELIMINARY PLAN FOR GROWTH
THE TAYLOR-ROBERTS PLAN

TITLE: A New & Accurate Plan of the City
of New York in the State of New York in
North America
DATE DEPICTED: 1797
DATE ISSUED: 1797
CARTOGRAPHERS: BENJAMIN TAYLOR
AND JOHN ROBERTS
Uncolored copperplate engraving,
24½ x 37½ inches
Collection of Arthur O. Sulzberger, New York

The closing years of the eighteenth century
set the stage for the phenomenal growth
and expansion of New York throughout the
nineteenth century. Following the American
Revolution, the city lay in ruins. The
rebuilding that would characterize much of
the city's future began with the return of
the citizenry. Old streets were repaired, new
streets were laid out, and swampy land was
filled in. The construction of streets and
buildings gathered such momentum that
within two decades of the peace, New
Yorkers realized that they would need a
comprehensive plan for the development of
the entire island of Manhattan.

The last important map to show
Manhattan as it actually existed is the
Taylor-Roberts Plan, published in 1797 as
"A New & Accurate Plan of the City of
New York." During the next quarter-
century, the significant maps dealt officially
or unofficially with planning and speculation. The Taylor-Roberts Plan delineates
New York emerging from the war. It was the
first relatively large map of the city printed
in America since the Lyne-Bradford Plan of
1731 (see p. 40), and the first separately
issued map of Manhattan printed in the new
nation. Like so many of the early maps of
the city, it is also exceedingly rare; only six
or seven examples are known to survive.

Benjamin Taylor became a city surveyor
in 1794 and his responsibilities included the
first efforts to bring fresh water into the

city. In 1797 he and John Roberts, a Scot
known for his "highly superior dexterity as
an engraver," published their remarkable
map of the city, which they characterized as
standing "in the bosom of a spacious bay."
I. N. Phelps Stokes described it as "One of
the most accurate and beautifully engraved
plans of the city, and particularly interesting
on account of its tiny bird's-eye views of
some of the most important buildings."

The Taylor-Roberts Plan sets forth the
considerable civic activity in Manhattan
since John Hills's map of 1785. In the area
burned by the British, most of the streets
had been paved and many straightened,
"intersecting each other at right angles,"
according to a visitor who admired the
new "straight, broad" thoroughfares like
Greenwich Street, which had also been
widened. The streets are laid out up to
North Street (now Houston), but there is
still very little development that far north.

Most conspicuous were improvements
on Broadway and Wall streets. Broadway had
suffered during the British occupation and
was in need of grading "so as to give it a
gentle descent . . . to Bowling Green." Wall
Street, then a residential as well as a business
street, became "one of the show places of
the town" after the Common Council
ordered numerous improvements, including
the removal of the city horse market.

The Taylor-Roberts Plan records the
decision of the Common Council in 1794
to change the names of streets that reminded the citizens of the British. Queen Street,
Prince Street, and King George Street all
were absorbed by other thoroughfares—
Pearl, Beaver, and William streets, respectively. Other offending street names got
new names: Prince became Rose, Little
Queen was changed to Cedar, and King to
Pine. Bit by bit, the city became
Americanized, and the renaming of streets
was an important stage in that process.

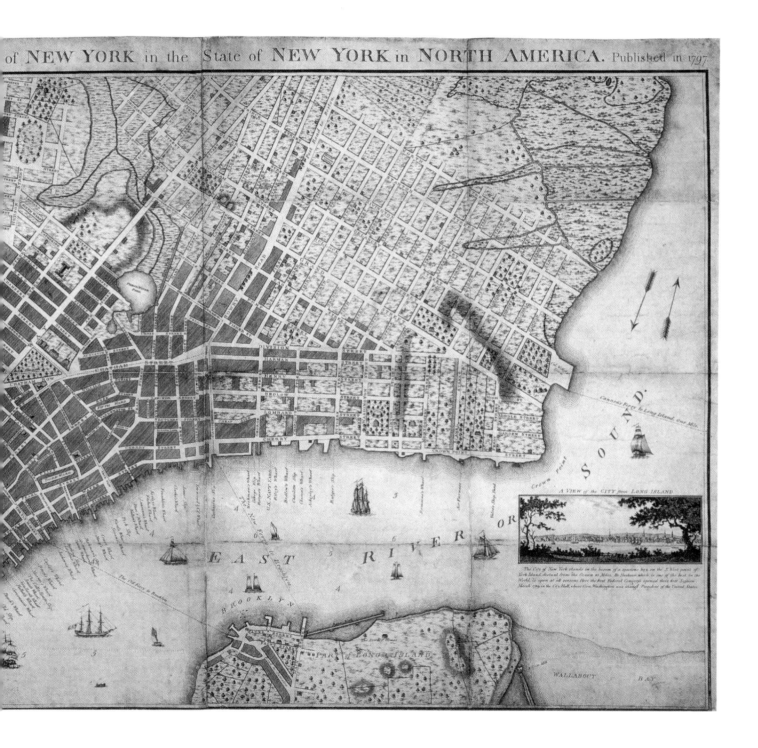

A VIEW of the CITY from LONG ISLAND

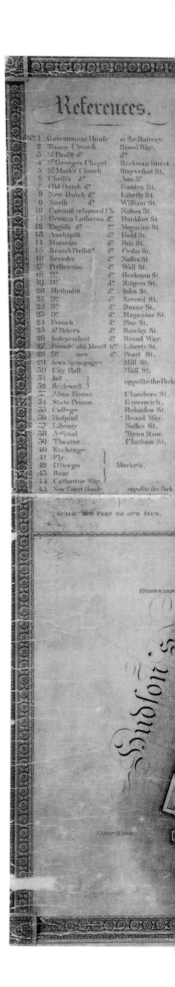

THE MANGIN-GOERCK PLAN

TITLE: Plan of the city of New York, drawn from actual survey
DATE DEPICTED: 1803
DATE DRAWN: 1803
CARTOGRAPHERS: JOSEPH FRANÇOIS MANGIN AND CASIMIR GOERCK
Uncolored copperplate engraving, four sheets 33 x 15½ inches each
New-York Historical Society

THE BRIDGES PLAN

TITLE: Plan of the city of New-York, with the recent and intended improvements
DATE DEPICTED: 1803
DATE DRAWN: 1807
CARTOGRAPHER/ENGRAVER: WILLIAM BRIDGES
Uncolored copperplate engraving, 12⅞ x 12¼ inches
Private collection

The Common Council of New York City should have become concerned about their first "regulating plan of the city" long before it was declared a disaster in 1803. The Mangin-Goerck Plan, drawn from an actual survey, was to have been an ambitious new map by two of New York's most promising surveyors: Joseph François Mangin and Casimir Goerck. In 1797, these two men proposed New York's first real-estate map, one that would show houses, lots, and include the names of their owners. In addition, it would delineate all the municipal buildings, churches, streets, squares, wharfs, and wards; "the leveling of the whole city will be added to the map."

Joseph Mangin was a talented French architect who had arrived in New York in 1795 and soon after was appointed a city surveyor. Some of New York's most famous early buildings are by Mangin, including City Hall which he designed with John McComb. Less is known about Casimir Goerck, his collaborator of one year, who died on December 11, 1798, leaving Mangin to complete the map alone.

Mangin and Goerck agreed to draft their six-foot-square map for the use of the Common Council and then publish copies on a reduced scale. With the approval of the council and an initial payment of two hun-

dred dollars, on December 11, 1797, they began work on the survey, expecting to complete the project in eighteen months. At the same time, the enterprising Mangin also started raising additional funds by selling subscriptions for a printed version.

The first sign of trouble occurred late in 1798 when Charles Loss, a fellow surveyor with an assignment to execute a plan of New York Harbor, asked to look at Mangin's map-in-progress. This request was summarily rejected by Mangin, who informed Loss that the map would not be of much use as it "is not the plan of the city such as it is, but such as it is to be." Instead of making the map he had proposed, Mangin had taken the liberty of making a plan for New York City's future.

Five years later, in November 1803, Mangin presented the high aerial map of the city to the committee of the Common Council. The committee was stunned by the odd, angular map before them. They had expected a straightforward real-estate map; instead they were confronted with a map that was primarily fanciful projection. The map "lately printed and ready for sale," they reported, "contains many inaccuracies and designates streets which have not been agreed to by the Corporation and which would be improper to adopt."

A Plan and Regulation of the
CITY OF NEW YORK,

83

Where Mangin had mapped existing streets, he had idealized them by converting uneven blocks and house lots into perfect geometric squares and rectangles. He also evened out the waterfront by delineating it with perfectly straight lines. As a result, some streets, like Front Street, ended up underwater on the map, but Mangin did have the good sense to supply a line that accurately delineated the existing waterfront. Mangin also supplied names for the numerous new streets he had created. Most were never adopted, but some, like South Street, made their first appearance on his map. He boldly named one of these ephemeral streets after himself, and another after his deceased partner: Mangin Street and Gorrek [sic] Street are located near the East River.

After unsuccessfully putting the map to use in a land dispute the street commissioner wrote as follows about Mangin's angular map: this is "an arrangement certainly to be desired but unfortunately it deviates so much from [previous maps] that the adoption of it would create great difficulties from its total derangement of a great number of Lots . . . owned by a variety of proprietors."

In fact, the committee found the map so inappropriate that it resolved "to return the money paid by each subscriber [and] endeavor to recall as many of said maps as have been sold." The map, however, was not completely suppressed; it was released to a few subscribers after a qualifying label supplied by the street commissioner was affixed to its surface. This label warned that the northern two-thirds of the map was invalid, the streets delineated in that part of the city not having been "ceded to the corporation" or "approved and opened under their authority." Without the sanction of the Common Council, the Mangin-Goerck Plan could not expect to have much of a future. The original, six-foot-square manuscript map has disappeared and very few copies of the smaller printed version were distributed; only about ten examples have survived.

There was, however, a brief revival of interest in the map in 1807 when William Bridges, the city surveyor who would later publish the great Commissioners' Plan of New York City (see p. 86), reengraved the Mangin-Goerck Map under his own name and on an even smaller scale to appear in Dr. Samuel Mitchell's *Picture of New York* (1807). There the map is cited but not identified: "A map of the city, published by order of the common council, in 1801 [i.e., 1803] . . . is the best exhibition of streets and intended improvements, including even the projected works to be completed on the East rivers, from the present shores to the line of limitation [about the present Twelfth Street]." Bridges' pirated map is more confusing than Mangin's because Bridges omitted the accurate line where Mangin had delineated the actual waterfront of Lower Manhattan. Bridges made no attempt to distinguish land from water; as a result, many of the streets on his map are at least partially underwater, but there is no way of knowing which ones.

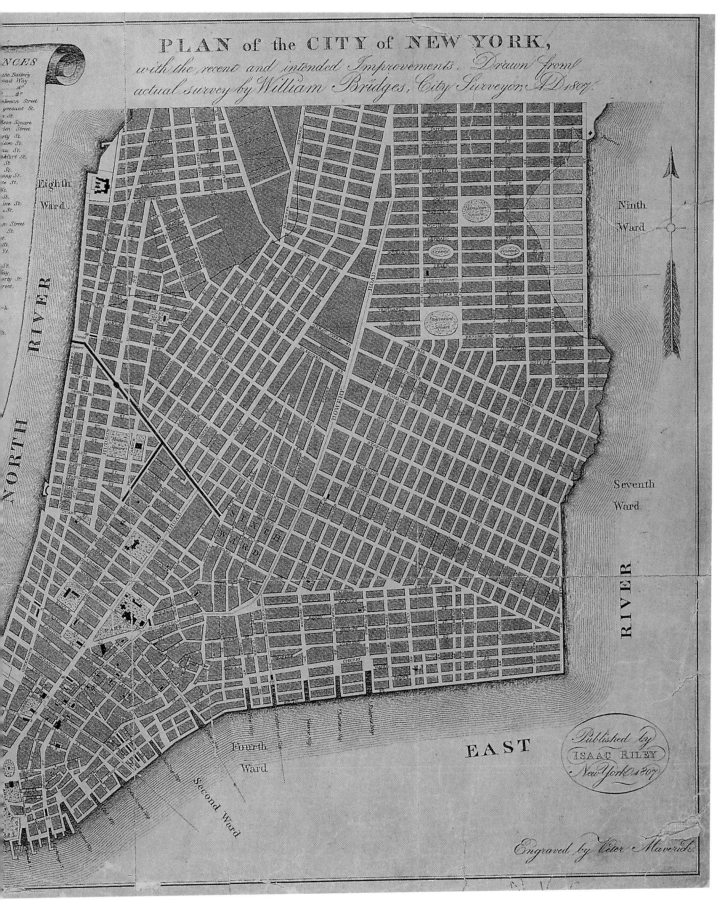

PLAN of the CITY of NEW YORK, with the recent and intended Improvements. Drawn from actual survey by William Bridges, City Surveyor, A.D. 1807.

Eighth Ward.

Ninth Ward

NORTH RIVER

Seventh Ward

SIXTH WARD

EAST

RIVER

Fourth Ward

Second Ward

Published by ISAAC RILEY New York 1807

Engraved by Peter Maverick.

THE COMMISSIONERS' PLAN

TITLE: A Map of the city of New York by the commissioners appointed by an act of the Legislature passed April 3rd 1807

DATE DEPICTED: 1811

DATE ISSUED: 1811

CARTOGRAPHER: JOHN RANDEL, JR.

Uncolored manuscript on paper, 106 x 30⁷⁄₁₆ *inches*

The New York Public Library

BRIDGES'S ADAPTATION OF THE COMMISSIONERS' PLAN

TITLE: This map of the city of New York and island of Manhattan as laid out by the commissioners

DATE DEPICTED: 1811

CARTOGRAPHER: JOHN RANDEL, JR.; ADAPTED AND PUBLISHED BY WILLIAM BRIDGES

PUBLISHED: WILLIAM BRIDGES, NEW YORK, NOVEMBER 16, 1811

ENGRAVER: PETER MAVERICK

Colored line engraving on copper, 91⅜ x 24⅝ *inches*

Library of Congress

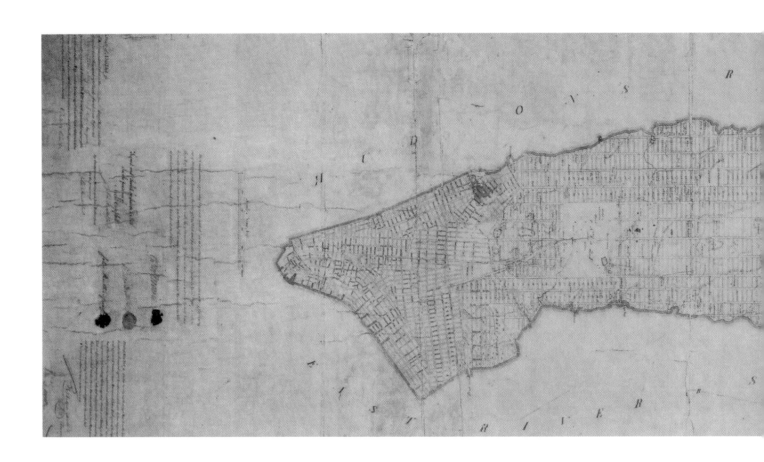

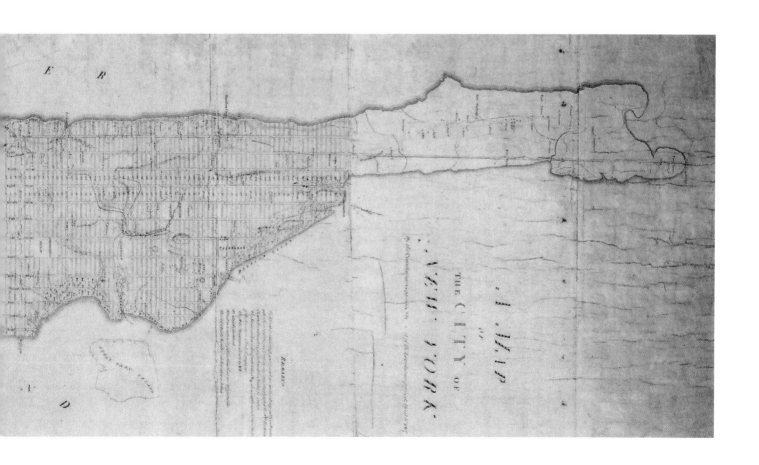

87

The single most important document in New York City's development is a map printed in 1811 called the Randel Survey or The Commissioners' Plan. It unveiled a plan to increase the size of the city by 11,400 acres and "provide space for a greater population than is collected on this side of China." Manhattan's familiar gridiron street pattern was introduced on the map, which I. N. Phelps Stokes, author of *The Iconography of Manhattan Island*, regarded as "marking the end of Old New York and the beginning of the Modern City."

In 1811, New York was still a "small but promising capital which," as characterized by Henry James in *Washington Square*, "clustered about the Battery and overlooked the Bay, and of which the uppermost boundary was indicated by the grassy waysides of Canal Street." North of Canal loomed a rugged wilderness broken only by an occasional farm or small community, such as the village of Greenwich (now Greenwich Village).

By 1804, New York's mayor and aldermen knew that the city was on the verge of rapid growth and began eyeing the undeveloped land. If their city was to expand in an orderly way, they needed a comprehensive plan. For two years, city officials struggled with property owners and conflicting political factions before realizing that such a grand project would be impossible to accomplish by New York City alone.

They turned to the state for assistance. In 1807, a special commission was appointed by the state legislature "to lay out streets, roads, public squares of such extent and direction as to them shall seem most conducive to public good." However, before Commissioners Simeon De Witt, John Rutherford, and Gouverneur Morris could begin, they required a proper survey of the entire island.

For this enormous undertaking, they hired John Randel, Jr., a man in his early twenties who had been a surveyor for Simeon De Witt, the surveyor general of New York State. De Witt was a noted cartographer in his own right who had distinguished himself during the Revolution by drafting military maps for General George Washington. Recognizing Randel's abilities, De Witt had already given him several assignments to survey state lands. His success in planning a complicated turnpike near Albany led De Witt, by then one of the commissioners, to recommend Randel for the Herculean task of surveying Manhattan Island.

In May or June 1808, Randel started the project, which would occupy him off and on for thirteen years. In a memoir, he recalled hiking from his residence in lower Manhattan to his headquarters at the corner of Christopher and Herring streets, at that time countryside. From there, he traveled to the distant parts of the island, which were often so thickly wooded that they were "impassable without the aid of an ax." In addition to these natural obstacles, over the years Randel and his workers had to retreat from the hostilities of rural property owners and squatters. The surveyors were sometimes arrested, and dogs were unleashed on them. An elderly woman who sold vegetables discovered them at work in her kitchen one day and forced them out under a barrage of cabbages and artichokes.

"I superintended the surveys," Randel said, "with a view to ascertain the most eligible grounds for the intended streets and avenues, with reference to sites least obstructed by rocks, precipices, steep grades, and other obstacles." The surveyors proceeded to measure every inch of Manhattan Island, and when they were finished, Simeon De Witt boasted that it had been accomplished "with an accuracy not exceeded by any work of the kind in America."

Randel brought the topographical maps he was drafting of various sections of the island to his regular meetings with the commissioners. The question of a street plan occupied much of their attention at these meetings: "whether they should confine themselves to rectilinear and rectangular streets, or whether they should adopt some of these supposed improvements, by circles, ovals, and stars." The gridiron was then the most popular street pattern and had already been employed in such cities as Philadelphia, Savannah, Charleston, and New Orleans. "This is a plan of which Americans are very fond," observed a visitor from Europe. "All the modern built towns are on this principle." It certainly had the advantage of being simple to lay out and easy for building construction.

When the commissioners decided on the gridiron for Manhattan, they "could not but bear in mind that a city is to be composed principally of the habitations of men, and that strait sided and right angled houses are the most cheap to build, and the most convenient to live in." Their plan consisted of a dozen north-south avenues each 100 feet wide, and at intervals of 200 feet were 155 numbered streets 60 feet wide.

By the fall of 1810, Randel had completed his survey, and the commissioners had arrived at their "comprehensive and permanent" system of streets. Then Randel drafted three large (approximately nine by two and one-half feet) and detailed topographical maps of the island on which he superimposed the orderly plan of avenues and streets. The natural geography of the island was originally to be a factor in devising a street system, but there is little evidence in the eight miles of numbered parallel and perpendicular streets and avenues delineated on Randel's map that the topography of the island was even a consideration. Lewis Mumford characterized the unimaginative plan as follows: "With a T-square and a triangle, finally, the municipal engineer, without the slightest training as either an architect or a sociologist, could 'plan' a metropolis."

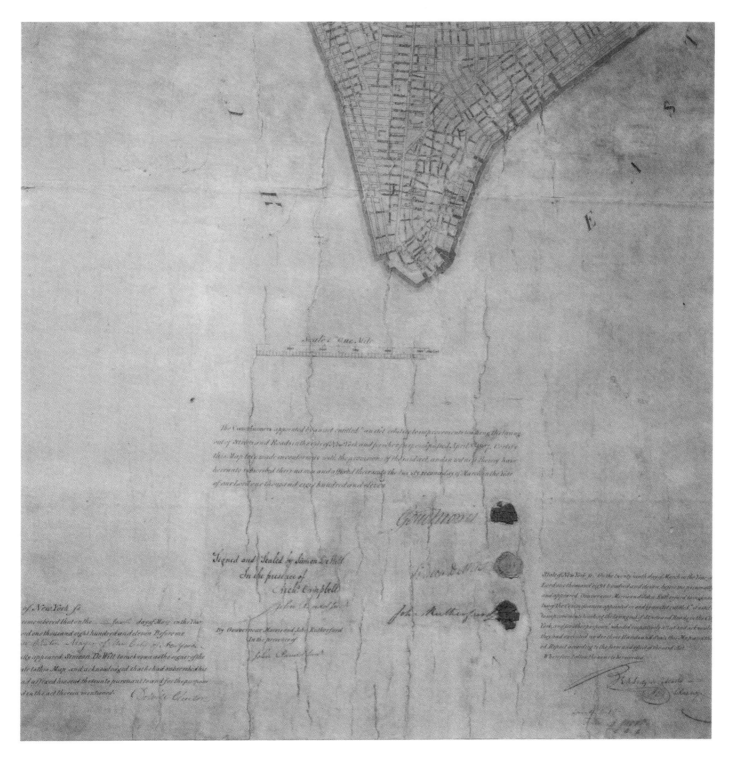

In the early nineteenth century, Manhattan was still an island of hills, and some civic-minded New Yorkers wanted those hills retained. "The great principle which governs these plans is, to reduce the surface of the earth as nearly as possible to dead level," wrote philologist and writer Clement Clarke Moore, who owned real estate where new streets were to be constructed. "The natural inequities of the ground are destroyed, and the existing water courses disregarded. . . .These are men . . . who would have cut down the seven hills of Rome."

Chancellor James Kent thought the city had been laid out on "a magnificent scale," but Randel's plan has attracted few other defenders over the years, and perhaps he should be thankful that his name appears nowhere on the engraved version of his manuscript map. In 1811, however, he was furious with the sequence of events that led to the publication of his survey. "I had commenced preparing a map for the engraver

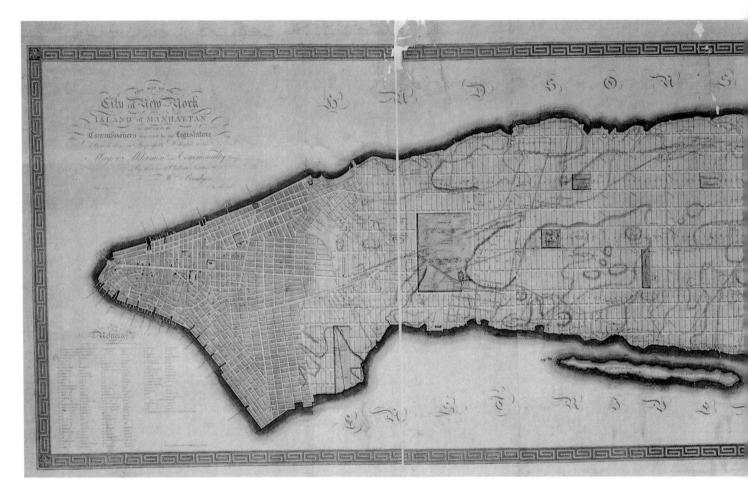

from the original papers," Randel wrote to one of the aldermen on May 8, 1811, "and had it in considerable forwardness when I understood that the corporation [of New York City] had given the privilege of publishing it to Mr. William Bridges."

When the eight-foot-long Commissioners' Plan was issued in 1811, the name "Wm. Bridges" occupied a conspicuous position on the map and was printed in larger letters than any other name, dwarfing the names of the three commissioners. Engraved by Peter Maverick, the map was accompanied by a fifty-four-page descriptive pamphlet. There is not a single reference to John Randel on the map or in the pamphlet. Bridges was the city surveyor whose only previously published map was a small copy of the Mangin-Goerck Plan in 1807 (see p. 82). Little is known about him, and his appropriation of Randel's survey was his most lasting accomplishment.

In a March 29, 1814, letter Randel accused Bridges of deceiving "the corpora-

tion (Alderman [Peter] Mesier informed me) by informing them that I would furnish you with the notes and papers of the commissioners to compleat the map." Bridges, however, did not have access to the official papers and, according to Randel, merely copied one of his three manuscript maps, which were by then part of the public record. Randel's assertion appears to be correct as the printed map is the same size as the manuscript and the two works are identical in every respect, except for the many errors Randel claimed Bridges made in the transcription. Bridges had successfully managed to issue and copyright Randel's map as a private venture.

Although Randel was cheated out of publishing the results of the most ambitious survey of his career, he nevertheless remained in Manhattan to execute the next phase of the enormous project. Once the map and plan were approved, the Common Council required elevations taken for each street, and at each intersection a marker

placed where future streets would be constructed. Between 1811 and 1821, Randel and his determined crew placed a three-foot nine-inch-long white marble marker engraved with the street's number at each intersection. Where rocks blocked the way, half-foot iron bolts were affixed to them. In total, 1,549 markers and 98 bolts eventually dotted the landscape of the island.

In later life, Randel occupied himself with a number of grand engineering projects and earned a reputation for eccentricity and a fondness for litigation. In 1823, he became chief engineer for the Chesapeake and Delaware Canal Company, where he conceived an ingenious method of using the Atlantic Ocean as the reservoir from which the canal was supplied; underestimated by some 82 percent the cost of constructing the canal; and made an enemy of Benjamin Wright, one of the canal's most important consulting engineers. Wright characterized Randel as "a complete Hypocritical, lying nincompoop (and I might say scoundrel if it

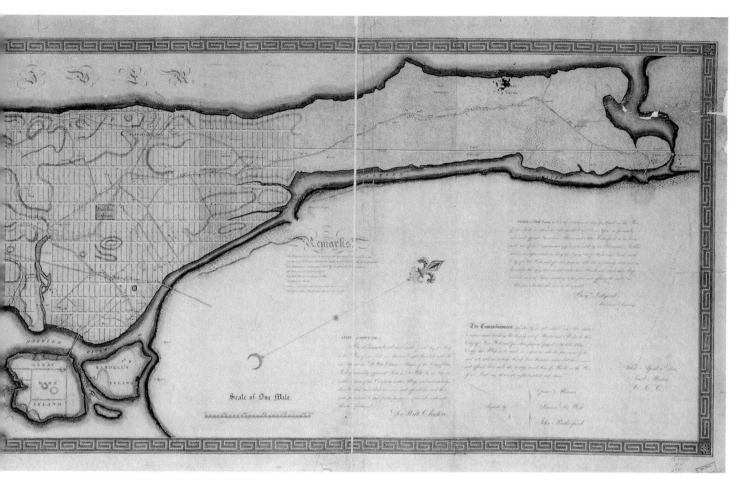

was a Gentlemanly word)."

Although it was one of Randel's plans that was eventually used in the construction of the canal, he was summarily discharged in 1825. The dismissal created an enormous clamor as Mathew Carey and others defended Randel by rushing into print such pamphlets as "Exhibit of the Shocking Oppression and Injustice Suffered for Sixteen Months by John Randel, Jun." (1825). The breach of contract suit that followed was in litigation until 1834, when Randel was awarded a staggering $226,885.84 in a decision that crippled the canal company and is still cited as "one of the most famous lawsuits" in Maryland history. With the windfall, Randel retired to a thousand-acre estate in Maryland.

In his last known letter, written in 1849 from the estate he named Randelia, he discoursed about the land in Manhattan above 155th Street. His first plan of the city ended at 155th, and he had designed an elegant extension of the city that would be accessi-

ble by elevated train (Randel was the first to envision the practical use of such trains). It would be "the most beautiful and comfortable suburban City you could desire to see," he wrote, with its avenues "200 feet wide, with Parks for trees and tasteful shrubbery, 80 feet in width in the middle." These plans were never executed, and in the same letter Randel complained that he had been "out of professional employment" for many of the years following the lawsuit. He died in 1865.

The plan for Manhattan that Randel and the commissioners devised is still virtually intact. A few significant changes have been made to it over the years—Broadway, for example, which was not included in the Commissioners' Plan, could not be eliminated, and Central Park was added in the 1850s—but the monotonous straight streets of New York City are the legacy of the "Randel Survey." "This plan," wrote Randel in 1864, "thus objected to before it [sic] completion, is now the pride and boast of the city." He pointed especially to the

opportunities for "buying, selling, and improving real estate." Many land speculators did profit from the plan, but others have considered it a failure—Lewis Mumford called it "civic folly." And John Reps has written: "The fact that it was this gridiron that served as a model for later cities was a disaster whose consequences have barely been mitigated by more recent city planners."

The map that Bridges published in 1811 has become an unaccountably rare item. The enterprising Bridges printed as many of the large maps as he could sell, and offered them in a variety of formats: uncolored and on sheets, $8; on rollers and varnished, $12.50; and a deluxe version on rollers and in color, $15.50. He lined up 345 subscribers, promised forty additional copies to city officials, and sold an indeterminate number in stationary stores. Despite the relatively large printing run, the map can now rarely be seen outside of a few museums and libraries.

A BETTER COMPREHENSIVE PLAN

THE NEW COMMISSIONERS' PLAN OF 1814

TITLE: The City of New York as laid out by the Commissioners, with the surrounding country
DATE DEPICTED: 1814
DATE DRAWN: 1814
CARTOGRAPHER: JOHN RANDEL, JR.
Uncolored manuscript on paper, 32 x 21 inches
New-York Historical Society

THE FINAL COMMISSIONERS' PLAN OF 1821

TITLE: The City of New York as laid out by the Commissioners, with the surrounding country
DATE DEPICTED: 1821
DATE DRAWN: 1821
CARTOGRAPHER: JOHN RANDEL, JR.
Colored copperplate engraving, 25¾ x 37½ inches
Library of Congress

"This map will be found on examination to be more correct than any that has hitherto appeared, and that part of it which contains the plan of the city cannot be made more accurate." The announcement of John Randel's New Commissioners' Plan on March 21, 1814, was full of promise, but it did little more than stir up a controversy with William Bridges over the official Commissioners' Plan, which he had published in 1811 (see p. 86). Randel's elaborate manuscript map of 1814 was not published until 1821, when it was printed in trompe l'oeil to appear like a surveyor's scroll, partially unrolled with other maps on a drafting table.

Titled "The City of New York as laid out by the Commissioners with the Surrounding Country by their Secretary and Surveyor," The New Commissioners' Plan is much smaller than the original Commissioners' Plan, but it encompasses a larger geographical area. Nevertheless, the grid plan that Randel had laid out is delineated in detail. "It appears to me more accurate than anything of the kind which has yet appeared," Gouverneur Morris, one of the original commissioners, told Randel. "Indeed until your actual measurements were completed, it was hardly possible to attain that accuracy which the totality of

the materials in your possession has enabled you to exhibit."

Randel seemed to be provoking Bridges by soliciting praise for his map from one of the commissioners. This, of course, raised questions about the accuracy of the map published for the commissioners in 1811. Such a challenge demanded a response from Bridges. On March 24, 1814, in the *New-York Evening Post*, he attacked Randel's "unprincipled, and most assuredly unprovoked conduct."

For almost three years Randel's anger had been simmering, and in the April 8, 1814, issue of the *Evening Post*, he delivered a 1,800-word diatribe on the city surveyor, accusing him of diverting "the public attention from your map to an attack on me." Randel began by attacking Bridges for stealing his map and went on to enumerate the errors that Bridges had made when preparing Randel's manuscript for publication: several hills were in the wrong places, fifty-eight buildings were omitted, another forty-five buildings were not in their proper location, and the Hudson and Harlem rivers flowed about two hundred feet too close to each other at certain points.

Many of these errors were corrected on Randel's new map, which he took pleasure in advertising in that same April 8, 1814,

issue of the *Evening Post* that featured his vitriolic attack on Bridges:

Randel's Map of Manhattan Island, is now exhibited for inspection at the Bookstore of Messrs. Eastburn, Kirk & Co. Wall-street. . . . This Map will show the exact position of each dwelling house, and the size in feet and parts of a foot of every block north of North-street, and Greenwich-Lane, which are not contained in the map published by Mr. Bridges—Also, the latitude, together with the longitude of places from the City Hall. It will be ready for delivery about December next.

Why was this attractive, accurate, and important map not printed that year? The only reason given suggests that its very accuracy may have thwarted publication. The War of 1812 was still raging as Randel prepared his map and delivered it to the engraver. "Under present circumstances," ran an announcement in the *Evening Post* (October 5, 1814), "it might be improper to furnish the enemy with an opportunity to procure by means of its agents such accurate information of the country." Washington, D.C., had been extensively burned by the British just two months before the announcement; at that time it

was feared that Manhattan was a likely target for additional military action.

From 1811 to 1821, Randel was employed by the Corporation of New York City to make elevations at each proposed street and to place markers at the future intersections. At the conclusion of this period, he finally published his 1814 map—but with a number of alterations. It still had the same dimensions as the original manuscript, but the delineation of Manhattan on the final map incorporated all of the changes to the grid that resulted from Randel's own fieldwork executed up to the year 1821. In addition, Randel had just completed for the Common Council an enormous manuscript map of Manhattan's farms (see p. 96), which included at a large scale all of the topography and projected streets of the island. Details from the farm map made their way onto the 1821 Commissioners' Plan, which is the most accurate and complete printed map of Manhattan's grid. It has a number of other features as well including a map of Philadelphia, although Randel is not known to have surveyed that city.

Randel credited the instruments he used for the great accuracy of his surveying. He invented some of these himself and adapted others for his particular needs; they are pictured at the top right of this map. "It is known, from experience," wrote Randel, "that a line measured twice with these instruments on such a field, will not in any case differ more than one inch in five miles."

Randel's 1821 map appears to be even rarer than The Commissioners' Plan of 1811. Not many additional copies of the map have turned up since I. N. Phelps Stokes located three examples some eighty years ago, including a copy printed on satin which was offered for sale by a nephew of John Randel.

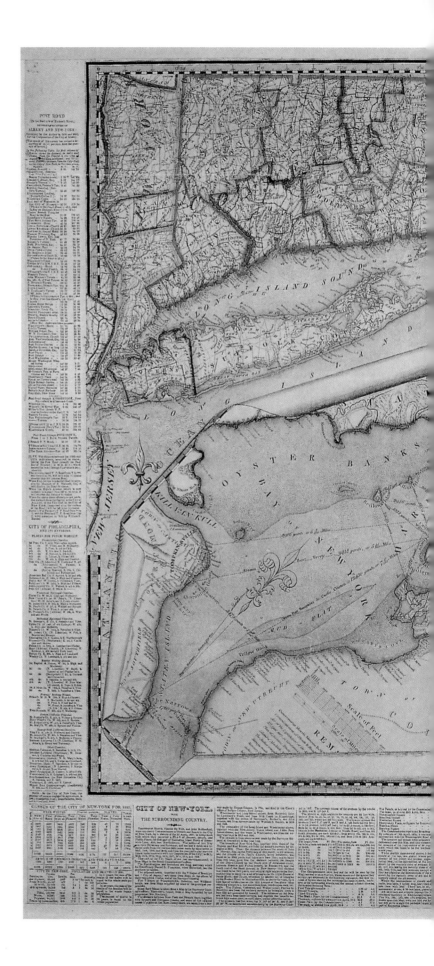

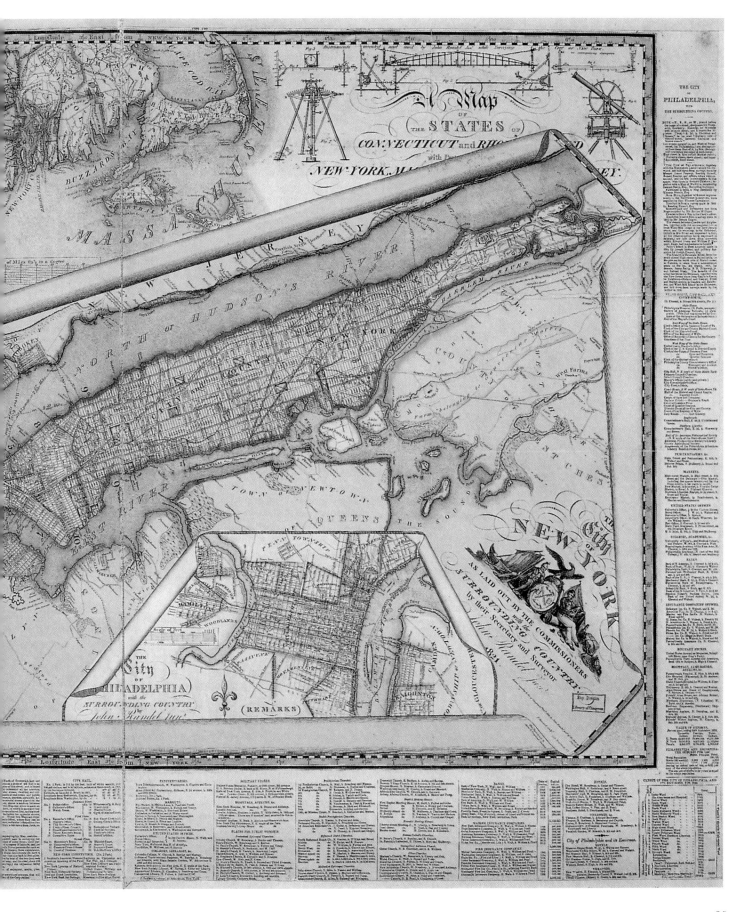

THE RANDEL SURVEY
RANDEL FARM MAP No. 27

TITLE: The City of New York as Laid out by the Commissioners Appointed by an Act of the Legislature....
DATE DEPICTED: c. 1819
DATE DRAWN: 1819–1820
CARTOGRAPHER: JOHN RANDEL, JR.
Pen and ink with watercolor on paper, 32 x 20 inches
Manhattan Borough President's Office

John Randel Jr.'s most influential map was the Commissioners' Plan, but his most monumental was a delineation of the farms of Manhattan. This huge topographical work incorporated most of the data Randel had accumulated in his years of surveying the island. It is made up of ninety-two numbered folio sheets (only one of the thirty-two-inch by twenty-inch sheets could be pictured here) executed on the enormous scale of one hunded feet to an inch. If assembled together—and the mapsheets never have been—they would create a map measuring eleven feet by fifty feet. Today they fill four bound volumes kept at the Manhattan Borough President's Office; Randel's field notes are at the New-York Historical Society.

The map had its genesis soon after William Bridges published the Commissioners' Plan in 1811. The following year, the Common Council recommended that Randel make "a map or maps protracted on a scale sufficiently large to exhibit accurately the Hills Valleys Rocks Houses. Creeks &c." Randel was too busy placing markers at the intersections of Manhattan's future streets to get started on the map right away. A contract for the map was not signed until 1818, and Randel did not actually begin drafting it until 1819.

During the first decade of the nineteenth century, when Randel was engaged in surveying, the greater portion of Manhattan consisted of farms and estates. In I. N. Phelps Stokes' *Iconography* (Vol. 6),

more than one hundred pages are devoted to detailed studies of each of the "Original Grants and Farms" where many of New York's oldest families owned property: the Beekmans, van Cortlandts, De Peysters, Emmetts, and De Lanceys. Accurate surveying information for these farms was essential for a city that had a plan to construct streets on the very land occupied by these farms. In fact, Randel had already drawn up a "list of the buildings in the streets and avenues, that will be paid for when removed by order of the Corporation."

Two years of meticulous labor were required to complete the map. During this period, the Common Council at least once extended Randel's deadline for completion, and the Committee on Surveys complained that the mapmaker was "more ambitious of accuracy than of profit." Stokes called the result "the only exact early topographical map of the island. This exceedingly important map shows the entire city above North Street, and indicates every individual lot and building, thus constituting the most complete and valuable topographical record of the period that exists." Randel himself recommended that his farm map "be examined by persons desiring more particular information than can be obtained from" his 1821 map of Manhattan (see p. 92).

It had been Randel's ambition to create a perfect and all-encompassing work, the culminating statement of the most important project in his career. "Upon it is delineated," he wrote, "all the avenues, streets,

public places, monumental stones, dwelling and out-houses, fences designating the bounds of real estate and public works; all hills, creeks, rocks, swamps, marshes, meadows, &c. with the elevation of all monumental stones placed on the 1st, 3rd, 5th, 8th, and 10th avenues, above a medium between high and low tide water."

Stokes was impressed that "distances scaled upon it will be found to compare exactly with later filed maps." One reason for this should have been obvious to Stokes: later mapmakers, recognizing the superiority of Randel's work, relied heavily if not exclusively on it when executing their own maps. When Colton expressed his debt to the maps on file at the Topographical Office, he was more precisely acknowledging Randel. And Viele, who is not known to have made many on-site surveys (except for the lands incorporating Central Park), must have drawn largely upon these farm maps when compiling his famous topographical map of the island. Stated simply, the Randel Farm Map is the most important topographical map of Manhattan ever executed.

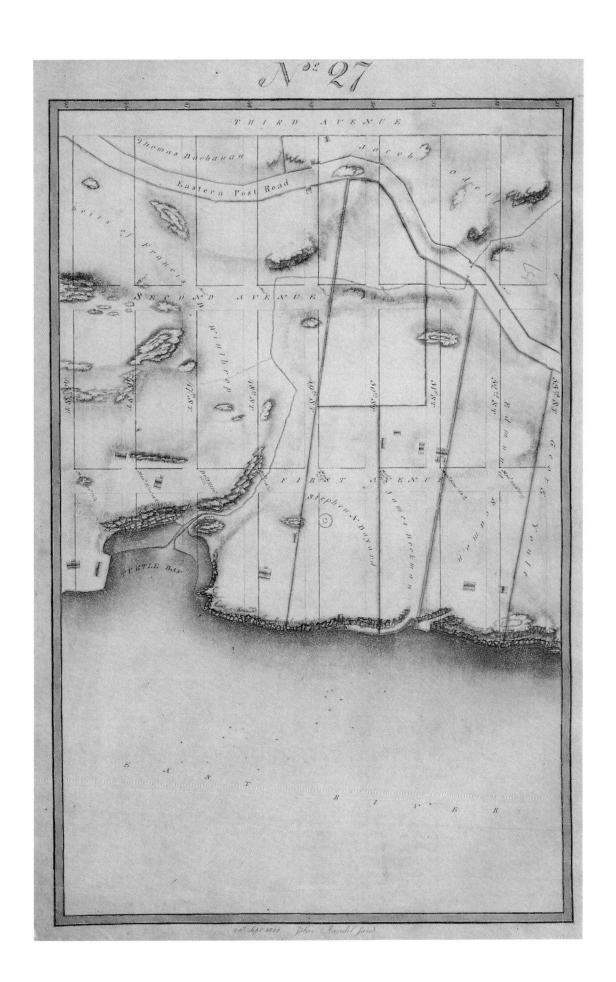

SURVEYING THE WATERFRONT
EWEN'S MAP OF BATTERY PARK

Untitled
DATE DEPICTED: 1827
DATE ISSUED: 1827 (unpublished manuscript)
CARTOGRAPHER: DANIEL EWEN
Pen and ink with watercolor, 32 x 20 inches
Manhattan Borough President's Office

New York Harbor had already established itself as the preeminent port in the Western Hemisphere when the Erie Canal opened in 1825. In addition to having the best natural harbor on the Atlantic coast, New York shippers had taken command of the seas after the innovative Black Ball Line began offering packet service to Liverpool in 1818. Unlike previous shipping companies, whose ships set sail only after their holds were filled with cargo, Black Ball's trim vessels operated on a strict schedule, even if it meant heading out to sea empty. They revolutionized shipping and soon other companies were imitating their practices. The completion of the Erie Canal, making New York City the destination of inland commerce, clinched New York Harbor's supremacy.

John Randel, Jr., had successfully surveyed the lands of Manhattan Island (see pp. 86–97), but he had not concerned himself with a detailed survey of the waterfront. Such a survey became essential as New York Harbor's importance in the world increased. In 1827, that duty fell to Daniel Ewen. He had been a city surveyor for ten years when he executed surveys of the waterfront showing the Hudson River up to Forty-second Street and the East River up to 155th Street. Included are the names of the previous owners of the shore properties which Ewen reconstructed from early deeds. Ewen's beautiful maps were never printed; the original, hand-drawn maps are collected in six large folio volumes on deposit at the Manhattan Borough President's Office. These maps provide the waterfront complement to Randel's farm mapsheets (see p. 96), which are also at the Borough President's Office.

The importance of such a detailed waterfront map is suggested by this account of the enormous harbor activity a short time after Ewen's survey: "The whole length of the wharfs, there rises up a forest of masts belonging to the vessels of many nations, and steamships engaged in trade among the various states of the Union. On the North River, the bay and its eastern arm, magnificent steamboats cross and recross without ceasing, coming and going at all hours of the day and night, laden with passengers, merchandise, and raw materials."

The mapsheet illustrated here delineates Battery Park at the southern tip of Manhattan. This park, built on landfill, occupies a strategic site where New York Harbor and the Hudson River converge. Its name derives from the gun batteries that were once in place there. Although established for military purposes, in 1823 the land was ceded to the city and became a popular public promenade. Philip Hone wrote in his diary of a walk there as "a luxury which the distance of my residence from the spot does not permit me frequently to enjoy, and a more delightful scene can nowhere be found."

Connected to Battery Park by a bridge was Castle Garden, for several decades New York's center for popular entertainment. Originally the site of Fort Clinton, built between 1808 and 1811 to protect New York Harbor from an invasion by the British, after the War of 1812 it ceased to have military value and was converted into a theater. It was at Castle Garden that P. T. Barnum staged the performances of Jenny Lind, the Swedish soprano, who was one of the most popular attractions of the nineteenth century. Tickets for her concerts at Castle Garden were in such demand that they were sold at auction.

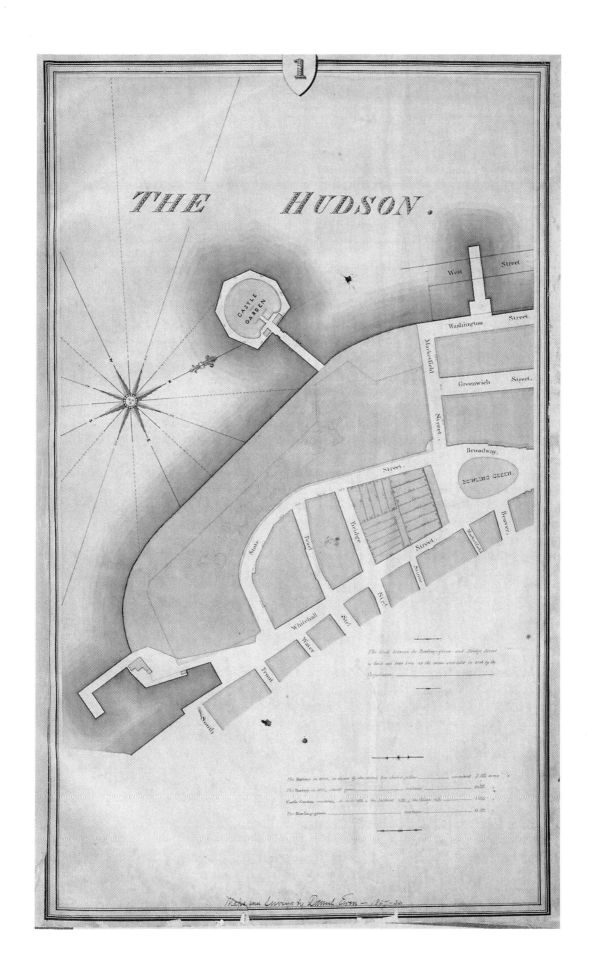

THE HUDSON.

CASTLE
GARDEN

West Street

Washington Street

Mannsfield

Greenwich Street

Street

Broadway.

Street

BOWLING GREEN.

Beever.

State

Pearl

Bridge

Street

Mannsfield

Slip

Stone

Whitehall

Slip

Water

Front

South

99

POSTWAR GROWTH
THE GOODRICH MAP

TITLE: A Map of the City of New York
DATE DEPICTED: 1827
DATE ISSUED: 1827
CARTOGRAPHER: ANDREW T. GOODRICH
Uncolored copperplate engraving, 28⅝ x 38½ inches
Private collection

"We are rapidly becoming the London of America," wrote John Pintard in 1826. "I myself am astonished & this city is the wonder of every stranger." The incredible physical growth of the city following the War of 1812 was the subject of the Goodrich Map, issued in several editions by Andrew T. Goodrich beginning in 1827. A decade after the conclusion of hostilities in 1815, New York City was busy implementing the Commissioners' Plan. New streets were being built and some three thousand buildings were under construction. The development northward was beginning to swallow up the once separate communities; the village of Greenwich was already part of New York City when Goodrich's map was published.

Among other things, road construction required the elimination of ponds and marshes and the extension of the waterfront. "It is apparent," wrote Goodrich, "that no inconsiderable portion of the city has been redeemed from the water by the persevering industry of man." Building the city according to the Commissioners' Plan meant leveling hills and filling "bodies of fresh water, that formerly covered many acres of what is now the very centre of the city." This "most tedious and expensive undertaking" was well underway when Goodrich issued his *Stranger's Guide* (1828), where he explained the demise of the Collect Pond: "Several large hills or mounds of earth that environed this pond, under various names, such as Bayard's Mount,

which elevated itself on the site of Grand and Rhynder streets, have all been leveled, and the ground thrown into the pond."

Although not officially commissioned by the city, the Goodrich Map was the standard plan of New York during an excessively productive decade (1827–36). The A. T. Goodrich Company was a well-established stationery store with a large private lending library. One of its many enterprises was map publishing, and this map of New York City was the most significant issued by the company. Goodrich proudly asserted that it "is considered as the most correct ever issued here . . . comprising, at one view, the ancient limits of the island, and the encroachments since made on the surrounding waters." Soon after it was published, a copy was presented to each alderman.

On this first edition, the "Parade" area, above Washington Square, is prominently shown. This was one of the very few public squares that the commissioners had designated on their 1811 map. The size of the square had already been reduced by the time the Goodrich Map was published; it appeared for the last time on this Goodrich map. On the second edition, Fifth Avenue continued northward directly through the land, eliminating the square. The commissioners had not been foresighted when they established too few parks and squares for the city. Central Park would eventually provide the solution to a developing problem that was being created as open spaces were lost.

FIRE AMID PROSPERITY
The Firemen's Guide

TITLE: The Firemen's Guide
DATE DEPICTED: 1834
DATE DRAWN: 1834
PUBLISHED: P. Desobry, New York, 1834
Lithograph, 16 x 19½ inches
New-York Historical Society

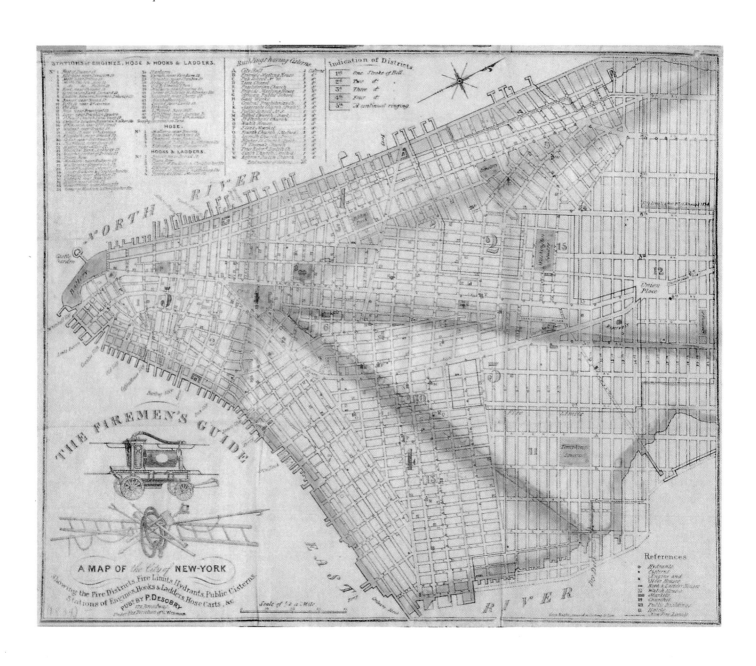

"The greatest calamities that have befallen New York have been its destructive fires," wrote fire historian Augustine E. Costello in 1887. Several times during the late eighteenth and first half of the nineteenth centuries, flames raged completely out of control and devastated parts of the city unchecked. The Firemen's Guide published by P. Desobry in 1834 and pictured here was a prototype of the fire insurance maps that were disseminated during the second half of the nineteenth century. Ominously, it was published in 1834, a year before the most devastating conflagration in New York's history and the largest in America up to that date. In fact, the Great Fire of 1835 was one of the most significant events in the city's history.

The Firemen's Guide was created by the former chief engineer of the New York Fire Department, U. Wenman, for volunteer firefighters who had to learn the fastest ways around the city. At one time, a copy of this map hung on the wall of every firehouse. Much information essential to a firefighter is delineated there, such as the location of sources of water throughout the city, including buildings with cisterns. Unfortunately, little of this information was much use on December 16, 1835, the coldest night in the city in thirty-six years. All of the hydrants had frozen; in addition, the river, cisterns, and wells were also frozen. Two feet of snow blanketed the ground, and there was a gale blowing.

Smoke was first noticed at a dry goods warehouse at Pearl and Hanover streets; within a half hour the entire block was on fire. "Never was there a more rapid extension of the flames . . . they have already extended to Water Street," reported the *Evening Post* at eleven o'clock that evening. "The engines can do nothing to stop the flames."

By one o'clock in the morning, "There is no knowing where the flames will be stayed—the hydrants are exhausted—the hose of many of the engines are frozen and useless, and the flames extending . . . the scene grows worse and worse." During the early morning hours, the Stock and Exchange Board, New York's just-completed business center, was in ruins and the recourse decided on by the chief engineer of the fire department was to blow up two buildings on Exchange Place to keep the fire from crossing Broad Street. This act of desperation successfully contained the fire.

On December 17, 1835, the most important business property in America smoldered in ruins. Fifty-two acres along with 674 buildings had been destroyed. "How shall I record the events of last night," wrote diarist Philip Hone, "or how attempt to describe the most awful calamity which has ever visited these United States." Journalist James Gordon Bennett wrote, "in one night we have lost the whole amount [the losses were placed at twenty million dollars] for which the nation is ready to go to war with France! Gracious Heaven! is it a punishment for our madness? Forgive us our sins as we forgive those that sin against us."

The gloom did not last long. The fire occurred during a period of prosperity; within days, the city was rebuilding, and soon thereafter, devastated land was trading at record prices: "twenty lots in the burned district were sold this day," wrote Philip Hone in his diary, "at most enormous prices, greater than they would have brought before the fire when covered with valuable buildings." Despite the tremendous losses—and the crippling of the entire insurance business—the city had little difficulty refinancing itself: "The bustle and activity of the laborers bringing in and adjusting to each other the materials of construction, the rapid erection of spacious buildings in different stages of progress, on each side of the numerous and irregular streets which run through the quarter, remind the spectator of what he had read concerning cities built up suddenly in waste places."

The most enduring benefit of the fire was Croton water. The firefighters were helpless without water, and the fire drove home to New Yorkers the urgent need for a good supply of water. Construction of the Croton Aqueduct System began in earnest in the spring of 1835. One year after the fire, Hone reported: "The whole is rebuilt with more splendor than before . . . and all this with no actual relief from the general or state government."

CROTON WATER REACHES THE CITY
Map of the Croton Water Pipes with the Stop Cocks

TITLE: Map of the Croton Water Pipes With the Stop Cocks
DATE DEPICTED: c. 1842
DATE DRAWN: c. 1842
LITHOGRAPHER: ENDICOTT
Uncolored lithograph, 13¾ x 10½ inches
New-York Historical Society

At dawn on October 14, 1842, one hundred cannons began firing. Sleepy New Yorkers were being awakened to the official opening of the Croton Aqueduct. For the first time, fresh water was flowing into Manhattan, putting to an end two centuries of frustration, disease, and death due to inadequate water supplies. "Nothing is talked of or thought of in New York but Croton Water," wrote Philip Hone in his famous diary. Throughout that October day there was much fanfare, including a five-mile-long parade, numerous speeches, and the opening of a magnificent fountain. Proud New Yorkers stood in City Hall Park marveling at the plume of water that rose a staggering fifty feet in the air. The spectacular celebration lasted for weeks.

It was the culmination of a seven-year municipal project begun in 1835 to resolve a crisis. As the city grew, the problems of sewage increased and traditional sources of water—from wells and private suppliers—dwindled or became polluted. Firefighters did not have enough water to subdue the fires that often raced through sections of the city unchecked. So when clean, fresh water diverted from the Croton River in Westchester County reached New York City in 1842, New Yorkers were exuberant.

The need for a superior water supply was never more acute than in the early 1830s. At that time, there were complaints that every breath of air was putrid and what water was available tasted rancid. In 1832, an Asiatic cholera epidemic killed 1 percent of the population (3,500 people), and two years later, there was an even larger epidemic. New Yorkers were in a state of desperation the day the city announced "an Act to provide for supplying the city of New York with pure and wholesome water." Twelve million dollars was appropriated to dam the Croton River, construct a forty-five-mile aqueduct, and then provide reservoirs from which the fresh water could be distributed throughout the city. The gravity of the crisis was underscored on December 16, 1835, when the city's worst conflagration devastated most of the business district. The biggest problem facing firefighters on that frigid night was the woefully inadequate water supply.

Acquiring the necessary land tracts between Croton and Manhattan proved formidable and expensive, but by May 1837, Chief Engineer John B. Jervis and his workers began constructing the necessary dam, tunnels, bridges, and foundations to convey the water to Manhattan. The biggest mishap occurred in January 1841 when warm weather, which melted a large accumulation of snow, combined with an sudden rainstorm, flooded the artificially created Croton Lake. The new dam that had to be built had a much better design and was three times the width of the original. Despite the setback, the aqueduct was completed on schedule. On June 22, 1842, the first Croton water streamed toward Manhattan.

"We observe with pleasure the new fountains in the midst of the city supplied from the Croton water works, finer than any which I remember to have seen in the center of a city since I was last in Rome," wrote Scottish geologist Sir Charles Lyell about a visit to New York in 1845. "A work more akin in magnificence to the ancient and modern aqueducts has not been achieved in our times. . . . The health of the city is said to have already gained by greater cleanliness and more wholesome water for drinking."

Once the water entered Manhattan, it came to rest in two huge basins located on Fifth Avenue between Fortieth and Forty-second streets, the present location of The New York Public Library. (Some of the original building blocks are still in place and serve as walls in the book stacks beneath the library.) The map illustrated here shows the system of pipes and valves for distributing the water throughout the city. These are "the huge veins and arteries," wrote one observer, "by means of which the Croton supplies life and health to the inhabitants."

"The water can be carried to the attics of every house," according to Lyell, "and many are introducing baths and indulging in ornamental fountains in private gardens." Bathing suddenly became the most popular activity in the city: "I've led rather an amphibious life for the last week," George Templeton Strong wrote in his diary in 1843, "paddling in the bathing tub every night and constantly making discoveries in the art and mystery of ablution. Taking a shower bath upside down is the latest novelty."

The completion of the Croton Aqueduct and the Brooklyn Bridge were the two most consequential civic projects of the nineteenth century. Both significantly changed the city. New life was pumped into the struggling island, allowing much new commerce and greater facilities for fighting fires. New York's population would not have doubled between 1835 and 1845 had it not been for Croton water.

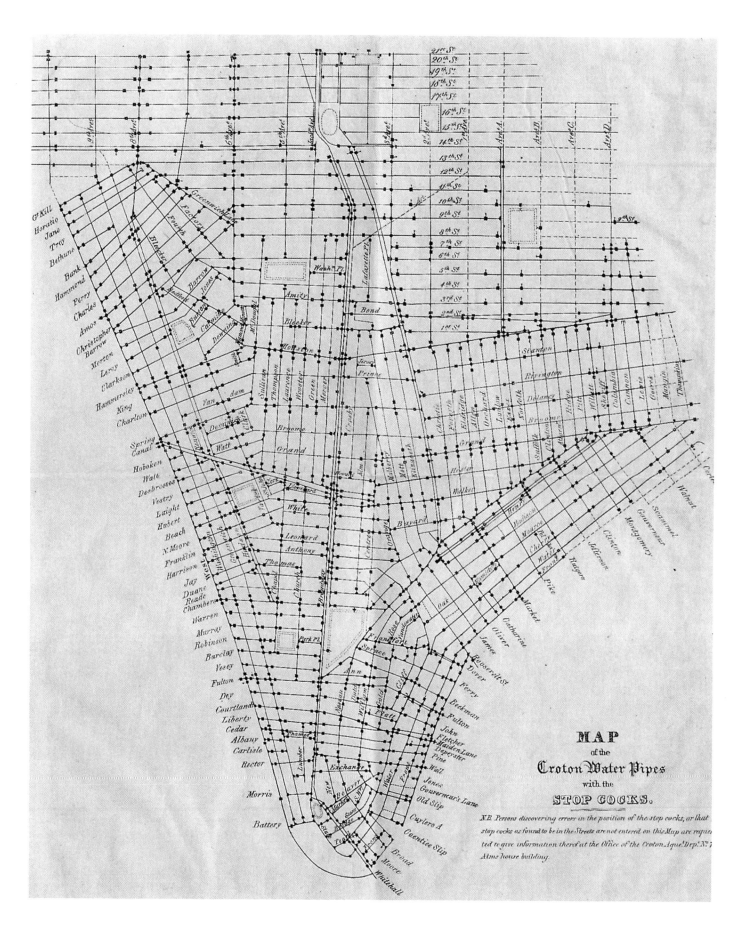

MAP
of the
Croton Water Pipes
with the
STOP COCKS.

N.B. Persons discovering errors in the position of the stop cocks, or that stop cocks as found to be in the Streets are not entered on this Map are requested to give information theref at the Office of the Croton Aque. Dep. No 7 Alms house building.

THE OLD JUXTAPOSED WITH THE NEW
COLTON'S TOPOGRAPHICAL MAP

TITLE: Topographical Map of the City and
Country of New-York, and the Adjacent Count
DATE DEPICTED: 1836
CARTOGRAPHER: DAVID H. BURR
PUBLISHED: J. H. COLTON AND COMPANY
NEW YORK, 1836
Uncolored engraving, 67⅛ x 29⅜ inches
New-York Historical Society

The Indians called Manhattan the "island of
the hills"; J. H. Colton took this appellation
one step further when he referred to
Manhattan's "Mountains and Hills" on the
legend of his "Topographical Map of the
City and County of New-York." Colton's
map shows how wild most of the island
remained north of the developing part of
the city, which then stopped at about
Twelfth Street. Other references on the
map also reveal the unspoiled condition of
most of the island in 1836: "Valleys, with
Running Streams," "Woods, Fruit Trees,"
and "Salt Marsh, Upland Marsh or Swamp."
The lands that would become Central Park
two decades later are among the most
rugged parts of the terrain.

Colton's Topographical Map is one of
the earliest productions of a mapmaker
who would dominate geographical publishing in America for sixty years and whose
name is associated with the finest atlases
produced in America in the nineteenth
century. The following appeared in the
New-York Commercial Advertiser on July 16,
1833, announcing the map: "J. H. Colton &
Co., no. 9 Wall Street, publish a new map of
the city drawn by David H. Burr from the
latest surveys of the city deposited in the
street commissioners office and from information obtained from several of the city
surveyors." The map is so up-to-date that it
includes the route of the underground
Croton water pipeline, which had just been
constructed.

"This is one of the most beautiful nine-

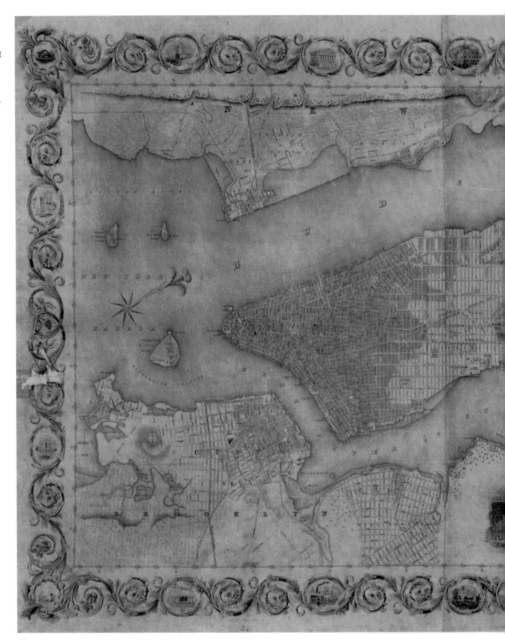

teenth century plans or maps of Manhattan,
and is full of interesting information,"
wrote I. N. Phelps Stokes, about the Colton
Topographical Map. "It is perhaps the best
example of really artistic mapmaking as
applied to Manhattan Island." Like most of
the maps executed in the years following
the Commissioners' Plan of 1811 (see p. 86),

Colton drew heavily on John Randel's survey, although Colton's is about half the size.
The grid is included up to 155th Street, but
a few changes are conspicuous. The commissioners tried to eliminate Broadway, as
this diagonal thoroughfare was not consis-
tent with the new grid pattern. However,
Broadway would not disappear just because

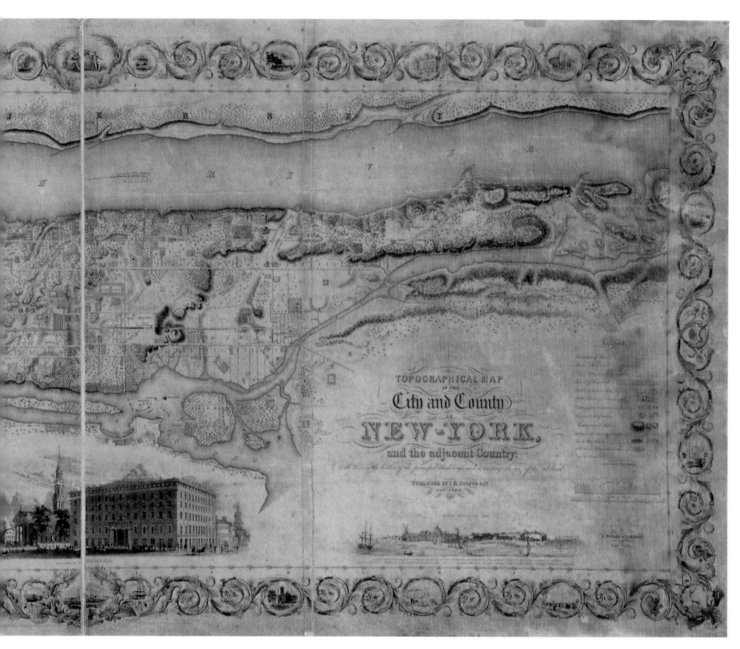

it was not recognized by the commissioners, and Colton delineated it on his map.
With Broadway back, several of New York's
most famous squares were made possible.
Times Square and Union Square were created by the angled course of Broadway slic-
ing decisively across the grid.

Colton contrasts the old city with the

new by juxtaposing one of the earliest
views of the city, the famous Jansson-
Visscher Map of 1655 (see p. 18), with a
view of Astor House, which had just been
completed as the map went to press. And
the mountains! Apparently there was just
one, Mount Morris, which still exists in
Mount Morris Park (now called Marcus

Garvey Park) at Fifth Avenue between
120th and 124th streets. Less a mountain
than a huge rock, Mount Morris looms
about seventy-five feet above Fifth Avenue.
For the little-traveled Colton, then at the
beginning of his great publishing career,
perhaps that is what he thought a mountain
looked like.

CHARTING THE BAY AND HARBOR WITH ADVANCED METHODS

THE HASSLER MAP

TITLE: Map of New York Bay and Harbor and The Environs
DATE DEPICTED: 1843
DATE PRINTED: 1845
CARTOGRAPHER: FERDINAND RUDOLPH HASSLER
Uncolored copperplate engraving, 24 x 34¾ inches
Private collection

One of the oldest traditions of mapmaking is the sea chart, and some of the earliest records that exist for many parts of the world are the charts that mariners used to pilot their vessels. Throughout the eighteenth century, mariners navigating New York Harbor primarily used British charts like those of DesBarres (see p. 52), but at the beginning of the nineteenth century these charts were becoming out-of-date. As the harbor's importance grew, and ships became larger, deeper, and faster, the need for more sophisticated charts was felt.

Scientific methods of charting were advancing significantly when The American Philosophical Society recommended a "Survey of the coasts" to Thomas Jefferson. After authorization from Congress in 1807, Ferdinand Rudolph Hassler, a Swiss mathematician, surveyor, and West Point professor, was appointed to direct the project. Thirty troublesome years would pass before his first chart was published; finally in 1843, Hassler issued his magnum opus, the magnificent chart of New York Harbor pictured here. It took so long to produce because there were many delays and much preliminary work to accomplish.

For example, there were precision instruments to have made. In 1811, Hassler set sail for London, where he supervised the construction of the various instruments necessary for the enormous task of surveying the entire Atlantic coast from Maine to Georgia. These included a theodolite of two feet in diameter, smaller theodolites, repeating circles, reflecting circles, artificial horizons, plane tables and alidades, meter bars, microscopes, thermometers, a balance, standard weights, standard volume measures, transit instruments, astronomical clocks, chronometers, telescopes, eyepiece micrometers, levels, compasses, and rules. Hassler was especially pleased with the two-foot theodolite: "It was executed under my own inspection by that distinguished artist, Mr. Edward Troughton of London, agreeable to our united views, and . . . with the great friendship with which he was pleased to favor me could alone inspire."

Hassler was occupied with his instrument makers on June 18, 1812, when Congress declared that a state of war existed with Great Britain. Despite the beginning of the War of 1812, on June 27 the Treasury Department instructed Hassler to remain in London until the completion of the object of his mission, "political changes notwithstanding." He did not return to America with his cargo of instruments until 1816.

Once the surveying finally got underway, an act of Congress further derailed progress by limiting employment in the U.S. Coast Survey to naval and military officers. As it turned out, many of the most-skilled surveyors were not officers, and Hassler and several of his colleagues on the project suddenly found themselves unemployed. The survey floundered after this, until fourteen years later when Hassler was recalled to service. Soon after the reappointment, a copperplate press was purchased and a staff of engravers and printers was hired. With high-quality copperplates acquired in France through the good offices of the Depôt de la Marine, the U.S. Coast Survey was at last ready to publish the results of decades of intermittent labor.

The Hassler Map was first published in six sheets in 1843, the year of Hassler's death. It is a landmark in surveying partly because by careful, systematic sounding and plotting, an unknown deep-water entry to the Lower Bay was identified and delineated. This channel was discovered by Lieutenant Thomas R. Gedney of the Navy and is still called Gedney's Channel. Through this channel a ship can enter the harbor "at any state of tide and with any wind." As the director of the project, Hassler received accolades for the discovery. In addition to the soundings, great atten- tion is paid to land topography. There are land-recognition profiles and directions for sailing by the main channels. The map illus- trated here is the smaller, one-sheet version published in 1845.

REAL-ESTATE INTERESTS DRIVE CARTOGRAPHY
DRIPPS I

TITLE: Map of the City of New-York Extending Northward to Fiftieth Street
DATE DEPICTED: 1850
DATE ISSUED: 1851
CARTOGRAPHER: MATTHEW DRIPPS
Lithograph, uncolored, 37 ¼ x 78 ½ inches
Private collection

One of the most speculative enterprises of the early nineteenth century was fire insurance. Devastating fires were prevalent throughout the century, and a large conflagration could easily bankrupt a number of insurance companies. In the early 1850s, a new kind of urban map began to be published in America: the real-estate map. It provided such detailed information important to insurance men as dimensions of blocks, configurations of buildings, and widths of streets. In 1851, when New York City was becoming complex, Matthew Dripps published two influential maps that delineated the hectic building activities in the city and distilled a great deal of information useful to the city's businessmen.

"How this city marches northward!" wrote George Templeton Strong on October 27, 1850. "The progress of 1835 and 1836 [when the city was rebuilding from the Great Fire] was nothing to the luxurient, rank growth of this year. Streets are springing up, whole strata of sandstone

have transferred themselves from their ancient resting-places to look down on bustling thoroughfares for long years to come. Wealth is rushing in upon us like a freshet."

These were "the first printed maps of New York that show, in detail, all the individual lots and buildings." Dripps was an unlikely man to stand at the beginning of such an important phase of New York mapping. An immigrant grocer with no training in geography, he established his map publishing business one year after disembarking in America from Ireland. Dripps I, "Map of the City of New-York Extending Northward to Fiftieth St." was Dripps's first significant map. The large scale—the map is more than seven feet long—allowed him to realize the remarkable detail. All of the city's important structures, parks, markets, and cemeteries are delineated and twenty vignettes of buildings decorate the border.

111

DRIPPS II

TITLE: Map of That Part of the City and Country of New-York North of 50th St.
DATE DEPICTED: 1850
CARTOGRAPHER: H. A. JONES
PUBLISHED: MATTHEW DRIPPS, 1851
Uncolored lithograph, 37¼ x 78½ inches
Private collection

Soon after Dripps published his monumental map of Manhattan below Fiftieth Street, also in 1851, he issued a companion map for the northern part of the island, Dripps II. At mid-century, the population of the city above Fortieth Street was sparse. Beyond Fiftieth, it was rural. In fact, a number of wealthy New Yorkers owned country estates along the rivers, and Dripps's map identifies the owners of the farms and private residences that dot the rustic landscape.

There are two intriguing features of Dripps II: it continues the street grid beyond 155th Street, the northern limits of the Commissioners' Plan; and it is the only map that delineated the first location of Central Park. On June 13, 1851, the "Common Council directed the street commissioner to lay out the streets north of 155th." On Dripps II, the street grid is extended—at least on a map—to the northern limits of the island. Lewis Mumford, in expressing his dissatisfaction with the original plan of 1811, wrote, "with a T-square and a triangle, finally, the municipal engineer without the slightest training as either an architect or a sociologist, could 'plan' a metropolis." The sudden appearance of 156th through 228th streets on Dripps II shows just how quickly these "municipal engineers" could accomplish their city planning.

Dripps's grid is singularly unimaginative, and, fortunately, it was never implemented. It consists of well-ordered, numbered streets up and across the island, nothing more—not even a park; and the planners completely ignored the very hilly terrain in that part of Manhattan. A different grid was eventually designed and used for northern Manhattan, one that incorporated curving roadways and parks.

That year, 1851, New Yorkers decided they needed a large park. When the commissioners laid out Manhattan in 1811, they made no provision for a large open space, and as the city developed northward, some prominent New Yorkers feared that dense concentrations of population were creating health problems throughout the city. It was then widely believed that many diseases were caused by bad air. The green-colored area on Dripps II between Sixty-sixth and Seventy-fifth streets and extending from Third Avenue to the East River identified Jones Wood, the first site for the park that would eventually become Central Park. George Templeton Strong described these "grounds" in 1851 as "very beautiful, and strangely intact for the latitude of Sixty-first [sic] Street."

In the 1840s, such civic leaders as William Cullen Bryant and Robert Minturn began lobbying for a large park to serve as "the lungs for the city." By the summer of 1851, 160 acres of wooded and landscaped land bordering the East River had been selected as the site, and the state had authorized the city to acquire Jones Wood. At this juncture, had the owners of the land—the Jones and Schermerhorn families—been cooperative, the plan might have gone through. These two families, however, were unwilling to sell the property at the rate offered and took the matter to court.

In January 1852—while Jones Wood was delayed in litigation—the Special Committee on Parks recommended the creation of a much larger park between Fifth and Eighth avenues, from Fifty-ninth to 106th streets: "Central Park will include grounds almost entirely useless for building purposes, owing to the very uneven and rocky surface." Over the next two years a political fight over the two sites raged. James Beekman led the fight for Jones Wood; he had much to gain if that area became the park, as the large tract of property he owned adjacent to the Wood would have quadrupled in value. In January 1854, a legal ruling resolved the question: Jones Wood was dropped from consideration in favor of the larger and more centrally located Central Park. In 1851, Matthew Dripps appears to designate Jones Wood a park on his map even though at that time the location of the city park was far from resolved.

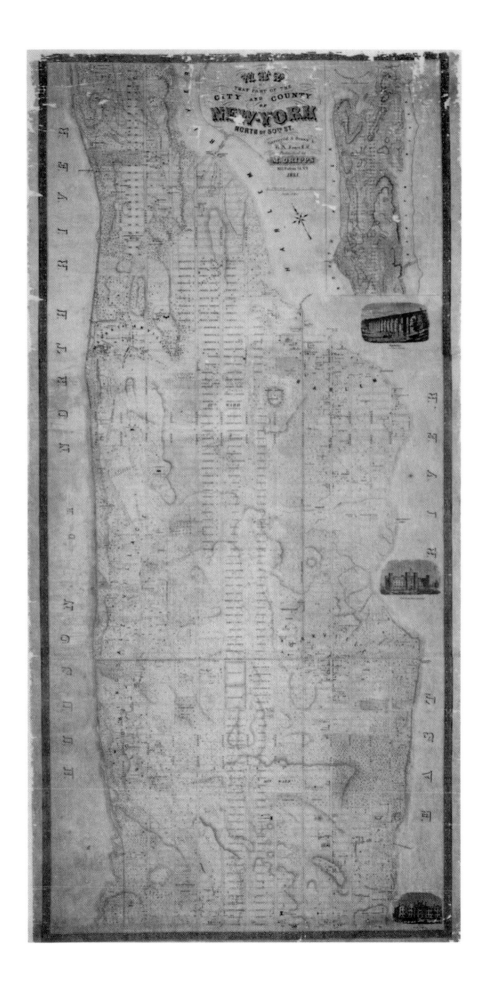

113

INSURANCE COMPANY SURVEYS
THE PERRIS MAPS

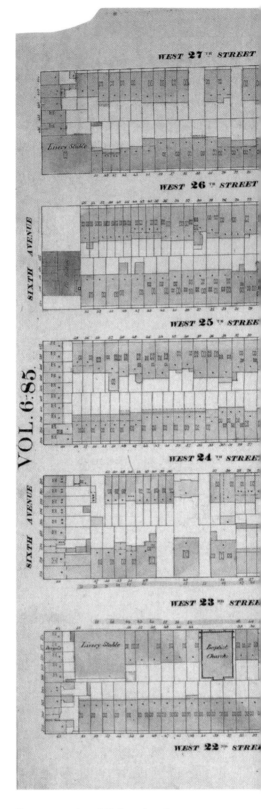

TITLE: Maps of the City of New York surveyed under directions of insurance companies of said city
DATE DEPICTED: 1853
CARTOGRAPHER: WILLIAM PERRIS
PUBLISHED: PERRIS COMPANY, 1853 (NEW YORK: KORFF BROS., 1852–1854)
Lithograph, 25 x 34¼ inches
The New York Public Library, Map Division

A new kind of map emerged at mid-century to keep pace with the accelerating development of the city. This was the property map, which had its beginnings in the insurance business. The devastating conflagration of 1835 had bankrupted most of New York's insurance companies. The new and often larger insurance companies that took their places found it increasingly difficult to examine personally the properties they insured for risk information. As the city rebuilt and expanded, these new companies required accurate, detailed, and current property maps.

George T. Hope of the Jefferson Insurance Company conceived a large-scale map that located and measured every structure in the city. Collecting the data for this ambitious map proved overwhelming for someone who could not devote all of his attention to the project. Hope employed British engineer William Perris to make surveys and draft the insurance map. Before long, Perris had established a veritable industry in publishing real-estate maps. Real-estate maps for Manhattan are still being published in the annual *Manhattan Land Book*; the representation of blocks and property on these maps closely resembles Perris's mid-nineteenth-century atlas.

These maps "are so little known outside the business for which they were designed," wrote Perris's son-in-law in 1874, "that few are aware there exists a plan of the city so carefully drawn . . . that the buildings therein can be described almost as well

hundreds of years hence." The reason for this remarkable precision was the painstaking method of delineating buildings and city blocks and the enormous scale of the resulting maps. Perris "worked with persevering care, measuring each house and angle accurately, until gradually, volume by volume, a map was produced of such dimensions as had never before been seen."

Perris's maps are not traditional, single-sheet maps but double folio mapsheets showing different sections of the city. The publication of Perris's first volume in 1853—covering the first four of the city's then twenty-two wards—consisted of maps drawn to a scale of fifty feet to an inch, making an ordinary residence almost one square inch. Each property was color coded to describe some facet of construction or function: a brick building, for example, is red; yellow indicates a frame structure; and green designates a warehouse. "To me, the little patches of red, yellow or green are not mere ground-plans," wrote Perris's son-in-law. "I have been round them all with a tape-line, and the picture of the block is before my eyes as I look at the pages." Once established, these color codes became standard practice in property maps for a century.

The maps were sold by subscription in atlas form. After the first four wards were mapped, the buildings in other wards were measured and mapped, and all the maps were constantly being revised and expanded. When fire destroyed a neighborhood or new buildings were constructed, the Perris

Company printed little colored map sections of the changed areas; these were to be glued onto the mapsheets to bring them up to date.

When the Perris Company presented a

114

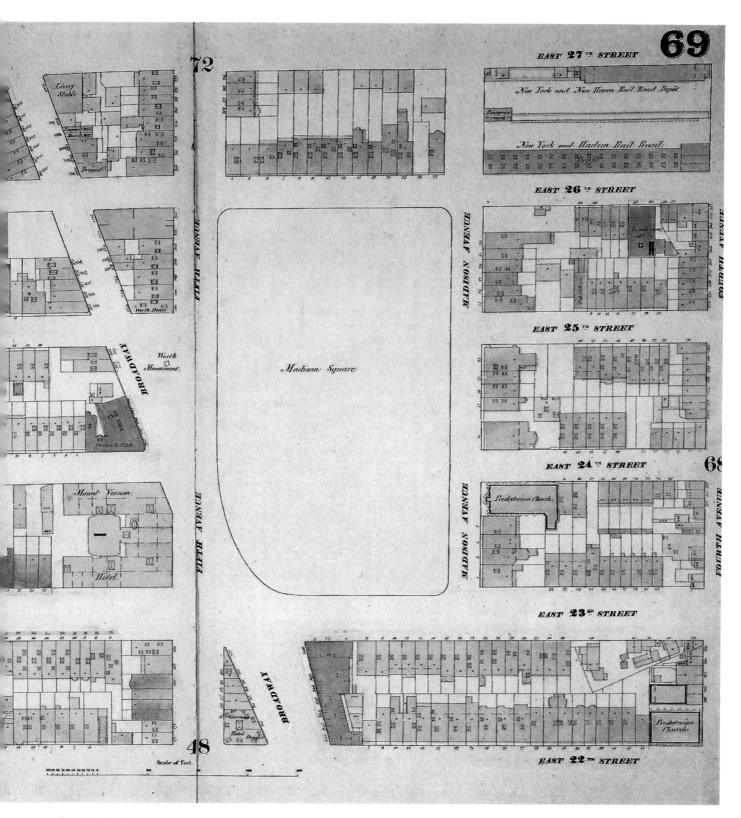

number of archival copies of their atlases to the New-York Historical Society in the nineteenth century, they praised their historical usefulness: "Had such a map been made in the last century, what a description

might we give of the old streets, now laboriously hunted up in scraps from the oldest inhabitant, and from bits of cherished writings which gradually turn up. No other city has such a map, so comprehensive, and so

regularly revised for the past twenty years." The mapsheet shown here is from the first edition of Perris's atlas and is the earliest of the large-scale maps published for fire insurance.

CENTRAL PARK
VIELE'S DRAINAGE PLAN

TITLE: Plan of Drainage For the Grounds of the Central Park
DATE DEPICTED: 1855
DATE DRAWN: 1855
CARTOGRAPHER: EGBERT LUDOVICUS VIELE
Hand-colored manuscript, 47 x 135¼ inches
Municipal Archives, New York City

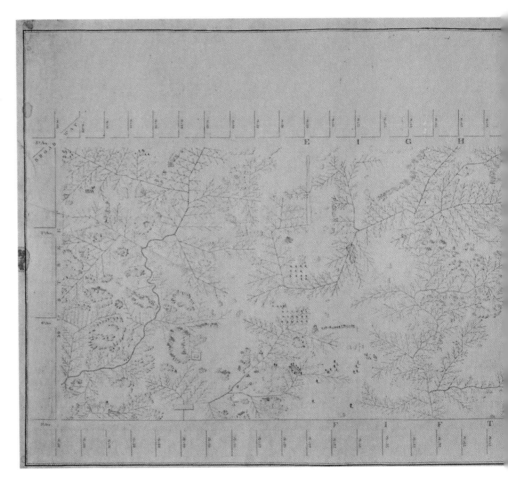

It must have astonished informed visitors to New York City in 1916 to read that Central Park was designed by Egbert Viele. Rider's *New York City* (1916 and later) was one of the most popular guides to the city, and it is still considered a useful resource for information about the city. On page 301, Fremont Rider described Central Park as "having been designed by Lieut. (later General) Egbert L. Viele, assisted by Olmsted and Vaux, landscape gardeners." Frederick Law Olmsted and Calvert Vaux are so famous for their design of the park that few people realize that once there was a controversy over its design. Viele was the first engineer-in-chief of the proposed Central Park, and he made the preliminary surveys and submitted a design for the park that was accepted by the first park commission.

In many ways, Viele was an obvious choice as engineer-in-chief. He was a trained engineer with extensive surveying experience. After graduating from West Point and fighting in the Mexican War, he became topographical engineer for New Jersey, conducting a complete topographical and geodetic survey for all of the state's lands. He also made a complete engineering report and survey of New York Harbor.

Viele was a member of one of New York's oldest Dutch families—the kind of family Washington Irving had described in his "Knickerbocker" history. As it happened, Irving was president of the Central Park advisory board, and it is said that he had approved Viele's plan for the park.

As chief engineer, Viele's first task was to survey the land designated for the new park. This was "a matter," said Viele, "of no little difficulty, requiring both courage and skill as well as a hardy constitution." Little had changed since the days when John Randel surveyed these same lands fifty years earlier. Viele and his crew of surveyors encountered the obstacles typical of surveying any wild piece of land. "The area designated was as unpromising an acreage as could be found in Manhattan, inhabited by roving animals and about five thousand squatters, most of them," Viele continued, "of foreign birth. Such was the danger of the situation that the designer of the park had to go armed while making his studies,

and in addition to this, to carry an ample supply of deodorizers."

The results of Viele's survey were drafted onto his "Plan of Drainage for the Grounds of the Central Park," which showed the site prior to any improvement or change. All of the hills, streams, and large rocks are delineated in great detail, along with the various settlements in the area. This survey and map were the necessary first step in designing the park, and this phase of the project gave Viele a satisfying feeling that he was "converting this cheerless waste into a scene of rural beauty."

Viele then drafted a design for the park. It followed more closely the natural terrain of the land than Olmsted and Vaux's later

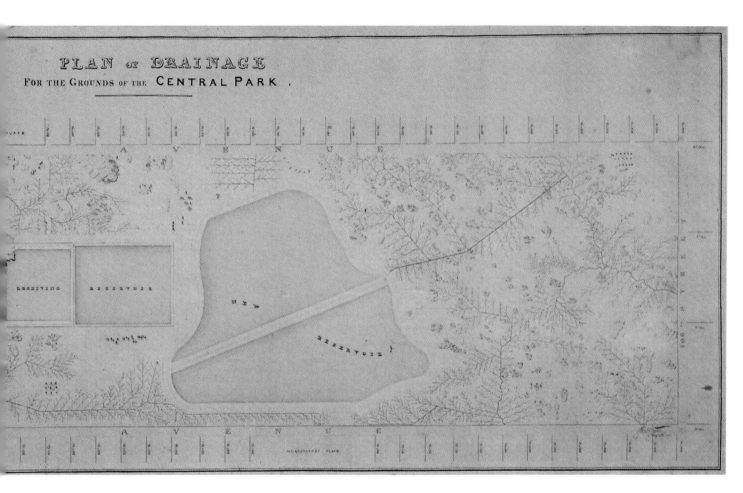

PLAN OF DRAINAGE FOR THE GROUNDS OF THE CENTRAL PARK.

design, but there are striking similarities between Viele's design and the park that was eventually built. It was Viele's idea to convert the reservoir to the shape of a lake rather than keep it a parallelogram, and the shape of Viele's Croton Lake has the familiar shape of the present reservoir. Many of the paths and transverses are placed similarly to those in the design eventually executed.

For a time, Viele was both engineer-in-chief and designer of the park, but that dual position began to come apart on April 30, 1857, when the state legislature established a new board of commissioners for the park. Missing from this new board were such Viele supporters as Washington Irving. The new board retained Viele as chief engineer

but made two appointments that marked the end of Viele's important role in the development of the park. Frederick Law Olmsted became the superintendent of construction and Calvert Vaux the chief designer of architectural structures.

"Being thoroughly disgusted with the manifest defects of Viele's plan," Vaux wrote, "I pointed out, whenever I had a chance, that it would be a disgrace to the city and to the memory of Mr. Andrew Jackson Downing [Vaux's mentor, who had first proposed the location of a large park in New York] to have this plan carried out." A new design competition was announced on October 13, 1857; the well-known outcome of the competition had a

far-reaching effect on New York City and the successful designers: Olmsted and Vaux. In the aftermath of the competition, Olmsted became the architect-in-chief of the park and Viele's position was abolished.

Viele claimed in the lawsuit that followed that his dismissal was invalid and that Olmsted and other competitors had, in fact, stolen his design. He won that lawsuit and always maintained that he was the true designer of Central Park. Viele's role in the cartography of Manhattan Island did not end here. He delineated a series of topographical maps of the entire island that are so important they are still in use today.

OLMSTED-VAUX'S "GREENSWARD"

TITLE: Greensward
DATE ISSUED: April 8, 1858
CARTOGRAPHERS: FREDERICK LAW
OLMSTED AND CALVERT VAUX
Pen-and-ink on heavy drawing paper, 3 x 8 feet
New York City Department of Parks, The Arsenal

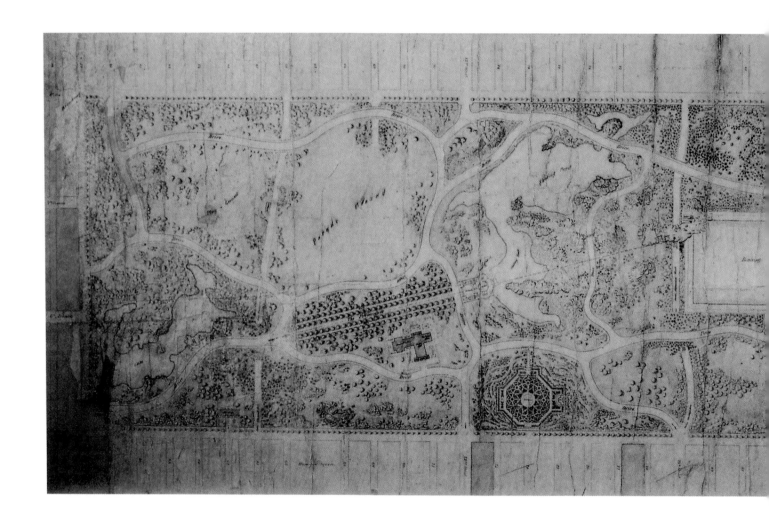

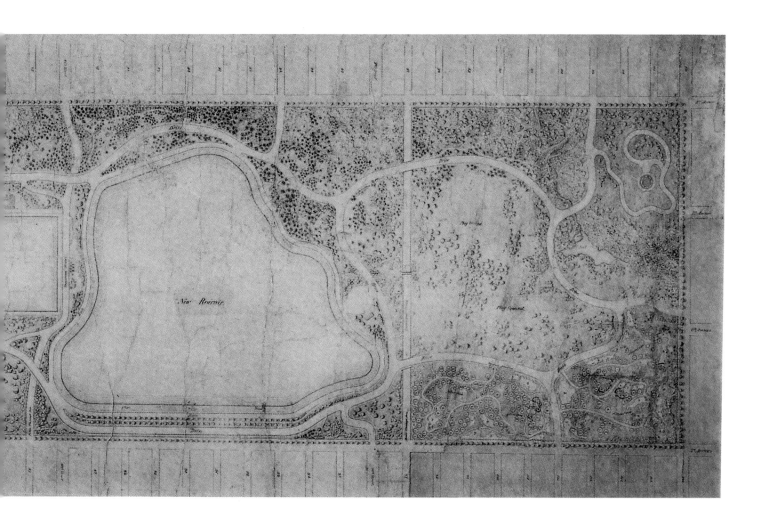

119

It is said that the design of America's most famous park began with a chance meeting in the summer of 1857. Frederick Law Olmsted was staying at the Griswald Inn in Essex, Connecticut, where he encountered Charles Wyllys Elliott, a landscape gardener who had just been named to the newly formed Board of Commissioners of Central Park. As the two acquaintances talked that August day, Elliott informed Olmsted that a superintendent was being sought for the proposed park. After listening to Olmsted's remarks on the subject of parks, Elliott encouraged him to apply.

Up to that point, the brief history of New York's great park had been a succession of misstarts and disagreements. John Randel had not provided ample space for parks in the Commissioners' Plan of 1811 (see p. 86). By 1836, the need for a large park had been recognized by William Cullen Bryant, followed a few years later by Andrew Jackson Downing, who was then America's leading landscape architect and the former teacher of Charles Wyllys Elliott. As publisher of *The Horticulturist*, Downing had printed the first articles promoting a park for the city: "Every American who visits London, whether for the first or the fiftieth time, feels mortified that no city in the United States has a public park—here so justly considered both the highest luxury and necessity in a great city."

Downing took his idea a step further when he drafted a plan for an ideal park for New York City. In fact, at the early stages of the park's development, Downing was unquestionably the obvious designer for the park. On July 28, 1852, however, he was drowned when the steamship Henry Clay caught fire on the Hudson River.

Much preliminary work on the park had already started at the time Olmsted applied for the job of superintendent of construction. The lands had been designated, a chief engineer—Egbert Ludovicus Viele—had been appointed, a complete survey of the land had been made, and a design by Viele for the park had been presented to Mayor Fernando Wood's consulting board and accepted. Had a new board not been created, Viele's name might have been the most prominent in the park's history.

With Olmsted's appointment on September 1, 1857, came the following duties: "He would be the executive officer of the Engineer with respect to the labor force, and would have charge of the police and would see that proper regulations were enforced with regard to public use of the park." Olmsted's presence greatly weakened Viele's authority.

When the board that had hired Olmsted then announced an open competition for a new design for the park, Viele's doom was sealed. Each competitor was provided with a copy of Viele's topographical map of the lands of Central Park (in spite of the widespread complaints about its inaccuracies) and given instructions that total construction costs could not exceed $1.5 million. At this juncture, the British landscape architect Calvert Vaux approached Olmsted and suggested that they collaborate on a design for the competition. Vaux had been Downing's partner, and he and Olmsted had become acquainted through Downing's *Horticulturist*, where Olmsted had been a contributor.

From the moment Olmsted appeared for work as superintendent, his relations with Viele were strained. Not wanting to exacerbate the problem, Olmsted asked his boss if he objected to his submitting a design for the competition. Viele is reported to have said no. With this obstacle out of the way, Vaux and Olmsted set to work on their plan during the evenings, after Olmsted had already put in a long day supervising the clearing of park lands.

In addition to their talent, Olmsted and Vaux had other advantages over the more than thirty competitors. Olmsted's job provided him with intimate knowledge of the terrain, and Vaux was better schooled and experienced in landscape architecture than anyone else in America. Vaux also had the advantage of having worked with Downing, so he was privy to the thoughts of the originator of the park.

They titled their plan "Greensward," and it was awarded first place. Their design received accolades for the ingenious way they had resolved one of the most difficult requirements of the design: the transverse crossings from east to west. Without them, the park presented a 2.5-mile obstacle to the city's commerce. With roads traversing the park, however, the flow of the park was segmented and interrupted. Vaux and Olmsted solved the problem by sinking the four roads below the level of the park. This was the most distinctive feature of their design, and it undoubtedly won them the prize.

It also made a lasting contribution to city planning by providing "unhampered circulation and safe crossings," as Lewis Mumford has pointed out: "In its system of circulation, Olmsted and Vaux's Central Park was superior to any conventional two-dimensional city plan; for, by using overpasses and underpasses whenever possible, it provided four independent traffic networks: footways for pedestrians, bridlepaths for horseback riders, carriage drives for wheeled vehicles, and crosstown transverses for city traffic."

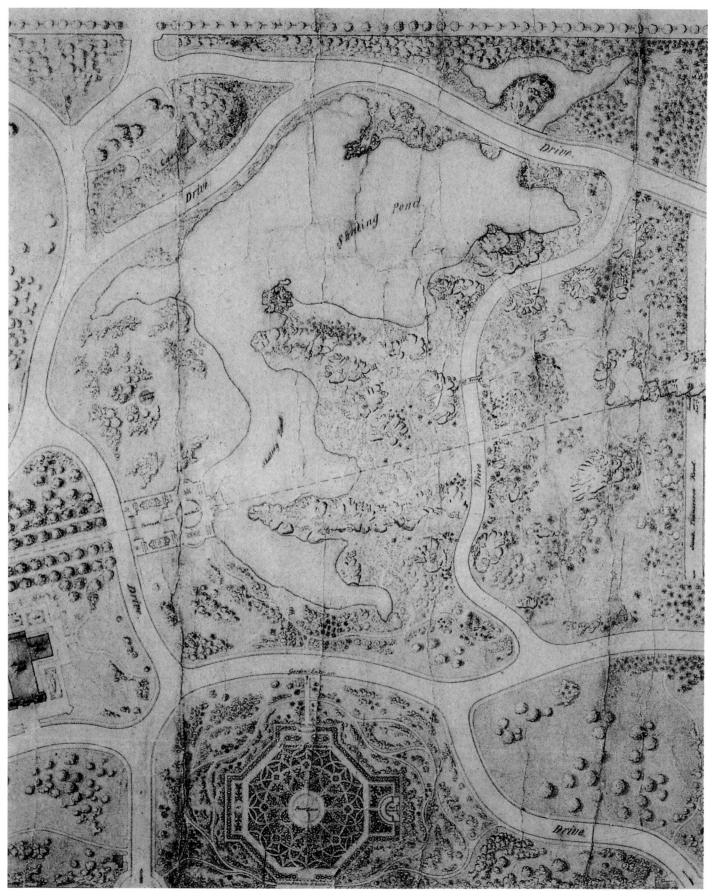

WATERY FOUNDATIONS TO GROWTH
VIELE'S WATER MAP

TITLE: Sanitary & Topographical Map of the city and island of New York . . .
DATE DEPICTED: 1864
DATE ISSUED: 1865
CARTOGRAPHER: EGBERT LUDOVICUS VIELE
Colored lithograph, 63 x 17½ inches
Library of Congress

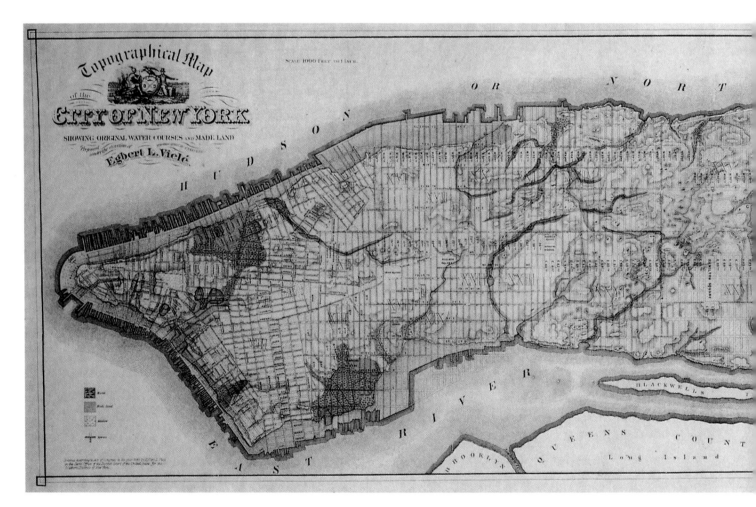

The most enduring nineteenth-century map of Manhattan is Egbert Ludovicus Viele's Water Map, which was first published in 1859 and is still in use today. It delineates the original watercourses, streams (underground and surface), meadows, marshes, ponds, ditches, canals, and the shoreline before landfill expanded the city's boundaries. Viele issued the hydrographical

and sanitary map to expose the problems being created as waterways were buried under newly constructed streets and buildings, destroying Manhattan's natural drainage system. Over the years, the map has been put to constant use by contractors, who study it to determine whether their building sites are former riverbeds that could still flood foundations.

This is not the purpose Viele envisioned when he presented the map to the U.S. Sanitary Commission and to a select committee of the State Senate investigating the city's health department. "How soon shall New York be prepared to enter [the ranks of the most disease-ridden cities in history]?" asked Viele at the Sanitary Association meeting. Epidemics were

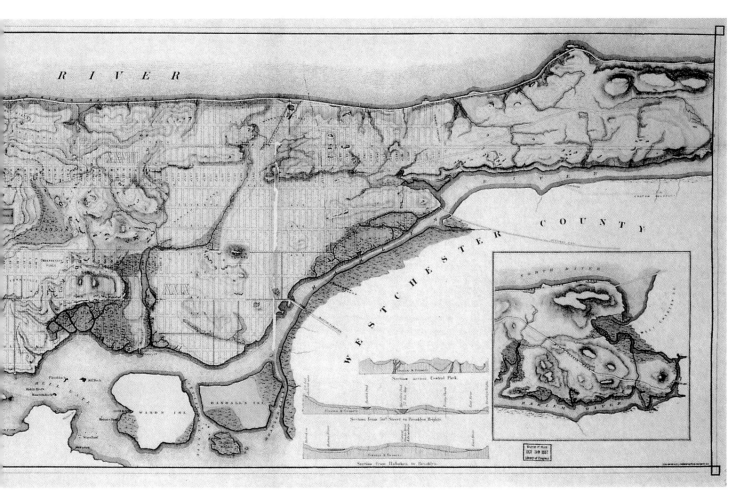

rampant throughout the city, and the death rate was on the rise when Viele likened New York in 1859 to Europe during the plague years: "There is now no doubt that the ravages of the plague . . . were due to precisely the same causes which foster the diseases [killing New Yorkers]."

Viele was convinced that cholera, malaria, and other diseases were caused by disrupting the ecology. As the city pushed northward according to the Commissioners' Plan (see p. 86), the island's vital arteries were being filled as hills were leveled and streams and ponds disappeared. "I know that it is generally supposed that when the city is entirely built upon all that water will disappear," Viele lamented, "but such is not the case." The waterways continued to have

a clandestine existence, becoming breeding grounds of pestilence and causing devastation. "It is a well established fact that the principal cause of fever is a humid miasmic state of the atmosphere, produced by the presence of an excess of moisture in the ground," stated Viele.

As a cavalry officer in the Rio Grande area of Texas after the Mexican War, Viele encountered yellow fever and malaria epidemics. "In all localities where there were original depressions in the topography," he observed, "the disease raged with the greatest violence, although there was no apparent presence of water or even moisture in the ground." Viele saw those same conditions in Manhattan as development altered the terrain. His theories, made years before mosquitoes were blamed for transmitting such diseases, led to his interest in sanitation.

Viele's map had its beginnings when he was appointed engineer-in-chief of Central Park. His first order of business was to map the land set aside for the park. Later he expanded the map to cover the terrain of the entire island. By examining earlier maps in the city archives, principally those by John Randel, Jr., he was able to recreate on paper a pristine, undeveloped Manhattan island.

Viele's Water Map was published three times in different formats and under various titles. In 1859, the lower half of Manhattan appeared as part of the State Senate report where Viele stated, "The Sanitary condition of any city or district or country is intimately connected with its proper drainage . . . that any inquiry into causes or remedies for sanitary evils . . . shall be based upon a thorough knowledge of the topography of the island." In 1865, a version showing the entire island was published to accompany the *Report of the Council of Hygiene and Public Health*. Finally, in 1874, he enlarged the map with corrections, changes and additions, and published it separately with the title "Topographical Atlas of the City of New York, including the Annexed Territory, Showing the Original Water Courses and Made Land."

Twenty years of surveying and studying went into perfecting this great map, and during those years Viele gained an intimate knowledge of New York's physical makeup.

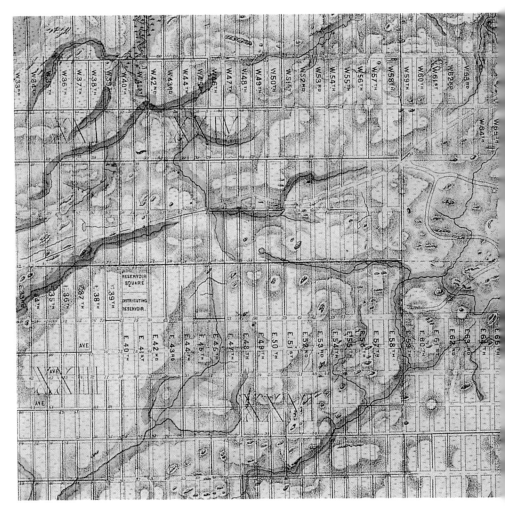

In the end, he made recommendations that he thought would improve the health of the city "by one hundred percent." First, he proposed wider streets for the lower part of the city, and second, "that the original water courses should again be permitted to have their deep and free outlets to tide water, in order to diminish the amount of humidity and decomposition that results from the artificial obstruction and diffusion of those streams."

Viele's recommendations to plan all future street and sewage systems in accordance with the island's natural drainage were ignored, but a different use for the map emerged. It became the invaluable guide to prospective purchasers of property and the faithful companion to architects, engineers, and builders who had to determine subterranean water and silt conditions to predict costs and practicability for building.

It is said that Paul Starrett, the builder of the Empire State Building and Stuyvesant Town, never prepared an estimate before consulting the Viele map. Without it, there was no telling what catastrophic pitfall lurked just below ground level. "I've found that it's accurate within feet," said Melvin Febesh, whose company laid the foundation for the Citicorp Center

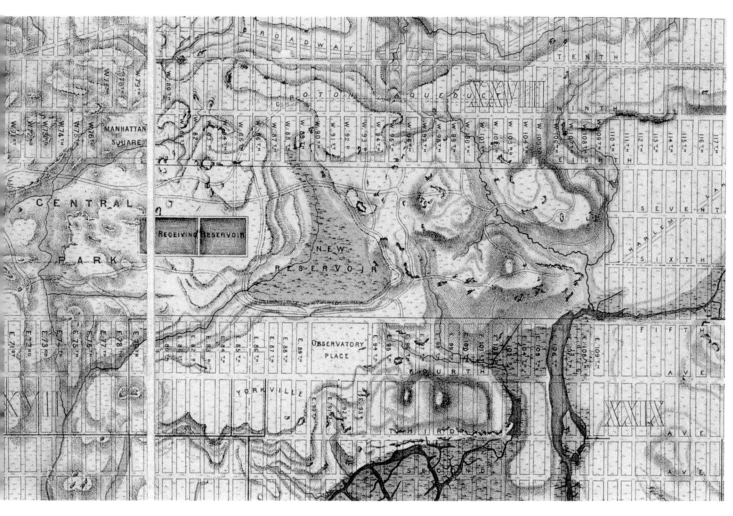

(Lexington Avenue and Fifty-fourth Street). In their digging they came across the stream indicated on Viele's map, which cut diagonally across their site.

When the site for the United Nations building was proposed in the 1940s, the engineers faced a special problem: landfill of unpredictable composition. One of the engineers wrote,

> Even before we can make the borings, we dig up all the old maps and surveys we can find. Our bible in this case is the Viele map of 1865, which shows the city as it then was, with its still largely natural shoreline. The

Viele map indicates, for instance, that Turtle Bay was to take up a large part of the present UN site, and in that section we can count on our borings to show filled-in land to a depth of thirty or forty feet. Along First Avenue, we expect to find, and are finding, that bedrock is only a few feet down, but along the river we'll have to push down through a good deal of gravel and mud.

Manhattan is the Indian word for "island of the hills." Trickling through the hills were trout streams and fishing holes. Certain New York City street names recall the time

when Manhattan was abundant with waterways. Maiden Lane got its name from the Dutch women who washed laundry in the brook along that street. Canal Street was a swampy place that at very high tides separated Manhattan into two islands. Gramercy Park was originally called Krom Moerasje, or Crooked Little Swamp by the Dutch. At Madison Avenue and Thirty-second Street in Murray Hill there was once a stream that cut through the Murray Farm and became Sunfish Pond, where panfish were caught.

THE NATION'S BUSINESS CENTER
LLOYD'S MAMMOTH MAP

TITLE: Lloyd's Mammoth Map of the Business Portion of New York City
DATE DEPICTED: 1867
DATE DRAWN: 1867
CARTOGRAPHER: J. T. LLOYD
PUBLISHED: J. T. LLOYD, NEW YORK AND LONDON, 1867
Colored lithograph, 77 x 48 inches
Library of Congress

"Look at that city," wrote President John Tyler in 1857, "and see her extending streets, her palatial mercantile establishments, with her vast congregation of vessels at her docks bursting forth like a crab from the shell." During the 1850s the wealth of the city increased 90 percent, and then, following the Civil War, New York City became the nation's business center. At the same time, the lower city was becoming less and less residential and more confined to the business of a rapidly expanding nation.

"Lloyd's Mammoth Map of the Business Portion of New York City" as of 1867 delineates Manhattan during this important decade of its development. New York's increasing stature in the world is symbolized by the gigantic size of the map; it measures more than six by four feet yet covers only the district from the Battery to Chambers Street, river to river. Illustrated here is a smaller version, which was probably issued as a prospectus by this New York and London publisher that was so proud of its maps that many of them featured the following pronouncement: "Any one finding an error on this Map will be entitled to a copy, gratis, by writing to the Publisher." Essentially a real-estate map, the blocks on Lloyd's Mammoth Map are divided into property lots. The enormous scale permitted Lloyd to name many businesses directly on their lots.

It is not certain why some businesses have been identified and others have not. The enterprising J. T. Lloyd publishing company undoubtedly solicited subscriptions by printing the names of participating businesses on the map. This would have encouraged a larger sale, an assumption not supported by the number of surviving copies. The Library of Congress and the National Archives own the only complete examples of the map, although The New York Public Library has an incomplete example with manuscript notations showing the proposed route of the Brooklyn Bridge and how its access roads would affect Manhattan's real estate.

The concentration of businesses in the lower part of the city was necessary at a time when communications were primitive. In fact, the very lack of telecommunications helped create the density of business activity in the lower part of the city. As more and more business leaders established themselves on or near Wall Street, lawyers, accountants, printers, and others located near them to provide expert information and services. The crowding of various businesses on Lloyd's map reveals the city before three inventions that would change the landscape of New York and the very way business was conducted: the "safety hoister" elevator, the first skyscraper, and the telephone.

EXPLANATION

WARD WARD Nº 1 .... WARD BOUNDARY

M.P. METROPOLITAN POLICE PRECINCT Nº 2 POLICE PRECINCT BOUNDARY

COVERED PIERS, SHEDS, TEMPORARY FRAME BUILDINGS &c.

PUBLIC BUILDINGS, CHURCHES, FACTORIES, ENGINE HOUSES, SCHOOLS &c.

P.P.O.Nº on U.S.M. ST. - LETTER RECEIVING BOXES ATTACHED TO LAMP POSTS

PARKS, PLEASURE GROUNDS, GARDENS, GRASS PLOTS &c.

FIRE ENGINE HOUSES COLORED RED.

24. RED NUMBERS INDICATE FIRE SIGNAL STATIONS.

POLICE STATION HOUSES COLORED YELLOW

LOTS BUILT UPON are SHADED (A NEUTRAL TINT) VACANT LOTS are LEFT WHITE

HORSE RAILROADS THE - ALONG THE TRACK INDICATES THE DIRECTIONS IN WHICH THE CARS RUN.

POST OFFICES are COLORED ORANGE

THE FIGURES on THE STREETS INDICATE THE HOUSE & STORE NUMBERS.

Price in Sheets, 50 cts.
Sent by Mail to any part of the World

NO MONEY TO BE PAID TO AGENTS IN ADVANCE.

LLOYDS MAMMOTH MAP
OF THE
BUSINESS PORTION
OF
NEW YORK CITY
1867
J.T. LLOYD

UNITING BROOKLYN AND MANHATTAN
THE GALT-HOY MAP

TITLE: The City of New York
DATE DEPICTED: 1879
DRAFTSMAN: WILLIAM I. TAYLOR
PUBLISHED: GALT AND HOY, NEW YORK, 1879
Uncolored lithograph, 42 x 72⅜ inches
Library of Congress

The Brooklyn Bridge was nearing completion in 1879 when William I. Taylor drafted his spectacular bird's-eye view of New York City. Unlike any other map of the city, this one includes practically every building on Manhattan Island. It was executed at a critical time in New York's history as many of the distinctive elements that gave the city its "titanic energy and force" were in place. Central Park had been completed in 1876; the first skyscrapers had been erected; and elevated trains were in operation.

I. N. Phelps Stokes called this a "remarkable map—a monument of patience and skill." It was issued by Galt and Hoy, a New York publisher of "Views of Cities and Summer Resorts," intended for the walls of important businesses. "The price of this view mounted on spring rollers is $12.50," reads a note on the map, which also advertises a more luxurious version "in black walnut or gilt case with handsome cornice. $15." A number of leading businesses are featured on insets, so it is likely that the map was created largely for advertising purposes. The Galt-Hoy Map has suffered the hardships of many large maps that were intended to hang on walls. Very few have survived; only two examples have been located in libraries, one at The New York Public Library and another at the Library of Congress. A later printing at the turn of the century was partially brought up-to-date with the addition of new structures, but the map still included

several edifices that had been demolished by the time it was reissued.

The most prominent structure on the map is the bridge that created a sensation at the end of the nineteenth century. At the time the Brooklyn Bridge was constructed (1867–83), it was considered a wonder of the world, and its engineer, John Augustus Roebling according to Rudyard Kipling, "the greatest artist of our epoch." Not only was the bridge the longest ever built up to that time, but its mile-long span joined two of the largest cities in America (Philadelphia was then the second in size; Brooklyn the third). The uniting of Brooklyn and Manhattan, preceded by the annexation of parts of the Bronx in 1874, marked the first steps in creating Greater New York City. The Galt-Hoy Map also delineated the annexed sections of the Bronx. Although the bridge was not completed until 1883, the mapmaker drew it finished and functioning.

The colossal scale of the bridge paved the way for other gargantuan structures. High buildings employing iron skeletons were not on the Manhattan landscape until the late 1880s, but by 1875 New York already had two buildings ten stories high: the Western Union Building on lower Broadway and the Tribune Building. Diarist George Templeton Strong described the Tribune Building as towering above the surrounding buildings "like a sort of brick and mortar giraffe." Elisha Graves Otis's

invention of the "safety hoister" elevator allowed the builders of the 1870s to begin the competition of what Walt Whitman called "heroic cloud touching edifices."

As the business district developed and residential construction steadily moved uptown, an elevated train system connected the various parts of the city. Second, Third, Sixth, and Ninth avenues were darkened with overhead tracks, and this map includes the just-completed extension of the Ninth Avenue line up to 110th Street. Parts of New Jersey are also incorporated; the Elysian Fields, a favorite resort for New Yorkers, is located at Hoboken.

New York City is remarkably placid in this view. There is no evidence of squalid slums, congested traffic, or the hectic activity that characterized the city. Like all bird's-eye views at that time, this one is idealized—"flattering urban portraits" is how Professor Gerald Danzer of the University of Illinois at Chicago described them: "They had to look accurate to be convincing, but not so honest as to reveal the problems and imperfections of their subjects. That is why the distance of the bird's-eye viewpoint and the perspective chosen by the artist were so advantageous."

THE PROMISE OF GREATER NEW YORK CITY
THE RISSE MAP

TITLE: General Map of the City of New York
DATE DEPICTED: 1900
DATE DRAWN: 1900
CARTOGRAPHER: LOUIS ALOYS RISSE
Uncolored lithograph, 94³/₁₆ x 109⅝ inches
Library of Congress

One of the chief attractions at the famous Paris Exposition of 1900 was a map of New York City measuring twenty-seven by thirty-one feet. The Risse Map, entitled the "General Map of the City of New York," was the largest of an American city ever executed, and it was the most impressive exhibit in the Palace of Civil Engineering and Transportation, where viewers stood in line to admire its expanse of cartography. The map pictured here is a smaller, printed version of the original, which was created entirely by hand. The manuscript map that caused such a stir in Paris has disappeared without a trace.

That Brobdingnagian map was the work of Louis Aloys Risse, the chief engineer of New York City's Topographical Bureau, who considered it a symbol of "an event without parallel in the world's history." On January 1, 1898, Greater New York City had been created by consolidating the largest and third-largest cities in America. "Never before," asserted Risse, "has there been anything like the amalgamation of two cities of the magnitude of New York and Brooklyn." The less-developed boroughs of Queens, Staten Island, and the remaining sections of the Bronx also became part of Greater New York. The *New York Tribune* proclaimed on New Year's Day, 1898, "the sun will rise this morning upon the greatest experiment in municipal government that the world has ever known."

New York City officials considered the Paris Exposition, the largest world's fair up

to that time, as a fitting occasion to unveil the map that delineated this monumental event. Ten thousand dollars was appropriated, and Risse was allotted six months to complete a new survey, map the existing streets, and make a plan for future development. If the city was looking for someone capable of creativity on a grand scale, Risse was the right person to direct the project. A few years earlier, in 1889, he had conceived, designed, and executed the Grand Concourse, giving the Bronx, then a modest and undeveloped city, a central thoroughfare modeled on but larger than the Champs-Élysée.

Risse employed several excellent draftsmen and engineers and set them working around the clock to complete on time "this great and artistic work, which, under ordinary circumstances would take two years." (I. N. Phelps Stokes erroneously reported that the drawing had taken ten years to complete.) In laying out the map, Risse evidently drew heavily upon Joseph R. Biên's *Atlas of the Metropolitan District* (1891) and the U.S. Geological Survey Quadrangle maps of the metropolitan area. He also gathered together all of the existing topographical maps of the boroughs and then adjusted them to the designated scale, six hundred feet to one inch. For Manhattan, Brooklyn, and the Bronx, this task proved manageable, "but an immense amount of intricate field and office work was necessary to bring light into the promiscuous

mess of maps and records representing the boroughs of Queens and Richmond." Various sections of the metropolis had to be hastily surveyed before they could be incorporated onto the map.

The resulting map was much more than the delineation of the streets and topography of the five boroughs: Risse's map set forth an ambitious tentative plan. At the time of its incorporation in 1898, Greater New York City had no official street plan. Despite the fact that the Board of Public Improvement did not have the official authority to change streets or map undeveloped parts of this newly created metropolis, as soon as Risse had mapped the existing parts of the city, he took the liberty of designing a majestic network of boulevards and parks that integrated the boroughs into a single entity.

In planning the large open areas within the expanded limits of Greater New York City, Risse provided many diagonal streets, most of which were never realized. Superhighways 100 and 125 feet wide are also included on the map. His work followed closely the accomplishments of the Bronx Park Commission's four-year program that began in 1884 and resulted in the acquisition of the land for the Pelham Bay and Bronx parks. In contrast to the fate of most of his highway proposals, a surprising number of Risse's park proposals were implemented. In Queens, Kissena Park, Alley Pond Park, and part of Cunningham Park made their first appearance on Risse's

map, as did Silver Lake, Clove Lakes Park, and much of Great Kills Park in Richmond.

Risse believed a population of twenty million could be accommodated in his city of parks, parkways, and boulevards. The waterfront was to be developed for shipping, recreation, and sanitation, and bridges were to be erected to strengthen the unity and interdependence of the different sections of the city. "This magnificent system," Risse wrote, "with its rectangular network of broad streets, diagonally intersecting boulevards, public squares and parks, canals, viaducts, and bridges [was] systematically laid out with reference to the future requirements of large cities."

At the opening of the Paris Exposition on April 14, 1900, the 837-square-foot map dominated the United States pavilion— partly because of its elephantine size, but also because it represented New York City's promise as the most important city of the new century. "The style, size, and exactness of the handmade lettering and the coloring of park, land, water, streets and buildings produce a most striking landscape picture of the city." An elaborate border consisted of fifty pen-and-ink sketches of the most prominent buildings and views of various parts of the city. This aspect of the map was facilitated by the private collection of New York City views that Risse himself had assembled as a hobby.

To exhibit the huge map properly, Risse

had an impressive frame constructed that lifted it off the ground at a slight angle. Viewers ascended a short flight of stairs to reach a platform where, from behind a bronze railing, they could examine from every perspective the one-hundred-square-mile delineation of Greater New York City. "It is safe to say," Risse ingenuously claimed, "that no other work of this kind in the Exposition attracted so much attention from the thousands of visitors or was so much admired by Americans and foreigners."

Of the eleven hundred exhibits from all parts of the world, Risse's map won the first-place award. "No comparison can be made with similar exhibits from other countries. The foreign maps produced by hand were in large measure small in size and inferior in workmanship. . . . The American and New York example of twentieth-century cartography had no rival at the Exposition." Risse himself became one of the exhibition's judges and later received the distinguished decoration of Office of Public Instruction from the French government for his many contributions at the exposition. This was quite an honor for the emigrant Frenchman, who had arrived in America to seek his fortune thirty-five years before.

The success of Risse's map led to various opportunities to exhibit it elsewhere. From Charleston came a request to use it at the South Carolina Interstate and West Indian Exposition, and from Buffalo, to fea-

ture it at the Pan American Exposition, for which the Topographical Bureau appropriated five thousand dollars for installation. I. N. Phelps Stokes reported in 1914 that the map had by then made its way to Bronx Borough Hall—then it disappeared. The Bronx city offices moved to a new building in the 1930s and the hall itself burned in the 1960s. Perhaps the map was destroyed at one of those times. Fortunately, we know what it looked like from the smaller version pictured here, which was printed for distribution to Topographical Bureau officials, and from a rare atlas made up of the sheets of the map.

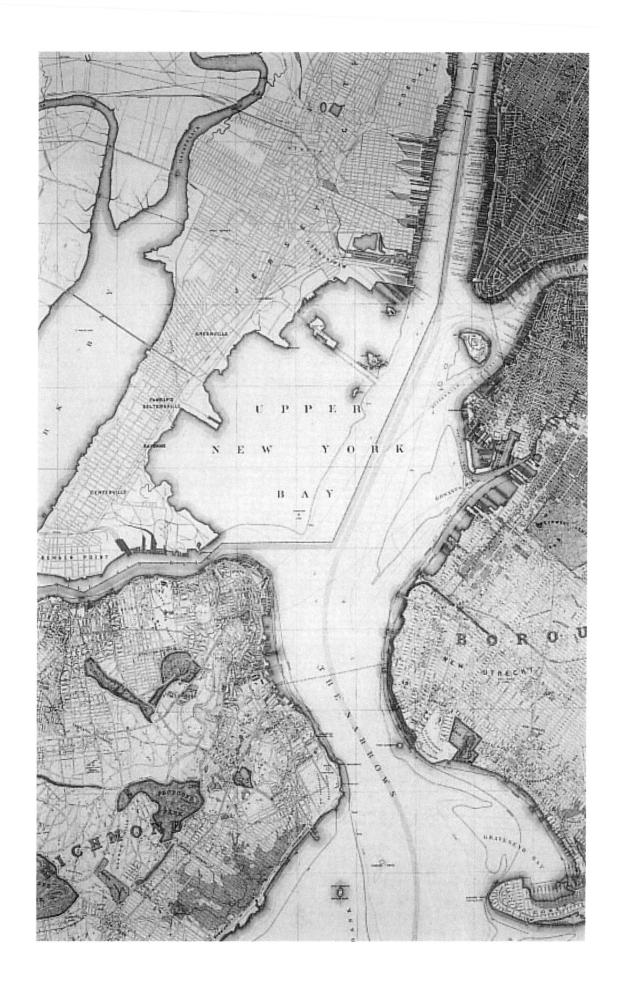

TIFFANY MAP OF THE IRT

Untitled

DATE DEPICTED: 1904

DATE ISSUED: 1904

Engraved sterling silver tray by Tiffany & Company, 37⅞ inches long

Museum of the City of New York

TAURANAC'S NEW YORK TRAVELER SUBWAY MAP

TITLE: New York Traveler Subway Map

DATE DEPICTED: 1990

DATE ISSUED: 1990

CARTOGRAPHER: JOHN TAURANAC

13 x 17 inches

Collection of John Tauranac

At the close of the nineteenth century, mass transportation within the largest city in the United States was limited to trolley lines that operated at ground level and noisy elevated trains. It was obvious to many New Yorkers that the city desperately needed an underground rail system to cope with the ever-increasing congestion. Between 1868 and 1900 at least seven companies failed to create a subway system. Finally, August Belmont, Jr., put together the financing ($37.7 million) and overcame the Herculean obstacles of building a railroad under functioning streets.

Subway service began on October 27, 1904, and the subway company was optimistically called the Interborough Rapid Transit (IRT) even though its initial route was limited to Manhattan. It operated north from the now-abandoned station under City Hall Park along Elm and

Lafayette streets to Astor Place, then north on today's Park Avenue South and Park Avenue to Grand Central Station. Then it zigged west on Forty-second Street on the tracks of today's shuttle to the newly named Times Square at Broadway, where it zagged north on Broadway to 145th Street. By 1905, construction reached the Bronx, and the IRT was living up to its name— and in 1908 three boroughs, including Brooklyn, were connected.

The route of that first subway is clearly delineated on a silver tray by Tiffany & Company, which Belmont apparently intended to present to John B. McDonald, the contractor of the system, whose image is engraved in a center roundel. A disagreement between McDonald and Belmont, which made headlines four days before the subway's opening, kept the tray in the Belmont family until it was given to the Museum of the City of New York. It depicts the subway at its first planned stage of completion. Assuming that the roundel with McDonald's likeness is meant to be at the top of the tray, to the modern eye the map seems flopped—it is a horizontal map with the south at the right, the north at the left, which requires the viewer to turn it upside down to avoid disorientation.

The subway was a far simpler system in this depiction than it would be after 1918, when the Z configuration in Manhattan had become an H configuration. This occurred with the creation of the Lexington Avenue line and the Seventh Avenue line. By that year, tracks were extended from Park Avenue to Lexington Avenue at Forty-second Street and north to the Bronx; from Times Square tracks were laid to Wall Street. The link between these two systems was the newly created Forty-second Street Shuttle.

The first subway map to be distributed was a private venture. In 1904, Wanamaker's, whose new department store boasted an entrance right at the downtown platform at Astor Place, published a simplified subway map heralding the coming of both the subway and the new store. By 1910, the presence of the subway was so important that hotels

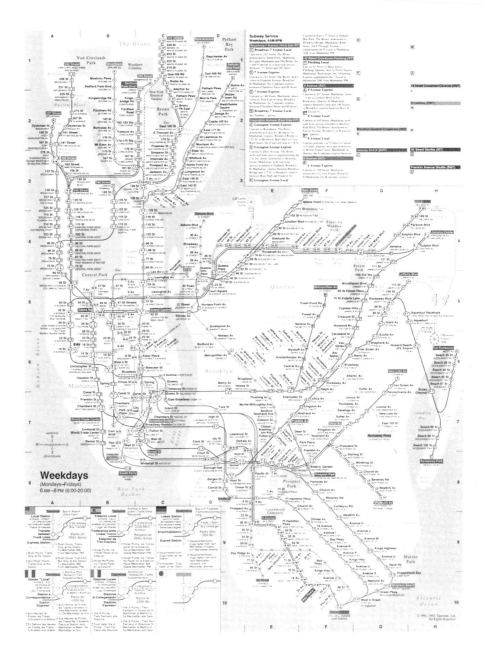

throughout the city were commissioning mapmakers to show how convenient their hotels were to the subway. The IRT itself did not print its own official map of the system until 1915.

The tradition of the privately printed subway map continues with John Tauranac's New York Traveler Subway Map, published in 1990. As the system became more and more complex, with transfer stations and twenty-four-hour service, it became harder and harder for maps to incorporate all the information clearly. Tauranac, a former mapmaker for the Transit Authority, grew

frustrated with the official subway map and decided to create his own maps of the system. "The subway system is filled with so many variations," he discovered, "that to present all the information lucidly in a single map is impossible." To resolve this problem he delineated subway operations in three maps on a single sheet, one illustrating weekday service (which is pictured here), another with evening and weekend service, and a third for late-night operations. His map now competes with those issued at infrequent intervals by the Transit Authority itself.

THE "RED SCARE"
THE LUSK COMMITTEE MAP

TITLE: Ethnic Map
DATE DEPICTED: 1920
CARTOGRAPHER: ADAPTED BY JOHN B.
TAYLOR FOR THE LUSK COMMITTEE
Printed map with manuscript additions by the
Lusk Committee, 16¾ x 46⅜ inches
New York State Archives, Albany

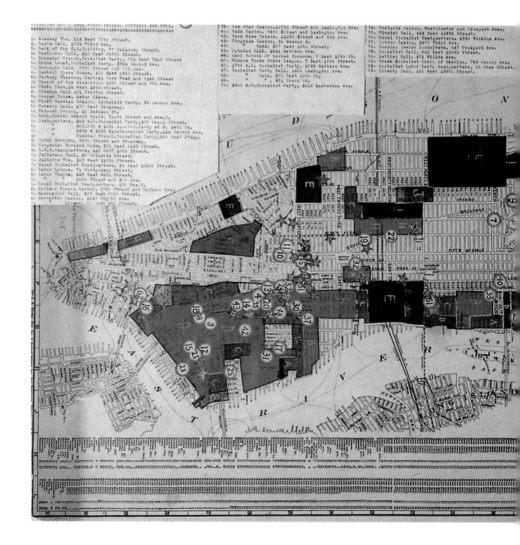

In January 1920, the Lusk Legislative Committee unveiled a map of New York that
located radical organizations throughout
the city. This "Ethnic Map" had been created by members of a committee established
by State Senator Clayton R. Lusk to inves-
tigate subversive activities throughout New
York State. Lusk believed "that the menace
of a bloody revolution was less remote than
people generally thought." He had just
been awarded $50,000 by the state legisla-
ture to ferret out political culprits.

One year of investigations had resulted
in several triumphs for the committee,
including the expulsion of five Socialist
members of the New York Assembly and
prosecutions of a number of people on
criminal anarchy charges. One of the
most publicized acts, however, ended in
embarassment. The Lusk Committee raid-
ed the offices of the Rand School of
Social Science, seized property, and, with
a court-ordered injunction, threatened to
close the school permanently. The school
fought the charges, and after a series of
court cases were resolved in the school's
favor, classes resumed.

"Any man who says the country is not
in danger is uninformed, unintelligent, or
disloyal," declared Senator Lusk. On
December 28, 1919, the *New York Post*
reported one of Lusk's successes: "Details of
a well-organized and violent Finnish revolutionary movement against the United
States Government, with branches throughout this country and possibly 300,000 sup-

porters were made public last night by the
Lusk Committee on Bolshevism."

"Chart of Red Nests Here Bares Peril,"
read the headline in the *New York Sun*
(January 17, 1920) when the Ethnic Map
was shown at a special legislative session of
the Lusk Committee at City Hall. The
map had been prepared by two members
of the Joint Legislative Committee
Investigating Seditious Activities: John B.
Trevor, the Special Deputy Attorney
General, and Clarence I. Converse, the

chief clerk. They had acquired a copy of
A.R. Ohman's "New Quick Reference
Street Indexed Map of the Borough of
Manhattan" (1917), calculated the percentage of foreign-born inhabitants in various
districts of the city, and then shaded the
neighborhood in various colors showing
where the offending citizens lived. The
Finns who then posed such a problem are
grouped with the Scandinavians and
identified in mustard color.

"Archibald E. Stevenson of counsel for

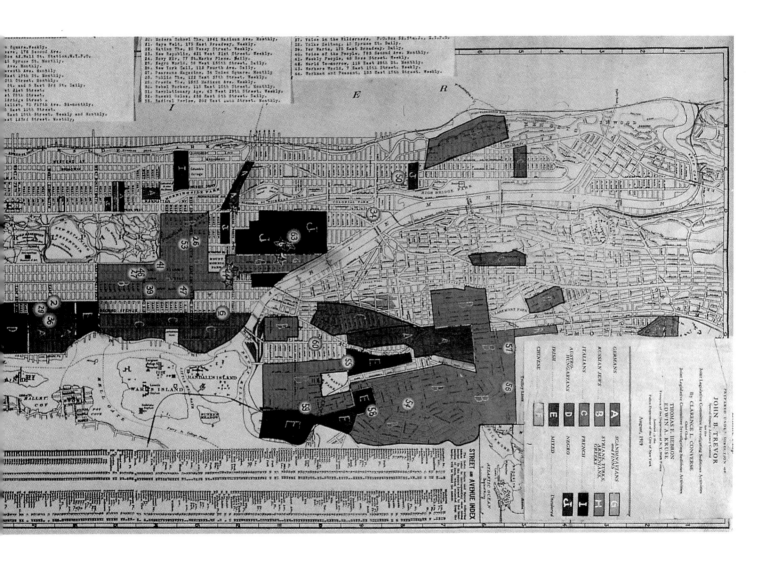

the committee," reported the *New York Post*, "brought the attention of members to the fact that all of the most heavily shaded portions were places where the greatest number of radical organizations were to be found." Settlement houses were often targeted as centers of revolutionary teaching.

The A.R. Ohman Map Company must have been very pleased that it was their map of Manhattan which had been doctored up by an important legislative committee and used at a highly publicized

session at City Hall. They wasted little time rushing into print the Lusk Committee map on a smaller scale (8⅛ by 26⅝ inches), and they retitled it "Map of the Borough of Manhattan and part of The Bronx showing location and extent of Racial Colonies" (1920). The map is identical to its predecessor in most respects, except that the name of the committee does not appear on it for some reason.

The Lusk Committee flourished for two years investigating seditious and radi-

cal propaganda, targeting such groups as the Russian Soviet Bureau, Industrial Workers of the World, and various branches of the Communist Party. The long-term effects of the committee's work were modest, and very few people were actually convicted or deported. In the end, there was considerable public outcry that the raids, investigations, and prosecutions were more harmful than the threat from the suspected radical groups.

137

CITY OF SKYSCRAPERS
THE BOLLMANN MAP

TITLE: New York
DATE DEPICTED: 1962
DATE ISSUED: 1962
CARTOGRAPHER: HERMANN BOLLMANN
Paper, 33¾ x 42½ inches
Private collection

Bird's-eye views of American cities like the Galt-Hoy Map of Manhattan (see p. 128) were popular during the second half of the nineteenth century, but this technique of delineating cities declined in the twentieth century. The time and research necessary to create such maps became impractical as cities became more complex. During the 1960s and 1970s, this kind of pictorial map was revived with the appearance of two remarkable maps of Manhattan. In 1962, German cartographer Hermann Bollmann published an ambitious pictorial map of midtown Manhattan, and in 1974, Curt Anderson issued an isometric map of a smaller section of the city.

Bollmann was a German graphic artist who was inspired to make picture maps after World War II as an effective way to delineate the towns devastated by war. His success led to more and more sophisticated maps, culminating in this isometric perspective of midtown Manhattan. By that time, Bollmann and his crew were depending heavily on ground and air photographs. Bollmann's map of midtown was based on some sixty-seven thousand photographs, seventeen thousand of which were aerial shots systematically taken from a camera specially designed for the purpose; fifty thousand others were taken from the ground. Once all of the data had been gathered, each building was hand-drawn to a scale of 1:4,800, until, block by block, entire sections of the city were recreated in exact detail.

At the time the Bollmann Map was created, half the skyscrapers (buildings of fifty stories or more) in the world were located in Manhattan, and these great edifices dominate the map. The landmark buildings are shown in meticulous detail and in three dimensions: Rockefeller Center, the Pan Am Building (now known as the Met Life building), the New York Hilton, and the Empire State Building. At the opposite end of the scale, lampposts, statues, and individual windows are all clearly shown.

The presence of so many high buildings close together created certain logistical problems for Bollmann's draftsmen. Exaggeration was sometimes employed to show the buildings to the best advantage. Streets were significantly widened out of proportion so that structures would not seem cramped together, and the heights of the buildings were increased. Vanishing point perspective was not employed in an effort to have all the buildings drawn to the same scale.

Bollmann has earned a reputation for being a truly artistic cartographer and has used his elaborate techniques to create pictorial maps of various cities around the world. He created his New York City map for the 1964 World's Fair. The map on exhibition there was huge, but there have been reprints on a smaller scale. The example reproduced here was issued as part of Bollmann's multilingual guidebook to the city.

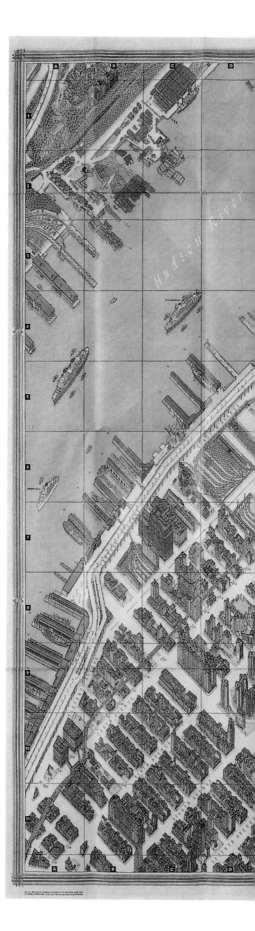

TIMES SQUARE CLEANUP
THE MIDTOWN VICE MAP

TITLE: Times Square; Office of Midtown Planning and Development, Office of the Mayor, 1973
DATE DEPICTED: 1973
DATE ISSUED: 1973
CARTOGRAPHER: OFFICE OF MIDTOWN PLANNING AND DEVELOPMENT
Paper, 40 x 30 inches (image size 27½ x 30 inches)
Shubert Archive

"There is no city in the world where there is so much vice, so many entirely abandoned, and reckless women . . . as in New York," wrote a journalist after the Civil War. Prostitution has always been present in New York, but sometimes it flourishes so openly that city officials feel compelled to crack down. That was the case in the 1970s when a new variety of brothel became popular—the massage parlor.

The City Council was partly responsible for the proliferation of massage parlors. In 1967, this body ended the licensing requirements that had limited massage parlors from becoming fronts for brothels; within ten years there were almost one hundred such establishments in the Times Square area. It was estimated that some twenty-five thousand prostitutes were at work in New York City during this period, some blatantly soliciting from street corners in Times Square.

This state of affairs alarmed Mayor John Lindsay, who made cleaning up Times Square a high priority of his administration, and he established an Office of Midtown Planning to confront the problem. "The principal problem," according to the director of that office, "is still the activities of prostitutes and pimps in hotels and dance halls." One of the instruments of attack was this map of midtown vice, which located the offending massage parlors, hotels where prostitution was practiced, purveyors of pornographic literature, peep shows, and adult movie theaters.

In March 1973, the City Council passed its massage-parlor bill, which required the purported masseuses to be licensed, a requisite that included eight hundred hours of training at an accredited massage school. Failing this, an aspiring prostitute needed a fifteen-dollar permit from the Department of Consumer Affairs certifying her "good moral character." Mayor Lindsay was jubilant when praising the bill as an effective tool in ridding New York of "phony massage parlors that are nothing more than fronts for houses of prostitution."

Massage parlors are no longer part of the Times Square landscape because the crackdown was immediate, successful, and enduring. "The first of the five midtown 'massage parlors' and pornography shops to receive eviction notices in the city's current Times Square cleanup campaign," reported the *New York Times* on March 24, 1973, "was padlocked yesterday and the others face eviction today."

As 1973 came to a close, Mayor Lindsay disclosed some impressive statistics about his year-long campaign against vice in Times Square. Between January and November, 1,431 prostitutes had been arrested and 98 percent resulted in convictions. In addition, four hundred men had been arrested for patronizing prostitutes, a new tactic with a 90 percent conviction rate. Arrests for selling pornographic materials numbered 529, and most of the unlicensed massage parlors were closed, as well as many hotels that catered to prostitutes. In all, arrests rose 20 percent during the mayor's crackdown. There are still a few remaining prostitutes, pornographic bookstores, and adult theaters in the area, but compared to the early 1970s, most of the most visible allurements have been eliminated from Times Square.

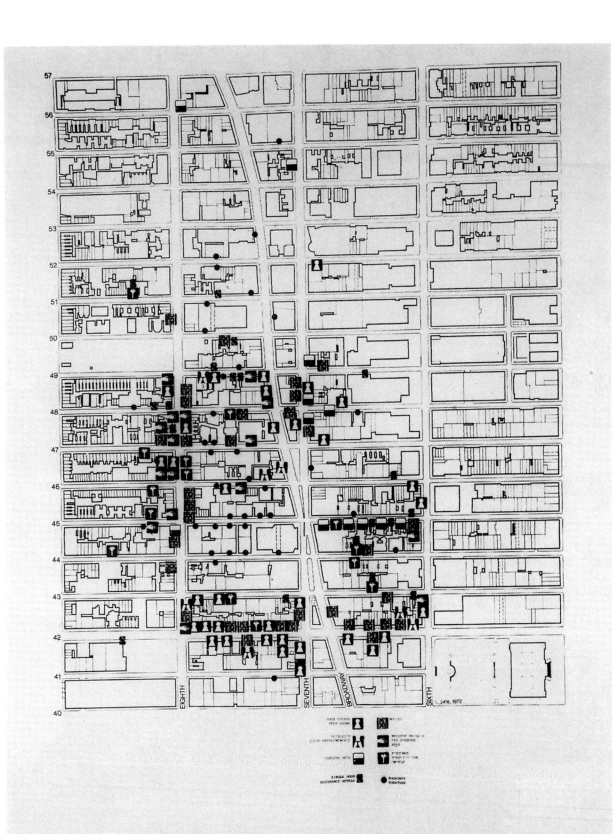

TIMES SQUARE

OFFICE OF MIDTOWN PLANNING AND DEVELOPMENT
OFFICE OF THE MAYOR   THE CITY OF NEW YORK
TIMES SQUARE DEVELOPMENT COUNCIL   1973

AVIATION IN THE SERVICE OF CARTOGRAPHY

AERIAL SURVEY OF MANHATTAN ISLAND

TITLE: Aerial Survey Manhattan Island, New York City (August 4, 1921)

DATE DEPICTED: 1921

DATE ISSUED: 1921

CARTOGRAPHER: FAIRCHILD AERIAL CAMERA CORPORATION

Two of four sheets of composite photograph, 8 feet long

Library of Congress, Washington, D.C.

SPOT METROVIEW OF MANHATTAN ISLAND

Untitled

DATE DEPICTED: c. 1990

CARTOGRAPHER: SPOT IMAGE CORPORATION

Photograph of satellite image

SPOT Image Corporation

Once photography and aviation had become sufficiently sophisticated, they were put to work in mapping. There were many obvious advantages: the air camera could accomplish in a few hours a task that would take an ordinary cartographer years to realize. The Fairchild Aerial Camera Corporation was an early leader in aerial mapmaking, producing their first pho-tomaps in 1918. On August 4, 1921, they created their first of two majestic aerial maps of Manhattan. In 1924, they also pro-duced a map of Greater New York City.

Aerial maps and views have long been a tradition in mapmaking, but before the air-plane, it often required the skills of the greatest artists to depict cities from significant heights and difficult angles. Albrecht Dürer and Leonardo da Vinci both experimented with such perspectives, probably executed by using a model.

The Fairchild Corporation's map of Manhattan looks seamless, but it is actually a mosaic of one hundred aerial pho-tographs all taken at an altitude of ten thousand feet. So many photographs were required because most of each image had to overlap with its neighboring images. Only the center portions of the photo-graph have value in a finished mosaic because only the centers are in true verticle projection. This overlapping of photographs allows for a stereoscopic effect, which gives the completed map a third dimension, or perspective.

"With a corps of engineers numbering more than 500, with the finest of existing maps of every description," the Fairchild Corporation wrote, "New York City experienced a decided lack when it wanted to visualize its engineering problems. The aerial map solved the problem." The detail in these maps is remarkable as every structure from construction sites to skyscrapers is apparent, every tree and bush is visible, unrecorded foot paths show up, even the congestion of traffic is clearly shown.

Forty years after Fairchild's photomosaic maps, NASA was sending back photomaps from space. The first photographs of the earth from space were taken in 1960, and in the decades that followed, these pictures from satellites have become increasingly detailed. Landsat spacecraft, launched by NASA, were for most of this period the satellites of choice for photomaps, but after the Chernobyl disaster in 1986, the satellite SPOT (Système Probatoire d'Observation de la Terre) took some of the most revealing photographs. "A new French satellite produced a more detailed view of the reactor," reported the *Washington Post*, "showing

damage to the ground next to the reactor and breaking Landsat's 14 year monopoly on such service."

The SPOT image of Manhattan reproduced here was taken during an orbit 517 miles from earth. The reason so many familiar features of Manhattan are visible from this distance is the camera resolution, which is designed to detect everything that is at least thirty-three feet wide. Where Landsat's images identify blocks of houses, SPOT's distinguish individual buildings. Central Park, Yankee Stadium, The New York Public Library, the various bridges, and Columbia University can all be easily seen, as well as individual apartment buildings.

The water in the Central Park reservoir is black, and most of the other colors in the image are not the ones usually associated with the landscape of Manhattan. To realize the best resolution, the satellites record and report in the near-infrared part of the spectrum, which is not visible to the eye. The process of passing the images through color filters and onto the film produces the color distortion called false color.

It is said that satellites create images more vivid than any map. In many ways this is true, as they reveal often-hidden details of the environment. Once these images were carefully protected by the military, but now several commercial enterprises sell satellite images of locations throughout the world.

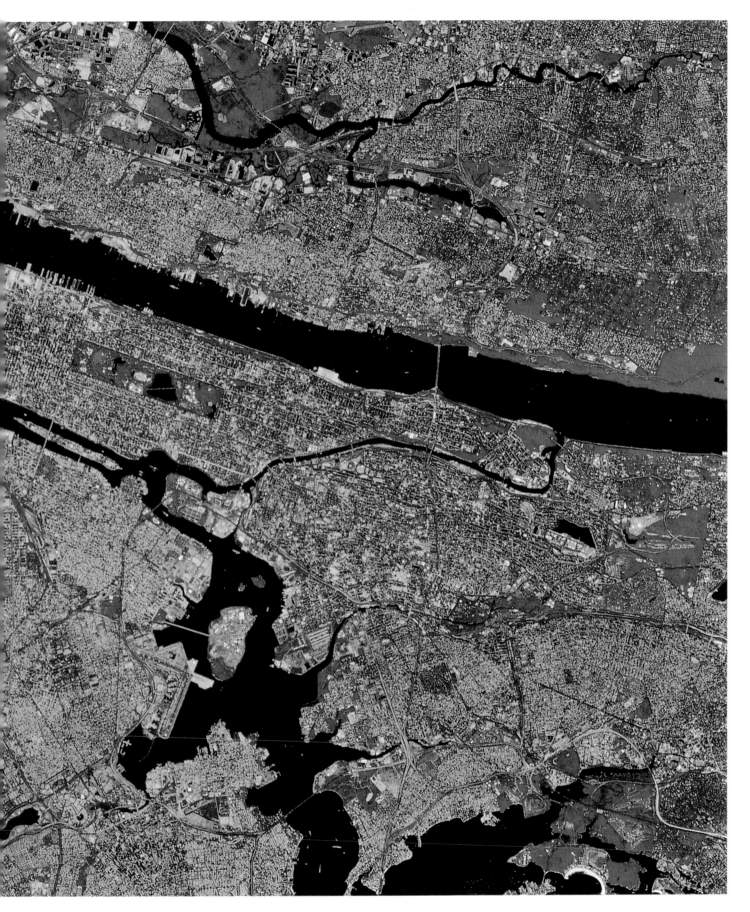

SELECTED BIBLIOGRAPHY

Ashton, Jean. "Manhattan on Paper: Windows on Nineteenth-Century New York: Perris and Browne Atlases," *Biblon* (Spring 1993), pp. 71–80.

Augustyn, Robert T., and Paul E. Cohen. "Maps in the Making of Manhattan," *The Magazine Antiques* (September 1995), pp. 336–347.

Archdeacon, Thomas J. *New York City, 1664–1710: Conquest and Change* (Ithaca, N.Y., 1976).

Blackburn, Roderic H., and Ruth Piwonka. *Remembrance of Patria: Dutch Arts and Culture in Colonial America 1609–1776* (Albany, N.Y., 1988).

Buisseret, David, ed. *From Sea Charts to Satellite Images* (Chicago, 1990).

Bridges, William. *Map of the City of New York and Island of Manhattan* (New York, 1811).

Campbell, Tony. *Early Maps* (New York, 1981).

Cohen, Paul E. "'Civic Folly': The Man Who Measured Manhattan," *AB Bookman's Weekly* (June 13, 1988), pp. 2511–2515.

Condon, Thomas J. *New York Beginnings: The Commercial Origins of New Netherland* (New York, 1968).

Cumming, William P., "The Montresor-Ratzer-Sauthier Sequence of Maps of New York City, 1766–76," *Imago Mundi* 31, pp. 55–65.

Deák, Gloria Gilda. *Picturing America* (Princeton, N.J., 1988).

Dunshee, Kenneth. *As You Pass By* (New York, 1952).

Evans, G. N. D. *Uncommon Obdurate: The Several Public Careers of J. F. W. DesBarres* (Toronto, 1960).

Grove, Pearce S., and Helen M. Wallis, "Discovery of the Rawlinson Copperplate Maps of the Americas and their Related Prints," *The Map Collector* 56 (Autumn 1991), pp. 12–21.

Harley, J. B. et al. *Mapping the American Revolutionary War* (Chicago, 1978).

Haskell, Daniel C. *Manhattan Maps: A Cooperative List* (New York, 1931).

Hemstreet, Charles. *Nooks & Corners of Old New York* (New York, 1899).

Homberger, Eric. *The Historical Atlas of New York City* (New York, 1994).

Hudson, Alice. "Manhattan on Paper: The Mapping of Property and Environment in Manhattan since the 1600s," *Biblion* (Spring 1993), pp. 39–70.

Jackson, Kenneth T., ed. *The Encyclopedia of New York City* (New Haven, Conn., 1995).

Kammen, Michael G. *Colonial New York: A History* (New York, 1975).

Keuning, Johannes. "Hessel Gerritsz" *Imago Mundi* VI, pp. 49–66.

Kroessler, Jeffrey A. *A Guide to Historical Map Resources for Greater New York* (Chicago, 1988).

Mercator Society of The New York Public Library. *English Mapping of America* (New York, 1986).

Miller, John. *New York Considered and Improved* (Cleveland, 1903).

Morison, Samuel E. *The European Discovery of America: The Northern Voyages* (New York, 1971).

Nebenzahl, Kenneth. *Atlas of the American Revolution* (Chicago, 1976).

Olmsted, Frederick Law. *The Papers of Frederick Law Olmsted* (Baltimore, 1977–1990).

Pedley, Mary. "Maps, War, and Commerce: Business Correspondence with the London Map Firm of Thomas Jefferys and William Faden," *Imago Mundi* 48, pp. 161–173.

Pomerantz, Sidney I. *New York: An American City 1783–1803* (New York, 1938).

Pound, Arthur. *The Golden Earth* (New York 1935).

Randel, John, Jr. "City of New York, North of Canal Street in 1808 to 1821," Common Council Manual (1866), pp. 547–556.

Reps, John W. *The Making of Urban America* (Princeton, N.J., 1965).

Ristow, Walter W. *American Maps and Mapmakers* (Detroit, 1985).

Rosenzweig, Roy, and Elizabeth Blackmar. *The Park and the People* (Ithaca, N.Y., 1992).

Rothschild, Nan A. *New York City Neighborhoods: The 18th Century* (New York, 1990).

Schilder, Gunther, and Jan van Bracht. *The Origins of New York* (Zurich, 1988).

Spann, Edward K. "The Greatest Grid," in *Two Centuries of American Planning*, ed. Daniel Schaffer (Baltimore, 1988).

——. *The New Metropolis* (New York, 1986).

Strong, George Templeton. *The Diary of George Templeton Strong* (New York, 1952).

Stokes, I. N. Phelps. *The Iconography of Manhattan Island, 1498–1909* (New York, 1915–1928).

Viele, Chase. "Egbert Ludovicus Viele," undated typescript in the Map Division of The New York Public Library.

Wall, Alexander J. "The Great Fire of 1835," *New-York Historical Society Quarterly Bulletin* XX (January 1936), pp. 3–22.

Wilson, James Grant, ed. *The Memorial History of the City of New-York* (New York, 1892).

INDEX

ILLUSTRATION CREDITS

Illustrations not listed below are held in anonymous private collections.

Biblioteca Medicea Laurenziana, Florence, Italy: 25

British Library, London: 29–31, 38–39

General Archives of Simancas, Spain: 7

Courtesy of Robert Goelet (Wit McKay, photographer): xii–xiii

Courtesy of the Harvard Map Collection: 3

Holkham Hall, Norfolk, England: 44–45

Courtesy of Leonard Milberg (Lynn de Marco, photographer): 20–21

Library of Congress, Washington, D.C.: 11, 14–15, 16–17, 90–91, 94–95, 122–125, 127, 129, 131, 133, 142–43

Manahatta Project (Markley Boyer and Eric W. Sanderson, cartographers), xxii–xxiii

Manhattan Borough President's Office: 97, 99

Martayan Lan, Inc. (Bob Lorenzson, photographer): 65, 67

Municipal Archives, New York: 116–17

Museum of the City of New York, Gift of August Belmont: 134

New York City Department of Parks (Bob Lorenzson, photographer): 118–19, 121

Courtesy of the New-York Historical Society: 49, 51, 75, 78–79, 82–83, 93, 103, 105–107

Map Division, The New York Public Library, Astor, Lenox and Tilden Foundations: 114–15

I.N. Phelps Stokes Collection, Miriam and Ira D. Wallach Division of Art, Prints and Photographs, The New York Public Library, Astor, Lenox and Tilden Foundations: 26–27, 41, 47

Manuscripts Division, The New York Public Library, Astor, Lenox and Tilden Foundations: 86–87

New York State Archives (Bryk and Provo Photographers): 136–37

New York State Library: 69

Public Records Office, London: 71–73

Regional Plan Association, New York (George Colbert and Guenter Vollath, cartographers): xiv

Richard B. Arkway, Inc. (Bob Lorenzson, photographer): 52–53

Shubert Archive, New York: 141

SPOT Image Corporation: 144–45

State Archives, The Hague, The Netherlands: 9

Collection of Arthur O. Sulzberger, New York (Lynn de Marco, photographer): 80–81

Collection of John Tauranac: 135

ABOUT THE AUTHORS

Paul E. Cohen is the author of *Mapping the West* (New York: Rizzoli, 2002) and the coeditor of *American Cities* (New York: Assouline, 2005). He is a partner in Cohen & Taliaferro LLC, New York City, dealers in rare books and antique maps.

Robert T. Augustyn is one of the owners of Martayan Lan Fine Antique Maps in New York City. He has written numerous articles and catalogues on the subject of antique maps.

Tony Hiss, author of thirteen books, was a staff writer at *The New Yorker* for over thirty years and is now a Visiting Scholar at New York University. His award-winning book *The Experience of Place* was followed most recently by *In Motion: The Experience of Travel*. The National Recreation and Park Association's National Literary Award praised Hiss for a lifetime of writing about "how our environments, modes of travel, and other aspects of the American landscape affect our lives."

Marguerite Holloway is the author of *The Measure of Manhattan: The Tumultuous Career and Surprising Legacy of John Randel, Jr., Cartographer, Surveyor, Inventor* (W. W. Norton, 2013), the first biography of Randel. Holloway is the Director of Science and Environmental Journalism at Columbia University's Graduate School of Journalism; she was a longtime contributor to *Scientific American* and has written for many other publications. She grew up in New York City.

Eric W. Sanderson is a Senior Conservation Ecologist at the Wildlife Conservation Society (WCS) in New York City, where he directs the Mannahatta and Welikia Projects on New York City's historical ecology. He led the team that created Mannahatta2409.org, an online forum to design and share futures for Manhattan. Sanderson is also the bestselling author of *Mannahatta: A Natural History of New York City* (New York: Abrams Books, 2009) and *Terra Nova: The New World After Oil, Cars, and Suburbs* (New York: Abrams Books, 2013).